THE GOVERNOR AND THE KING

THE GOVERNOR AND THE KING

Irony, Hidden Transcripts, and Negotiating Empire
in the Fourth Gospel

ARTHUR M. WRIGHT JR.

Foreword by Frances Taylor Gench

☙PICKWICK *Publications* · Eugene, Oregon

THE GOVERNOR AND THE KING
Irony, Hidden Transcripts, and Negotiating Empire in the Fourth Gospel

Copyright © 2019 Arthur M. Wright Jr. All rights reserved. Except for brief quotations in critical publications or reviews, no part of this book may be reproduced in any manner without prior written permission from the publisher. Write: Permissions, Wipf and Stock Publishers, 199 W. 8th Ave., Suite 3, Eugene, OR 97401.

Pickwick Publications
An Imprint of Wipf and Stock Publishers
199 W. 8th Ave., Suite 3
Eugene, OR 97401

www.wipfandstock.com

PAPERBACK ISBN: 978-1-5326-4993-6
HARDCOVER ISBN: 978-1-5326-4994-3
EBOOK ISBN: 978-1-5326-4995-0

Cataloguing-in-Publication data:

Names: Wright, Arthur M., Jr., author. | Gench, Frances Taylor, foreword.

Title: The Governor and the King : Irony, Hidden Transcripts, and Negotiating Empire in the Fourth Gospel / Arthur M. Wright Jr.

Description: Eugene, OR: Pickwick Publications, 2019 | **Includes bibliographical references and index.**

Identifiers: ISBN 978-1-5326-4993-6 (paperback) | ISBN 978-1-5326-4994-3 (hardcover) | ISBN 978-1-5326-4995-0 (ebook)

Subjects: LCSH: Bible. John—Criticism, interpretation, etc. | Rome—In the Bible. | Irony in the Bible. | Bible. John—Social scientific criticism. | Sociology, Biblical. | Opposition (Political science) in the Bible.

Classification: BS2615.6.R65 W7 2019 (paperback) | BS2615.6.R65 (ebook)

Manufactured in the U.S.A.   04/03/19

Unless otherwise indicated, Scripture quotations are from the New Revised Standard Version Bible, copyright © 1989 National Council of the Churches of Christ in the United States of America. Used by permission. All rights reserved worldwide.

To Beth, whose ceaseless encouragement, support, and love has helped see this project through to completion. I love you.

"My kingdom is not from this world. If my kingdom were from this world, my followers would be fighting to keep me from being handed over to the Jews. But as it is, my kingdom is not from here." (John 18:36)

Contents

Foreword by Frances Taylor Gench | ix
Acknowledgments | xi
List of Abbreviations | xiii

Chapter 1
Introduction | 1
    The Fourth Gospel and the Roman Empire in Scholarship | 3
    Historical Context of the Fourth Gospel | 17
    James C. Scott and Hidden Transcripts | 23
    Overview of Irony as a Literary Device | 30
    Hidden Transcripts and Irony | 40
    Thesis | 41

Chapter 2
The Gospel of John and the Roman Imperial World | 43
    Models of Empire | 43
    The Roman Imperial World | 53
    Conclusion | 73

Chapter 3
The Arrest Scene | 74
    Introduction | 74
    Irony and the Arrest | 76
    The Jewish Police and the Roman Cohort as Agents of Imperial Power | 77
    The Arrival of the Arresting Party (18:1–3) | 80
    Jesus and the Arresting Party (18:4–6) | 90
    The Second Exchange between Jesus and His Captors (18:7–9) | 101
    Peter's Violent Resistance (18:10–11) | 103
    The "Arrest" (18:12) | 105
    Irony, Hidden Transcripts, and Negotiating Roman Rule | 106

Chapter 4
The Roman Show Trial | 112
  Introduction | 112
  Scene 1: Jesus Is Handed Over to Pilate (18:28–32) | 122
  Scene 2: Questioning the "King of the Jews" (18:33–38a) | 132
  Scene 3: Releasing Barabbas (18:38b–40) | 141
  Scene 4: Torture and Jesus' Investiture as King (19:1–3) | 146
  Scene 5: The Presentation of Jesus as King (19:4–8) | 152
  Scene 6: Origins of Power (19:9–11) | 159
  Scene 7: Judgment (19:12–16a) | 166
  Irony, Hidden Transcripts, and Negotiating Roman Rule | 180

Chapter 5
Jesus' Crucifixion and Burial | 186
  Introduction | 186
  The Meaning of the Cross in Imperial Rome | 187
  Scene 1: Crucifying Jesus (19:16b–18) | 193
  Scene 2: The Inscription on the Cross (19:19–22) | 196
  Scene 3: Dividing the Spoils of Crucifixion (19:23–25a) | 200
  Scene 4: New Relationships at the Foot of the Cross (19:25b–27) | 206
  Scene 5: Jesus' Death (19:28–30) | 210
  Scene 6: Blood and Water (19:31–37) | 215
  Scene 7: Interment of the King (19:38–42) | 222
  Crucifixion, Burial, and Hidden Transcripts | 227

Chapter 6
Conclusion | 231
  Summary and Conclusions | 231
  Suggestions for Further Study | 236
  Negotiating Empire Today | 238

Bibliography | 241

Foreword

THE FOURTH GOSPEL, THROUGHOUT most of the history of its interpretation, has been regarded as a largely apolitical document—as Clement of Alexandria dubbed it, the "spiritual Gospel," without much to contribute to historical or political reflection. Only in recent years have scholars begun to direct attention to its political dimensions, and this study rides the wave of this intriguing and momentous development, advancing an important discussion. Indeed, it was a great pleasure to serve on the dissertation committee, along with John T. Carroll and Warren Carter, that supervised Arthur Wright's stimulating project, *The Governor and the King: Irony, Hidden Transcripts, and Negotiating Empire in the Fourth Gospel*. Wright's study takes seriously the complex relationship between the Fourth Gospel and the Roman Empire, attending carefully to its political implications. I am delighted that it is now available to a larger audience in published form, for it is distinguished in two important respects. First, it brings general developments in the emerging field of imperial studies to bear on a close and detailed reading of the distinctive Johannine Passion Narrative, an especially important section of the Fourth Gospel for any consideration of its engagement with Roman imperial realities. Second, it bridges interpretive methods, bringing the Fourth Gospel's celebrated use of irony (the focus of a great deal of literary/narrative-critical work on John) into conversation with historical-critical work on Roman imperial reality, demonstrating the significant intersection between the two. Irony, as Wright notes, is often political because it has power to support or subvert perspectives and opinions. The study effectively demonstrates that the story of Jesus's arrest, trial, and execution in John 18–19 displays part of a Johannine hidden transcript that resists and contests elements of Roman imperial power, thereby informing early Christian navigation of life in the Roman imperial world in important and nuanced ways. At the same time, it discloses a deep-rooted imperializing impulse within Johannine Christianity itself, which imitates and reinscribes elements of the system it resists.

Wright's work is notable for the quality of interpretive detail that it provides in its reading of the Johannine Passion Narrative, and for its deft attention to the literary use of irony to shape historical perspectives on Roman imperial realities. Wright also contributes to a significant broadening of historical discussion of the Fourth Gospel beyond concentration on conflict with the synagogue, thereby providing vital food for thought for people of faith who continue to navigate life in their own contexts of imperial power, in which they too are enmeshed. In so doing, they can be informed by both the insights and the dangers of political dimensions of John's Gospel disclosed in this compelling study. I celebrate its publication and its contribution to ongoing discernment of the shape of faithful Christian public life.

Frances Taylor Gench
Union Presbyterian Seminary
Richmond, Virginia

Acknowledgments

I CANNOT BEGIN TO imagine completing this project without the wealth of support that I have received from a number of people. Friends and family have offered encouragement, conversation to hone my ideas, and proofreading advice along the way. Several groups of people have loved, supported, and walked beside me along this journey. I am especially thankful for the Alkulana community, the Big Chill group, and dear friends in Richmond and Nashville who I call "family." The members of Tabernacle Baptist Church in Richmond, Virginia have provided me with a loving community in which I can wrestle with matters of Scripture and faith as we attempt to follow Jesus together. I am so grateful for you all.

When I was a student at Averett University in Danville, Virginia, Dr. Mark Nickens was the first to inspire me to attend seminary and pursue biblical studies. The example he set as a professor and the time that he invested in my personal, spiritual, and professional growth have led me to this point. I am grateful to have had him as a wise mentor along the way.

I am also grateful for the community at the Baptist Theological Seminary at Richmond (BTSR) of which I have been a part these past several years. I am thankful for colleagues there who have supported my professional growth and rooted for me to finish this project. The students at BTSR have been gracious with me as I have waded into the deep waters of the teaching profession. I have thoroughly enjoyed our time together and conversations in and out of the classroom. I have learned so much from you already.

Union Presbyterian Seminary and its faculty and staff nurtured my academic development and my spiritual life for many years. In the PhD program at Union, I was blessed with wise, patient professors and wonderful friends. As I worked on this dissertation, I was blessed to have a supportive, talented committee guiding me along the way. John Carroll and Warren Carter provided wise counsel with regards to the overall argument of my project and with numerous editorial matters. This project is better because of their involvement. John and Warren: thank you.

I am eternally grateful to my principal advisor, Frances Taylor Gench, for her patience, guidance, and encouragement along the way. She helped me to dream up this project from the beginning and has been a steady guide as years have passed. Frances, you inspire me with your teaching, your scholarship, and your heart for serving the church. Thank you for inspiring my love of this "Maverick Gospel" and seeing this project through to the end.

My parents have been selfless in their support of my academic pursuits and have always encouraged me to pursue my dreams. To this day my brother Rob inspires me to work harder, to be a better, more generous person, and to drink my coffee black. I still look up to him. I am thankful that my young children, Julian and Adrian, will probably not remember this period of my life, when I have spent long stretches of time working in the library. I recognize the sacrifices made and am amazed at the wonderful young people they are becoming. Most of all, I offer my deepest thanks to my wife, Beth. It is safe to say that I could not have done this without your love and support. You fill my heart with joy and continue to inspire me in so many ways. Thank you for encouraging me and for believing in me all along the way.

Finally, to the one they called the light of the world: I don't know where this journey leads, but I will continue to follow. I pray that this work glorifies you and sheds light—even if just a little bit—on what it means to be your disciple in this world.

List of Abbreviations

AB	Anchor Bible
ABRL	Anchor Bible Reference Library
ANRW	*Aufstieg und Niedergang der römischen Welt: Geschichte und Kultur Roms im Spiegel der neueren Forschung.* Edited by H. Temporini and W. Haase. Berlin, 1972–
ATANT	Abhandlungen zur Theologie des Alten und Neuen Testaments
BDAG	Danker, Frederick W., Walter Bauer, William F. Arndt, and F. Wilbur Gingrich. *Greek-English Lexicon of the New Testament and Other Early Christian Literature.* 3rd ed. Chicago: University of Chicago Press, 2000.
BDF	Blass, Friedrich, Albert Debrunner, and Robert W. Funk. *A Greek Grammar of the New Testament and Other Early Christian Literature.* Chicago: University of Chicago Press, 1961.
Bib	*Biblica*
BibInt	*Biblical Interpretation*
BSR	*Biblioteca di Scienze Religiose*
CBQMS	Catholic Biblical Quarterly Monograph Series
CR	*Christian Reflection*
ExpTim	*Expository Times*
FCNTECW	Feminist Companion to the New Testament and Early Christian Writings
JBL	*Journal of Biblical Literature*

JSJ	*Journal for the Study of Judaism in the Persian, Hellenistic, and Roman Periods*
JSNT	*Journal for the Study of the New Testament*
JSNTSup	Journal for the Study of the New Testament Supplement Series
JSOTSup	Journal for the Study of the Old Testament Supplement Series
JTS	*Journal of Theological Studies*
LCL	Loeb Classical Library
L&N	Louw, Johannes P., and Eugene A. Nida, eds. *Greek-English Lexicon of the New Testament: Based on Semantic Domains.* 2nd ed. New York: United Bible Societies, 1989.
LXX	Septuagint
MTZ	*Münchener theologische Zeitschrift*
NCB	The New Century Bible Commentary
NIB	*The New Interpreter's Bible Commentary*
NICNT	New International Commentary on the New Testament
NovTSup	Supplements to Novum Testamentum
NRSV	New Revised Standard Version
NRTh	*La nouvelle revue théologique*
NTS	New Testament Studies
SBLSymS	Society of Biblical Literature Symposium Series
Scr	*Scripture*
SemeiaSt	Semeia Studies
SHBC	Smyth & Helwys Bible Commentary Series
SNTSMS	Society for New Testament Studies Monograph Series
SP	Sacra Pagina
WBC	Word Biblical Commentary

Chapter 1

Introduction

WHEN THE ROMAN GOVERNOR Pontius Pilate appears on the scene in the Fourth Gospel, his presence dominates the action until Jesus is crucified. Whereas Jesus has been the primary focal point of the narrative to this point, Pilate suddenly steals the spotlight and becomes the central focus of the action. As Jesus arrives at the praetorium in John 18:28, the narrative ceases to follow him and begins to track Pilate's movement instead as the Roman governor moves back and forth between the Jewish authorities outside and Jesus, the condemned man, within. Not only is Pilate the dominant figure at this point in the Gospel, but the Roman interrogation of Jesus that he conducts in John is lengthier and more involved than in the Synoptics.[1] The Gospel rushes rapidly through Jesus' appearance before the Jewish authorities, arriving quickly at Jesus' extended Roman "trial" before Pilate.[2] The emphasis on Jesus'

---

1. In Mark, Jesus' interaction with Pilate is narrated in a mere fifteen verses (Mark 15:1–15). Matthew uses sixteen verses to describe the Roman proceedings (Matt 27:11–26). In Luke, this takes up twenty-two verses, split by a brief scene in which Herod questions Jesus (Luke 23:1–7, 11–25). John devotes twenty-eight verses to a description of Jesus' appearance before Pilate. Raymond E. Brown notes the interrogation by Pilate in John is three times longer than in Mark (*Death of the Messiah*, 1:757–58).

2. For reasons that will be discussed at length on pp. 67–68 below, "trial" is not a particularly useful designation for Pilate's interactions with Jesus in the Fourth Gospel. Because the so-called "trial" is conducted primarily for the sake of political interests—and not to ensure a fair hearing for Jesus—I prefer the designation "show trial," or more simply at times, "Jesus' appearance before Pilate" or the "Roman proceedings." Where I do use the term "trial," I use quotation marks to disrupt typical assumptions

appearance before Pilate is so strong in the Fourth Gospel that it forms the centerpiece of John's passion narrative.

Even the arrest of Jesus earlier in the narrative is steeped in a visible Roman presence that the Synoptic Gospels lack. Whereas the Synoptics describe how armed representatives of the Jewish authorities come to arrest Jesus in the garden, only John includes an entire cohort of Roman soldiers (as many as six hundred strong) in the group that takes Jesus into custody.[3] John also includes a specifically political motivation for arresting Jesus in the first place. While meeting together to discuss how to deal with Jesus, the chief priests and Pharisees declare, "If we let him go on like this, everyone will believe in him, and the Romans will come and destroy both our holy place and our nation" (John 11:48).[4]

All of these references demonstrate that the arrest and "trial" scenes in the Fourth Gospel are flooded with Roman imperial presence and political concerns and should prove fruitful for an exploration of the relationship between John and the Roman Empire. Although the Fourth Gospel in particular has not often been considered a political document, the heightened Roman element in the arrest and "trial" scenes vis-à-vis the Synoptic Gospels, along with the political justification for Jesus' arrest, are among the reasons that Stephen D. Moore declares John the "most political of the gospels."[5] This project explores the political nature of the Fourth Gospel and its relation to the Roman Empire by examining the arrest, "trial," and crucifixion scenes. I argue that the Gospel exhibits what James C. Scott calls a "hidden transcript" of resistance that subverts some elements of Roman imperialism. Notably, the irony present in the scenes critiques elements of imperial power and authority while appealing to readers to share the Johannine worldview. Above all, these sections of the Fourth Gospel espouse a vision of the lordship of Jesus Christ over and against the lordship of the Roman Emperor. At the same time, these scenes also mimic elements of Roman imperial power by asserting Jesus' kingship, power, and worldwide empire.[6]

---

about the nature of Jesus' appearance before Pilate and to indicate my skepticism that "trial" is an appropriate term for the show trial in which Jesus, the Jewish authorities, and Pilate participate.

3. Matt 26:47–56; Mark 14:43–50; Luke 22:47–53; John 18:1–12.

4. Unless otherwise indicated, all quotations from the New Testament or Hebrew Bible are from the NRSV.

5. Moore, *Empire and Apocalypse*, 50.

6. Homi K. Bhabha maintains that colonized groups typically adopt and mimic

The Fourth Gospel and the Roman Empire in Scholarship

1. The "Spiritual Gospel" and the Johannine Community

What is the relationship between the Fourth Gospel and the Roman Empire? Lukan scholars have long discussed and debated the question of the Third Gospel's relation to the empire, but until recently, Johannine scholarship has paid relatively little attention to this question.[7] Even though the Fourth Gospel's narrative tells the story of a Galilean peasant who is ultimately crucified by a Roman governor, for much of the history of its interpretation, studies have neglected to attend to this narrative's political dimensions. Instead, scholars have approached and understood this Gospel in three major ways: as the "spiritual gospel"; as a document that was written at a particularly difficult juncture in the Johannine community's relationship with the Jewish synagogue community; and strictly as a narrative in which the story itself and the way it impacts the reader is of utmost significance.

From an early point in the Gospel's reception history, leaders of the church referred to it as the "spiritual gospel." Clement of Alexandria, for example, suggested that John, the latest of the four gospel writers, wrote in direct contrast to the Synoptic Gospels, which had already presented the "external facts" of Jesus' life.[8] Reading the Gospel today, it is not difficult to understand why so many have read and interpreted the Fourth Gospel as a "spiritual gospel."

The Johannine text presents Jesus' origins, not through birth stories, but with a soaring, cosmic vision of the preexistent Word. Throughout,

---

aspects of the colonizer's ideology and culture (*Location of Culture*, 85–92). While colonized persons mimic significant elements of the colonial power, they also display ambivalence in this regard. There are inevitably significant differences in their imitation of the colonizer's ideology; they are "almost the same, *but not quite*" (Bhabha, *Location of Culture*, 86). Within the Fourth Gospel, we see mimicry as themes of empire are reinscribed. Most notably, Jesus is presented as a king/emperor who commands worldwide dominion and power. Yet Jesus' kingdom differs from Rome's in significant ways (John 18:36).

7. For a thorough overview of the discussion surrounding Luke's Gospel, see Oakes, *Rome in the Bible*, 1–41. Some of the most significant studies in this area include Conzelmann, *Theology of St. Luke*; Walaskay, *And So We Came to Rome*; Robbins, "Luke–Acts"; Esler, *Community and Gospel in Luke-Acts*; and Cassidy, *Jesus, Politics, and Society*.

8. Eusebius, *Hist. eccl.* 6.14.7, quoted in Koester, *Word of Life*, 4.

it depicts Jesus as the one who is sent from God, who does the works of God, and who reveals God's own self.[9] The Fourth Gospel goes further than the Synoptic Gospels in equating Jesus with God, even while maintaining a distinction between the two.[10] The Johannine Jesus does not tend to get involved in relatively mundane matters: he performs only a few miracles and tells no parables. Instead, Jesus speaks in long, sweeping discourses that are primarily about his own identity. The narrative also places heavy emphasis on the Spirit: people must be "born of the Spirit" (John 3:6); worship should be conducted in "spirit and in truth" (4:24); the Spirit "gives life" (6:63); and in his Farewell Discourse, Jesus talks at length about the Holy Spirit (the Paraclete). Thus, it is argued that the Fourth Gospel has much to say about theology and the spiritual significance of Jesus, but little to contribute to discussions of a social or political nature. It has often been viewed primarily as a resource for individual spiritual reflection and for catalyzing personal belief in Jesus.

For similar reasons, many scholars have concluded that the Gospel of John contributes little to a discussion of history. If it has been regarded as the "most spiritual gospel," it has also been regarded as the least historical of the Gospels, with very little of its material deriving from the historical life of Jesus. Because John differs so radically from the Synoptic Gospels, especially in its presentation of Jesus, many scholars have assumed that it primarily exhibits the influence of various streams of religious thought on the Johannine evangelist and does not contain reliable historical data. Attempts have been made to identify these influences, whether Greek, gnostic, or Jewish, and then to demonstrate how they shaped the Gospel's theology.[11] However, all of the canonical Gospels are deeply theological narratives, and none of them attempts to present history in a strict sense. Each evangelist presents a story of Jesus that is shaped by particular theological perspectives and agendas, and all of the Gospels are useful for understanding history to some extent. Thus, recently, the Society of Biblical Literature has sponsored a "John, Jesus, and History" group whose goal is to demonstrate the relevance of the Fourth Gospel to the study of the historical circumstances surrounding the life

---

9. See, for example, John 1:1–18; 5:36; and 14:1–11.

10. For examples within the text where this distinction between Jesus and God is evident, see John 1:1 and 14:28.

11. Moloney, *Gospel of John*, 12. For examples of such a perspective, see Bultmann, *Gospel of John*; and Dodd, *Interpretation of the Fourth Gospel*.

of Jesus, as well as the teaching and actions of Jesus himself.[12] Moreover, scholars now generally accept that, whatever the relationship between the Fourth Gospel and the life of the historical Jesus, the text is useful for illuminating the historical circumstances of the Johannine community in which the Gospel was written.

However, for much of its history of interpretation, scholars have paid insufficient attention to historical circumstances that inform an interpretation of John, focusing their efforts on the "history of ideas" in John rather than on the history of the Johannine community. David Rensberger notes that scholars have long been interested in the polemical context of many of Paul's letters, for example, but in the Gospel of John, evidence of conflict and historical circumstances that might have evoked such conflict lies beneath the surface of the text.[13] But over the past few decades, a significant shift has taken place in Johannine scholarship, as reconstruction of the historical context of the Johannine community and its bearing on interpretation have dominated much of the discourse on the Fourth Gospel. J. Louis Martyn and Raymond E. Brown are largely responsible for effecting this shift in perspective.[14]

Martyn and Brown were able to argue compellingly that the Johannine community—the community in which the Fourth Gospel was produced—had recently experienced a painful separation or expulsion from the local synagogue community. Both scholars called attention to three references in the text that refer to expulsion from the synagogue (9:22; 12:42; 16:2) and argued that Johannine believers had recently been forced out because other Jews deemed their beliefs incompatible with monotheistic faith. Martyn argued that the text of the Fourth Gospel could be read as a "two-level drama": many scenes within it simultaneously recount episodes from the life and ministry of Jesus while offering a glimpse of the life of the Johannine community as well (especially 5:1–47; 7:1–52; and 9:1–41). In Martyn's view, the story of the man born blind in John 9 describes an event in Jesus' ministry, but the evangelist has incorporated it into the Gospel in such a way that it also reflects the struggles and developing Christological insight of the Johannine community in the late first century. As the man born blind experiences conflict with the Jewish authorities and expulsion from the synagogue community, readers can

12. For publications of this group, see Anderson et al., *John, Jesus, and History, Volume 1*; and Anderson et al., *John, Jesus, and History, Volume 2*.

13. Rensberger, *Johannine Faith*, 15–16.

14. See Brown, *Community*; and Martyn, *History and Theology*.

also glimpse the Johannine community's conflict and its own eventual expulsion from the synagogue.[15]

Brown's hypothesis shares many similarities with Martyn's, but adds a significant inciting event to the picture: he argues that groups of anti-temple Jews and Samaritan converts entered the Johannine community and effected a shift in the group's theology, specifically toward a more elevated Christology.[16] This triggered a reaction within the synagogue community that led to the expulsion of Johannine believers. Brown also goes further than Martyn by reconstructing the entire history of the Johannine community. While admitting the hypothetical nature of his reconstruction, he sketches the evolution of the community from its origin, through its growth, conflict with the synagogue, a period of internal conflict (reflected in the Johannine epistles), and finally its integration into the larger early Christian church. Brown also discerns a number of connections between the text and the circumstances of the Johannine community near the end of the first century: namely, a number of the characters within the text are representative of groups outside the Johannine community. For example, Brown argues that texts such as 12:42–43, in which many Jewish authorities believe in Jesus but do not publicly confess him, reflect the presence of "Crypto-Christians" in the Johannine community's late first-century context who were afraid to publicly announce their faith because of their fear that they would be expelled from the synagogue.

Both Martyn and Brown highlight the conflict between Johannine believers and the synagogue community. Both consider expulsion from the synagogue to be a defining moment for this early Christian group. In their view, this traumatic event in the life of the Johannine community accounts for a number of distinctive features in the text, including the Fourth Gospel's dualistic and sectarian worldview and the severe rhetoric against "the Jews."

Martyn and Brown's groundbreaking work charted a course for Johannine studies for several decades, as the widely accepted "expulsion hypothesis" focused scholarly attention on the Johannine community's

---

15. Martyn, *History and Theology*, 3–41.

16. Brown, *Community*, 43–47. Many Samaritans anticipated a *Taheb*, a "teacher" and "revealer" who was preexistent and would come from God. Brown speculates that this Samaritan expectation of a messiah figure heavily influenced the Johannine perspective on Jesus.

conflict with the synagogue.¹⁷ This hypothesis still figures prominently in much scholarship on the Fourth Gospel. However, the level of certainty once conferred upon it has begun to erode. Many scholars now question whether the three references to expulsion in the Gospel (9:22; 12:42; 16:2) can bear the weight of the precise claims that Martyn and Brown made, given the fact that there is meager external evidence to support these claims.¹⁸ Given the Fourth Gospel's harsh polemic against "the Jews," it is possible that conflict may have existed between some Johannine believers and others in the synagogue community, but it is difficult to ascertain the exact nature or source of such conflict.¹⁹ As with any ecclesial conflict, past or present, much is a matter of perspective. Readers only have access to one side of the conflict, viewed through the lens of the Fourth Gospel, and the contours of it are vague. We may be able to catch a glimpse of the perspective of members of the Johannine community, but we do not have access to the perspective of the synagogue community. Nor do we know whether conflict and expulsion were realities or merely perception. It is possible that members of the Johannine community willfully separated themselves or felt they were being "expelled" because of theological differences. Furthermore, it is possible that a separation did not occur at all, but rather that the Fourth Evangelist wished to encourage and create separation between Christian believers and the rest of the Jewish community by narrating conflict in the text.²⁰ Nevertheless, the work of Martyn and Brown has had a lasting influence in that it "forced biblical scholars to think seriously about the circumstances in which the Gospel of John was produced."²¹ Johannine scholarship now routinely takes into account the historical circumstances that lie behind the Gospel, and a number of scholars continue to find the Martyn-Brown hypothesis a compelling point of departure for interpreting the Gospel.

---

17. Even relatively recent publications presume as historical fact many of the features of the Martyn-Brown hypothesis. See, for example, Richey, *Roman Imperial Ideology*, 2–13; Reed, "Rethinking John's Social Setting," 93–106.

18. For a sampling of the recent discussion and the growing criticism of the Martyn-Brown hypothesis, see Reinhartz, *Befriending*, 37–53; Kysar, "Expulsion," 237–45; Carter, *John: Storyteller*, 155–94.

19. John 7:14–24 and 8:39–47 present examples of Johannine polemic against Jewish authorities.

20. Carter, *John and Empire*, 19–45.

21. Thatcher, "Anatomies of the Fourth Gospel," 8.

However, in the 1980s, as narrative criticism became popular in New Testament scholarship, a number of scholars began to study the narrative of the Fourth Gospel in earnest.[22] Narrative critics resisted the general tendency to pose historical and theological questions to the text, or to view the text as a "window" through which one might glimpse the Johannine community, and focused instead on literary features of the text and the impact upon readers of those literary features. Narrative criticism brought a "fresh methodological breeze" to the study of the Fourth Gospel.[23] Many new insights emerged from the study of narrative devices such as characterization, plot, irony, rhetoric, and conflict development.

2. The Fourth Gospel and the Roman Empire

This brief survey of major scholarly approaches to the Fourth Gospel oversimplifies, of course, for other approaches have been engaged throughout the history of its interpretation. However, attention to the impact of the Roman Empire on the Gospel's composition and content has been lacking until recently. The Roman Empire is the dominant historical context in which the entire New Testament emerged, including the Fourth Gospel. This fact alone suggests that consideration of the nature of the relationship between the empire and the Fourth Gospel is in order. Yet there are a number of other indications that the imperial context of this Gospel is in need of attention.

Musa Dube observes that "Imperial domination is central . . . to John's gospel as a whole."[24] The Fourth Gospel reflects an awareness of the realities of imperial power and rule in numerous ways. For example, it is unique among the Gospels in that it reports the Jewish authorities' fear that the popularity of Jesus will evoke a violent Roman response. The chief priests and Pharisees meet together and ironically declare the problem: "If we let [Jesus] go on like this, everyone will believe in him, and the Romans will come and destroy both our holy place and our nation" (John 11:48).[25] The powerful threat of Rome's military might was pervasive throughout the empire, even in territories in which legions were not

---

22. See especially Culpepper, *Anatomy*.

23. Conway, "There and Back Again," 77.

24. Dube, "Reading for Decolonization," 62.

25. See also 11:47–53. John differs from the Synoptic Gospels in that it describes the motivation for Jesus' death as fear of Roman violence.

stationed. During the Jewish revolt in 66–70 CE, Roman legions arrived from neighboring Syria and elsewhere to crush the uprising.

The Fourth Gospel is also flush with Roman titles, many of which were appropriated by early Christians and by the Fourth Evangelist and applied to Jesus. Appellations such as "Savior" (σωτήρ; John 4:42) and "Son of God" (υἱός τοῦ θεοῦ; e.g., 1:34) described the Roman Emperor in the first century.[26] Their use to describe Jesus suggests that they may be more appropriate designations for him than for the Roman emperor. Another title, "king" or "emperor" (βασιλεύς), is shared by both Jesus (1:49; 12:13, 15; 18:33, 37, 39; 19:3, 12, 14–15, 19, 21) and Caesar (19:15) in the Gospel of John.

The Fourth Gospel reflects an awareness of imperial realities in other, less obvious ways, as well. When Jesus and the Samaritan woman converse at the well, he declares to her, "You are right in saying, 'I have no husband'; for you have had five husbands, and the one you have now is not your husband" (John 4:17–18). Throughout the history of Johannine interpretation, this has usually been understood as a reference to the woman's illicit sexual history. Recently, however, some scholars have made a compelling case that the woman's personal history parallels the Samaritan national history as detailed in 2 Kings 17:24. That account suggests that when the Assyrians conquered the region in the eighth century BCE, they brought colonists from five foreign nations into Samaria, which resulted in intermarriage and worship of false gods. Thus, the Samaritan woman's personal history of marriage to five husbands and cohabitation with a sixth (Rome) may well symbolize the colonial history of Samaria.[27] The text thus reflects the reality that lies behind the surface-level distinction between Samaritans and Jews: the two groups lived in conflict and with distinct cultural markers as a result of the historical effects of imperial occupying forces.[28]

---

26. A number of sources attest the use of "savior" for Roman emperors. Josephus reports that Vespasian and Titus were both welcomed into cities with the honorific title "savior" (*J.W.* 3.459; 4.112–13; 7.70–71, 100–103, 119). An impressive number of other first-century emperors were lauded as "saviors," including Augustus, Tiberius, Nero, and Trajan. Hadrian, like Jesus, was called "savior of the world." See Koester, "Savior of the World," 665–80. For uses of the title "son of god" for Roman emperors, see Richey, *Roman Imperial Ideology*, 99–100. For the use of this title in inscriptions in Ephesus, see Tilborg, *Reading John in Ephesus*, 38–39.

27. See, for example, Koester, "Savior of the World," 675–76; and Schneiders, *Written That You May Believe*, 139–40.

28. Dube makes a similar argument in "Reading for Decolonization," 62–63.

Given these indications of the Johannine evangelist's awareness of the realities of Roman domination, it is important to ask: what is the Gospel of John's relationship to the Roman Empire, and how might this inform a reading of it? Historically, scholars have discerned little or no significant relationship between the two. Recently, however, a handful of scholars has begun to explore in earnest the intersections between the Roman Empire and the Gospel of John.

3. David K. Rensberger

David K. Rensberger made an early and significant contribution that effected a shift in the prevailing view that the Fourth Gospel lacks political implications.[29] Rensberger, building upon the work of Martyn and Brown, attempts to tease out some of the political implications of the Gospel and the historical context within which it was written. He also argues that Jesus' own interactions with Pilate in the "trial" scene served as a model for the Johannine community in its dealings with Romans.[30] In Rensberger's view, the Gospel advocates neither violent resistance against Rome nor quiet accommodation to imperial rule. Instead, it offers the Johannine audience a vision of Christian life within society as one of steadfast witness to the reality that Jesus—not Caesar—is the true king of the world. Rensberger was one of the first to contend that the Fourth Gospel assisted the Johannine community with the difficult task of negotiating Christian life within the Roman Empire.

Rensberger's study is also significant in that it presents a very different reading of Pontius Pilate in the Gospel. Prior to Rensberger, scholars tended to view John's Pilate as a weak, vacillating character who does not want to execute Jesus, but who caves to the demands of the powerful and coercive Jewish authorities.[31] Rensberger says that "by virtually universal consent, Pilate is seen in John as a more or less sympathetic figure, a man who wants to be fair, who would gladly acquit Jesus, but who through lack of resolve and susceptibility to political pressure all too easily becomes the tool of 'the Jews' and their malevolence."[32] Rudolf Bultmann,

---

29. Rensberger, "Politics of John," 395–411; and Rensberger, *Johannine Faith*.

30. Rensberger, *Johannine Faith*, 87–100.

31. For example, Barrett, *Gospel According to St. John*, 531–46; Bultmann, *Gospel of John*, 657–59, 665; Brown, *Gospel According to John*, 2:863–64, 872, 885–96; and Schnackenburg, *Gospel According to St. John*, 3:241–67.

32. Rensberger, *Johannine Faith*, 92.

for example, presented Pilate as a pitiable character who attempts to adopt a neutral stance in the conflict between Jesus and the Jewish authorities.[33] Similarly, Brown found that Pilate was "typical . . . of the many honest, well-disposed men who would try to adopt a middle position in a struggle that is total."[34] R. Alan Culpepper concluded that, "as in the other gospels, Pilate is coerced into authorizing Jesus' death" by the persistent Jewish authorities.[35] The Roman governor certainly appears to waver on how to handle the proceedings, and even seems to attempt to free Jesus, although he accedes in the end to Jewish demands.

In contrast, Rensberger insists that Pilate is the one character in this dramatic scene who emerges victorious: he elicits an ironic and tragic exclamation from the lips of the Jewish authorities: "We have no king but Caesar" (19:15). He is not a weak character after all, but instead strong, calculating, and cold. Pilate is indifferent to the fate of Jesus and contemptuous of the Jews, and uses this show trial not to ascertain Jesus' innocence or guilt, but to humiliate the Jews. He mocks the Jewish authorities throughout the proceedings, and in the end disgraces them by evoking their declaration of faith in the Roman emperor. This stunning statement on the lips of the Jewish authorities, that Caesar is their true king, finally satisfies Pilate. He has no further use for Jesus and sends him to be executed.

Rensberger's reading of Pontius Pilate in the Fourth Gospel has much more historical plausibility than previous interpretations. Several accounts from the first century suggest that Pilate was a powerful—not weak—governor who was often antagonistic toward the Jews. Josephus records how Pilate installed ensigns bearing Caesar's image in Jerusalem early in his rule, leading to mass protests from the populace (*Ant.* 18.55–59; *J. W.* 2.169–74).[36] Later, Pilate seized funds from the treasury of the Jerusalem temple in order to construct an aqueduct. When Jews protested, Pilate sent disguised troops into the crowds to assault the protesters (*Ant.* 18.60–62; *J. W.* 2.175–77). The Gospel of Luke alludes to another violent incident in which Pilate had Galileans killed in the temple (Luke 13:1–2). Given Pilate's historical reputation, Rensberger's interpretation of Pilate makes better sense of how the figure of Pilate would have reso-

33. Bultmann, *Gospel of John*, 655–65.
34. Brown, *Gospel According to John*, 2:864.
35. Culpepper, *Anatomy*, 142.
36. Throughout, citations from the works of Josephus are from Thackeray et al., *Josephus*.

nated with Johannine readers. Nevertheless, regardless of the historicity of John's presentation of Pilate, Rensberger makes a compelling case that Pilate is in firm command of the Johannine "trial" scene, and that there are political implications for Johannine readers.

4. Stephen D. Moore

Several authors have approached the Fourth Gospel from a postcolonial perspective, which lends itself naturally to a discussion of imperialism and the relationship between the Fourth Gospel and the Roman Empire.[37] Moore has made a significant contribution with *Empire and Apocalypse: Postcolonialism and the New Testament*, in which he argues that the "trial" scene in the Fourth Gospel poses a harsh critique of Roman imperial ideology in general, and Roman torture and justice in particular.[38] Moore insists that the location of the torture of Jesus in the middle of the Johannine "trial" rather than at its conclusion (as in the Synoptics) is significant; it suggests that the evangelist offers a critique of imperial torture, a cornerstone of the Roman order which imposes the will of the empire upon a colonized subject.[39] The scourging of Jesus in John is judicial torture because it occurs before his sentence is passed; it is not a "prelude to crucifixion" as in Mark or Matthew, or a "lesser punishment" that the Lukan Pilate hopes will avert Jesus' crucifixion. "Torture," Moore says, "is none other than the central mechanism designed to keep every Roman subject—slave, peasant, every other non-citizen, and, in certain cases, even citizens themselves—firmly in their respective, and respectful, places in relation to Roman imperial authority."[40] In Moore's view, the Johannine text pointedly draws attention to, and condemns, this brutal and inhumane means of imperial control.

Perhaps equally important, however, is that Moore highlights resistance to Roman imperial ideology in the Johannine text, while also noting tensions in the text that make it impossible to argue that the Fourth Gospel is wholly resistant to Rome. In many ways, for example, the ideology of the Gospel mimics the ideology of the Roman Empire. Like Rome,

---

37. See, for example, the collection of essays in Dube and Staley, *John and Postcolonialism*.
38. Moore, *Empire and Apocalypse*, 62.
39. Moore, *Empire and Apocalypse*, 60.
40. Moore, *Empire and Apocalypse*, 62.

Jesus and God also have an "empire" (John 3:3, 5; 18:36).[41] Jesus is granted imperial titles, such as "Savior of the world" and "King" (e.g., 4:42 and 12:13). Johannine Christianity, like early Christianity in general, could not help but model its understanding of the world and power dynamics on the Roman Empire. Moore says that "the Johannine resistance to Roman colonization might be said to be an alternative program of colonization yet more ambitious than the Roman: the annexation of the world by non-military means."[42] In Moore's view, the Johannine Jesus intends to do exactly what the Romans intend to do: conquer the world. Jesus himself declares that he has already completed the task: "I have conquered the world!" (16:33). John's Jesus, whose ministry focuses on Israel, begins his program of colonization with the Jewish homeland, with the ultimate intention of replacing Rome's entire empire with God's. The Fourth Gospel thus offers an implicit approval of conquest and hegemony as acceptable elements of imperialism.

Further, although a critique of some aspects of Roman imperialism is evident, the Fourth Gospel never explicitly envisions an end to Rome's empire or to Caesar's reign, according to Moore. Moore claims that, unlike Revelation, which unequivocally depicts the end of Rome (e.g., Rev 18:1–24), and the Synoptic Gospels, which implicitly envision the same (e.g., Mark 13; Matt 24–25; Luke 21), the Fourth Gospel assumes that Caesar will reign perpetually.[43] Moore says, "John's rejection of a death-sentence verdict for Rome . . . makes it the gospel of the imperial status quo."[44] John even entertains the idea that Caesar can serve as an agent of God's will, for the Gospel insinuates that the emperor carries out God's judgment on the Jews through the destruction of the Jerusalem temple (cf. 11:48).

Moore's contribution is significant in that it convincingly demonstrates that the Fourth Gospel offers specific critiques of certain elements of Roman imperialism. He also makes the case that the Gospel is not wholly opposed to Rome or its imperial ideology. Even as it critiques aspects of the empire, the Fourth Gospel mimics elements that it finds

41. The Greek term βασιλεία, commonly translated as "kingdom," can also be rendered "empire."

42. Moore, *Empire and Apocalypse*, 70.

43. Carter observes that many New Testament texts speak of God's judgment upon Rome and imply the end of Roman rule (*Roman Empire and the New Testament*, 18–19).

44. Moore, *Empire and Apocalypse*, 74.

useful for expressing its own worldview. For example, Jesus is depicted prominently as "king" (βασιλεύς) in the passion narrative (e.g., 19:3, 19), mimicking the title and function of Caesar himself (19:15). Moore's assessment fails to note, however, that the Fourth Gospel does anticipate the eventual end of the Roman Empire. The depiction of Jesus as the "Son of Man" (1:51; 3:13–14; 5:27; 6:27, 53, 62; 8:28; 9:35; 12:23, 34; 13:31), who receives "dominion and glory and kingship" (Dan 7:14) over all the peoples of the earth, does portend Rome's demise.[45]

5. Warren Carter

Warren Carter's *John and Empire: Initial Explorations* is the most comprehensive study to date of the Fourth Gospel's engagement with the Roman Empire. Carter writes extensively about the way in which the Gospel assists its audience in negotiating the realities of life under Roman imperial rule. He begins by arguing against traditional ways of reading John—individualistic, spiritualized readings, as well as "sectarian-synagogal" approaches—and insists that the determinative historical reality in the Fourth Gospel is not expulsion from the Jewish synagogue community, but rather more simply, and more importantly, the Roman Empire.

Carter's contribution is significant for several reasons. For one thing, he argues that the Johannine community is in all likelihood still associated with the synagogue community, rather than recently separated from it. He maintains that the Johannine Christians, like the synagogue community in which they participate, are significantly accommodated to life within the Roman Empire.[46] Carter argues that the Fourth Gospel exhibits a "rhetoric of distance" that urges "Jesus-believers to a less-accommodated and to a more-distinctive way of life as an antisociety or alternative community" against the synagogue, and especially Rome.[47] In his view, the polemic that the Fourth Gospel exhibits is not "descriptive," for it does not describe what has already happened between Johannine Christians and the synagogue. Rather, the polemic is "performative" in that the evangelist hopes it creates distance between the synagogue and the Johannine community. Carter demonstrates several ways in which the Gospel manifests this "rhetoric of distance."

---

45. See pp. 133–34 below.

46. This argument builds upon Carter's earlier work in *John: Storyteller*, esp. 155–74.

47. Carter, *John and Empire*, 82.

Carter's work is also significant because he views the Fourth Gospel as a "hidden transcript" of the Johannine author and supporters that resists Roman imperial domination.[48] Hidden transcripts represent the discourse of subordinate people when they are not in the presence of ruling authorities. Because direct confrontation with imperial power often leads to violent retaliation, open revolts and outright resistance are often avoided by subordinated and oppressed people. Instead, they may hide or disguise their resistance to domination in the form of what James C. Scott calls "hidden transcripts." As part of a Johannine hidden transcript, Carter argues that the Fourth Gospel challenges active participation in Roman imperial power and offers its audience a vision of reality different from Rome's. Thus, the Fourth Gospel, far from being apolitical or even conciliatory toward the Roman Empire, does offer resistance in the form of political discourse that occurs outside the presence of the ruling authorities.

6. Tom Thatcher

Tom Thatcher's recent volume, *Greater Than Caesar: Christology and Empire in the Fourth Gospel*, also offers a perspective on the Fourth Gospel in which the Roman Empire represents a significant piece of the contextual puzzle for interpreting the Gospel. He, too, argues that the Fourth Gospel is part of a hidden transcript of the Johannine community that responds to Roman imperial power. He suggests that the content of that hidden transcript represents a "countermemory," a way of presenting the events of the past and present in opposition to the official imperial version by a "reimagining" of how things happened.[49] For example, in the Gospel, Jesus does not die as a "treasonous sinner" on the Roman cross, but rather as one who willfully and intentionally embraces crucifixion by means of his own authority and power.

Thatcher also argues that John's response to the Roman Empire is embedded in the Gospel's Christology, in John's understanding and presentation of Jesus in the text. In Thatcher's view, the Fourth Evangelist presents Roman imperial power in the text as a "three-headed dog," composed of Caiaphas and the Jewish authorities, the Roman governor Pilate, and the Roman cross. The Fourth Gospel "slays" this "three-headed"

---

48. I will discuss James C. Scott's concept of "hidden transcripts" at length later on. See pp. 23–30 below.

49. Thatcher, *Greater Than Caesar*, 126–28.

Roman presence through the presentation of Jesus, specifically with a consistent motif highlighting that he is "greater than" these manifestations of imperial power.[50] For example, in his chapter devoted to Jesus' appearance before Pilate, Thatcher shows how Jesus is presented as the one who is in control of the proceedings, not Pilate. Thatcher has augmented recent "empire studies" by clarifying the presence of Roman imperial power in the Fourth Gospel (including the Jewish authorities as an example of imperial power) and by articulating the relationship between the Gospel's Christology and the empire.

7. Contribution

This study of the arrest, "trial," and execution scenes in John 18–19 seeks to expand upon these significant contributions to Johannine scholarship. It takes seriously the complex relationship between the Fourth Gospel and the Roman Empire, as well as the political implications of the Gospel, and it seeks to further clarify what those implications are. Like Carter and Thatcher, I view the Fourth Gospel as part of a "hidden transcript of resistance" to Roman imperialism. The resistance that it exhibits is not open, direct, and violent confrontation with imperialism, but rather subtle, nuanced resistance that offers a different vision of reality. I will also argue that this resistance mimics aspects of Roman imperial power in significant ways.

This project will focus specifically on the arrest, "trial," and execution scenes in John 18–19. These chapters deal most directly with Jesus' interactions with Roman imperial power in the Fourth Gospel, and thus are especially significant for understanding the Gospel's relation to Rome. The contribution that this project seeks to make is by means of a specific focus on ways in which aspects of John 18–19 function as part of the Johannine hidden transcript, with a special emphasis on the evangelist's use of irony to achieve that end.

Irony, which will be described at length, was particularly prominent in discussions of the Fourth Gospel in the first half of the 1980s. During the peak of literary interest in the Fourth Gospel, irony was of particular interest to scholars who were concerned with the effect that John's use of this literary device had on readers. When discussions of irony intersected with historical concerns, scholars described its relationship to the expulsion theory and the Johannine community's polemical relationship

---

50. Thatcher, *Greater Than Caesar*, 15–16.

to other Jews.⁵¹ This project will show that, whatever the Johannine community's relationship to the synagogue, the evangelist's use of irony was significant also for Christians living within the Roman Empire. It was one strategy for negotiating life within the empire and a powerful tool of resistance to many realities of imperial rule.

This study of irony in the Fourth Gospel will shed much-needed light on an overlooked topic within recent Johannine studies. Discussions of the Fourth Gospel and the Roman Empire are beginning to gain traction within the scholarly community. This project will further that scholarly conversation by connecting the discussion with the pervasive use of irony in the Fourth Gospel. It will assess the impact of the use of irony in the arrest, interrogation, and execution scenes in John 18–19 on the original audience and its guidance in their negotiation of life within the Roman Empire. This project also fills a need for a book-length project on these scenes, and the arrest scene in particular, which has received scant attention to date in discussions of the relationship between the Gospel and the empire. The final chapter will also discuss implications of this study for Christian engagement with the Fourth Gospel today. The remainder of this chapter will clarify aspects of the Fourth Gospel's historical context, and then describe the concepts of hidden transcripts and irony at length.

Historical Context of the Fourth Gospel

It is not possible to establish a conclusive answer to the question of the Fourth Gospel's authorship. Modern scholarship has rightly undermined the traditional view that it was written by Jesus' disciple John, the son of Zebedee, but has been unable to establish much by way of consensus beyond that. In addressing the question of authorship, Robert Kysar wisely proposes that "this figure stands too far back in the shadows of history for us to make out anything more than a vague outline."⁵² Adding to the difficulty is the fact that the Gospel was probably composed in stages, with multiple sources and contributors over a period of time.⁵³ For this reason,

---

51. See, for example, Duke, *Irony in the Fourth Gospel*, 149–50. Duke argues that the Jews are the most prominent and consistent victims of the Fourth Gospel's irony, and that this polemic fits well with the expulsion theories espoused by Brown and Martyn.

52. Kysar, *Maverick Gospel*, 34.

53. The text of the Fourth Gospel itself seems to suggest that more than one person

the primary concern of this project is with the completed redaction of the Gospel and its impact upon its original readers.

This form of the Gospel was probably completed sometime late in the first century. Manuscript evidence and quotations in several second-century writings suggest that the Fourth Gospel was widely known and in broad circulation by the mid-second century. This makes it likely that it was completed by at least the earliest part of the second century.[54] Internal evidence suggests composition sometime after 70 CE.[55] Like Brown, I find a date between 75 and 110 CE likely.[56]

What of the location of writing and the context of the Fourth Gospel? Church tradition connects its composition with Ephesus, and that location remains an intriguing possibility.[57] Ephesus did have a rather large Jewish population, and a number of scholars think it the best candidate, but others have suggested Syria, Alexandria, and even Palestine as

---

was involved in the composition of the document. The closing verses end with "This is *the disciple* who is testifying to these things and has written them, and *we* know that *his* testimony is true. But there are also many other things that Jesus did; if every one of them were written down, *I* suppose that the world itself could not contain the books that would be written" (21:24–25, italics mine). The "disciple whom Jesus loved" appears several times throughout the Gospel (e.g., 13:23–26; 19:25–27; 20:2–10; 21:7, 20–23). The "we" suggests a group reflected elsewhere in the text (e.g., 1:14, "we have seen his glory"; and 3:11, "we speak of what we know"). Finally, the "I" who speaks here fits well with the probability that chapter 21 is a later addition to the Fourth Gospel. Warren Carter suggests that behind the Fourth Gospel lies "a source ('the disciple'), an author or authors ('we' the evangelist), and an editor, or redactor ('I')." See Carter, *John: Storyteller*, 181. For speculation regarding the composition history of the Gospel, see also Bultmann, *Gospel of John*, 6–7; and Brown, *Gospel According to John*, xxxiv–xxxix.

54. P52, a papyrus fragment found in Egypt, has been dated to approximately 125 CEs, necessitating an earlier dating of the Fourth Gospel. The gnostic Heracleon wrote a commentary on the Gospel around the middle of the second century. Irenaeus, Melito of Sardis, Tatian, and Justin Martyr all also quote or seem to be aware of the Fourth Gospel before the end of the second century, suggesting that it had been in existence for a while and circulated widely.

55. The Fourth Gospel presupposes the destruction of the Jerusalem temple in 70 CE, both in 2:13–22 and in 11:47–53.

56. Brown, *Gospel According to John*, lxxxvi. There are, of course, numerous other suggestions, some of which are too precise, in my opinion, given the paucity of evidence. Regardless, I do not think that such a specific date is essential, at this juncture, for interpreting the text.

57. Irenaeus suggested this around 180 CE (*Haer.* 3.1.1). While his assertion is intriguing, his attribution of the Gospel to the "beloved disciple" makes his suggestion that it was composed in Ephesus suspect as well.

possible locations of composition.⁵⁸ It is even possible that the community was not entirely stationary. There is unfortunately little evidence in the Gospel itself to make any conclusive judgments regarding location.⁵⁹ Whatever its location, however, one fact is certain: the Fourth Gospel was written within the expansive territory ruled by Rome. Nothing in the Gospel hints of a location outside the empire.⁶⁰ Thus, realities of Roman imperial rule affected both the author(s) and readers of the Fourth Gospel. Coping with and negotiating issues and circumstances related to domination were thus part of the fabric of life for these early Christians.

Establishing the situation to which the Fourth Gospel responds is perhaps more instructive and significant for interpretation than is the identification of any particular author or place. First, however, some clarification is in order. By "Johannine community," I refer, in a broad sense, to the Christian community in which the Fourth Gospel was written and to whom it was addressed, most likely from its earliest to its final redaction. The earliest Johannine believers were probably both Jews and gentile "God-fearers." There is no reason to imagine that the Johannine community was a completely homogenous group, even though it is likely that its members had much in common. Members probably held

58. See O'Day, "Gospel of John: Introduction," 506–7; and Brown, *Introduction*, 368. There is also some discussion regarding whether or not the Fourth Gospel was even intended for readers in only one particular location. It is possible that the Gospel was written and intended for wider circulation, to address needs of Christian communities wherever they were located. See, e.g., Bauckham, *Gospels*. If this is true, it is worth noting that, given the diverse nature of early Christianity, the Gospel was still written from a particular viewpoint within Christianity. It has its own distinctly Johannine perspective on theology and the challenges and tasks facing Christians. See Cassidy, *New Perspective*, 4; and Kysar, *Maverick Gospel*, 26.

59. I appreciate Warren Carter's suggestion to locate the reading of the Fourth Gospel in Ephesus, the center of Roman imperial power in the province of Asia Minor, not because it was certainly written there, but rather because it was likely read there. Locating the Gospel within the context of Ephesus gives a stronger basis for making specific claims about the realities that Johannine Christians faced in the Roman imperial world. As Carter says, "An Ephesian context positions the Gospel and its audience in the Roman imperial world, a world much bigger than a solitary synagogue, in the era of the Flavian emperor Domitian (81–96 CE) and in the capital of the Roman province of Asia." See Carter, *John and Empire*, 53, as well as Tilborg, *Reading John in Ephesus*, who also locates the reading of the Fourth Gospel in Ephesus, not because it was necessarily written there, but in order to understand the interplay between particular words and phrases in the Gospel and inscriptions in Ephesus.

60. Cassidy also gives up on the frustrating attempt to locate the Gospel: "Wherever John's location when he published his Gospel, he published it within the geographical and political context of Roman rule" (Cassidy, *New Perspective*, 4).

diverse viewpoints, and the author or authors of the Gospel reflected a particular strain of thought within the community. Thus, by "Johannine community" I do not refer to a static, monolithic entity, but rather to the dynamic, living, breathing, diverse community to which the Fourth Gospel was addressed.

As noted above, the hypothesis that this Johannine community had recently been expelled from the synagogue community has faced serious challenges of late. It is simply no longer possible to state with certainty that the Johannine community was in conflict with the synagogue community.[61] While it is possible that some may have chosen to leave or perceived conflict with the synagogue community, there is no clear evidence that Johannine believers had been expelled. In the absence of such evidence, it is probable that many Johannine Christians maintained an ongoing relationship with the broader Jewish community.[62] Thus, the tensive relationship that the Fourth Gospel displays between Christ followers and other Jewish figures may be a creation of the evangelist and exist only at the level of the narrative itself.[63] The Fourth Gospel simply does not provide an easy or uniform answer to the relationship between Johannine believers and the broader Jewish community.

The larger Roman imperial context in which the Johannine community found itself is more significant for this project. Whatever the relationship between Johannine believers and the synagogue, neither the Johannine community nor the synagogue was isolated from the broader world of the empire. Synagogues were not reclusive, withdrawn communities, and were themselves places in which people had to make decisions

---

61. I appreciate Reinhartz's critique of Martyn's hypothesis, which demonstrates that it is possible to find at least three "models" for the relationship between Johannine Christians and the synagogue community if one adopts a two-level reading. In addition to the possibility of expulsion from the synagogue community, she highlights the sympathetic mourning by "many of the Jews" for Lazarus (11:19), as well as the fact that the Gospel reports that "many of the Jews were deserting and were believing in Jesus" (12:11). The two-level reading strategy employed by Martyn does not generate one simple solution to the question of the relationship between Johannine believers and the synagogue. It is possible that members of the Johannine community related in different ways to the greater synagogue community. See Reinhartz, *Befriending*, 37–53.

62. Carter observes that as late as the fourth century CE, John Chrysostom, the archbishop of Constantinople, was attempting to dissuade Christians from attending synagogues, which suggests that some were still doing so (*John and Empire*, 25).

63. Carter argues that this is the case, and that the Fourth Gospel seeks to disrupt the participation of believers in synagogue life (*John and Empire*, 19–45).

about how to negotiate the political realities of life under Roman rule.[64] Carter provides several examples of imperial negotiation in synagogues located in Asia Minor.

In one example, a Jewish group accepted the generosity of a wealthy gentile woman, Julia Severa, to build their synagogue at Akmoneia in the 80s or 90s CE. Even though this woman was a high priestess of the imperial cult, they were still receptive to her beneficence, and even honored her with an inscription in the synagogue. That they did not reject her support because of her cultic involvement shows their accommodation to this particular reality of Roman imperial rule. It is also noteworthy that this gentile woman concerned herself with the life of the synagogue. The Jewish community must have maintained a significant level of civic involvement to have attracted the attention and generosity of such a patron. This particular Jewish community was not a withdrawn group, but rather participated in meaningful ways in Roman imperial society.[65]

In another example from much earlier, around the turn of the century, Jews living in Asia offered a declaration to honor Emperor Augustus as a response to his goodwill in allowing Jews to observe their religious practices. Josephus records this inscription on a temple dedicated to the Emperor:

> Caesar Augustus, Pontifex Maxiumus with tribunician power, decrees as follows. *Since the Jewish nation has been found well disposed to the Roman people* not only at the present time but also in time past, and especially in the time of my father the emperor Caesar, as has their high priest Hyrcanus, it has been decided by me and my council under oath, with the consent of the Roman people, that the Jews may follow their own customs in accordance with the law of their fathers, just as they followed them in the time of Hyrcanus, high priest of the Most High God, and that their sacred monies shall be inviolable and may be sent up to Jerusalem and delivered to the treasurers in Jerusalem, and that they need not give bond (to appear in court) on the Sabbath or on the day of preparation for it (Sabbath Eve) after the ninth hour. And if anyone is caught stealing their sacred books or their sacred monies from a synagogue or an ark (of the Law), he shall be regarded as sacrilegious, and his property shall

---

64. We even see hints of this in the Fourth Gospel when the Jewish leaders worry that Rome will come to destroy the temple and when they collaborate with the Romans to execute Jesus. See John 11:47–53 and chapters 18–19.

65. Carter, *John and Empire*, 32–33.

be confiscated to the public treasury of the Romans. *As for the resolution which was offered by them in my honour* concerning the piety which I show to all men, and on behalf of Gaius Marcius Censorinus, I order that it and the present edict be set up in the most conspicuous [part of the temple] assigned to me by the federation of Asia in Ancyra. (*Ant.* 16.162–65; italics added)

This inscription illustrates Jewish participation in imperial society by calling attention to a testimonial honoring the emperor, and also hints at ongoing Jewish participation and acceptance in the empire.

In addition to documenting Jewish interaction with the broader imperial society, both of these examples highlight the fact that Jews and Christians who participated in synagogue life had to make decisions about how to live under the realities of Roman rule. Can a Jewish synagogue accept the financial support of a priestess of the imperial cult? Can Jewish authorities honor the Roman emperor, who, like the Jewish God, claims lordship over the entire world? Other issues required decisions as well, such as whether to participate in certain religious and civic rituals and festivals. In the examples given above, Jewish leaders answered affirmatively. Accommodation to imperial realities certainly provided many advantages.

Johannine Christians also had to negotiate realities of life in the empire. Questions of lordship (e.g., who is the true lord of the world?), divine right to reign, responses to military might and harsh rule, taxation, and social structures all constituted issues with which the Johannine community would have had to contend. In the New Testament, it is clear that different Christian groups responded in different ways to these challenges of living within the Roman world. Revelation, for example, takes a clear stance against the Roman Empire and any positive engagement with its civic, religious, economic, and political life.[66] First Peter, however, exhorts its audience to "accept the authority of every human institution, whether the emperor as supreme, or of governors" and to "honor the emperor" (1 Pet 2:14-15, 17; cf. Rom 13:1-7).[67] Carter maintains that, because they were likely still involved with the synagogue community,

---

66. It is apparent, however, that many Christians in the various churches addressed by Revelation do not take this approach (e.g., the church at Thyatira addressed in 2:18–29).

67. Carter argues that this includes the requirement to participate in sacrifices and cultic observances. See Carter, "Going All the Way," 14–33.

Johannine Christians were relatively accommodated to Roman rule.[68] Yet, at least some within the Johannine community—the Fourth Evangelist and supporters at the very least—must have opposed elements of Roman imperialism because, as we will see, the Fourth Gospel displays some resistance to empire. Some scholars have also argued that at least some Johannine Christians experienced persecution.[69] There is no reason to believe that all Johannine believers experienced identical circumstances or responded in similar fashion to imperial rule. The Fourth Gospel has the capacity to assist believers in varied circumstances to negotiate life in the empire while also resisting Roman domination. To some it might offer hope and encouragement within the Roman imperial context. To others it might provoke a more antithetical relationship to the empire. While expressions of resistance surface in many ways throughout the Gospel, the remainder of this chapter will indicate the specific focus of this project's contribution to an understanding of Johannine negotiation and resistance.

JAMES C. SCOTT AND HIDDEN TRANSCRIPTS

Because open rebellion was relatively uncommon within the Roman Empire in the first century, some scholars have maintained that, for the most part, its inhabitants were quietly and happily adjusted to life under Roman rule.[70] The extremes of violent revolution and peaceful acquiescence, however, are not the only options available for persons living under dominating imperial rule. Accordingly, political scientist and anthropologist James C. Scott's concept of "hidden transcripts" has been of interest in New Testament studies in recent years. In the absence of overt, violent opposition to the Roman Empire within early Christianity, it provides scholars with a way of talking about resistance to imperialism that is not violently rebellious, but nevertheless active. I will employ Scott's model to argue that, in the Fourth Gospel, we can see manifestations of a Johannine hidden transcript that assisted early Christians in negotiating life under the domination of the Roman Empire.

---

68. See, for example, Carter, *John and Empire*, 45.

69. See, for example, Cassidy, *New Perspective*, 110–13; and Brown, *Gospel According to John*, 2:691.

70. See, for example, Ando, *Imperial Ideology*.

During the Roman era, there were, to be sure, some overt resistance movements against imperial rule. The province of Judea, in particular, was at times a hotbed of resistance activity. The Jewish revolt of 66 to 70 CE and the Bar Kochba revolt in the early second century (ca. 132-35 CE) were both failed attempts to liberate the province from Roman rule. Such overt resistance was observable and readily recorded by elite writers. Thus, Josephus reports a number of such uprisings and resistance movements during the early centuries of the Roman Empire. When Herod came to power in 40 BCE, Judeans and Galileans alike waged guerrilla warfare against Herod's administration and the Roman troops under his command (*J.W.* 1.314-30; *Ant.* 14.430-54). Following Herod's death in 4 BCE, a number of revolts sprang up in Jerusalem, Galilee, and Perea (*J.W.* 2.56-65; *Ant.* 17.271-85). Furthermore, when the Romans installed the first governor of the Judean province in 6 CE, two leaders organized resistance to reject payment of the tribute to Rome, which would have implicitly acknowledged the lordship of Caesar (*J.W.* 2.118).[71]

In the Fourth Gospel, however, there are no calls to arms against the Roman Empire and its agents, nor does it explicitly envision any sort of violent downfall of the empire.[72] Does that mean that the author or authors of the Fourth Gospel and its audience were complacent and content with their lives within the empire? Did the Gospel offer no critique or assistance for Johannine followers endeavoring to negotiate realities of life within the empire? This is where Scott's model is helpful in providing a way forward. It reminds us that overt resistance is the tip of an iceberg—whatever is visible to the eye masks a much larger reality that lies covertly beneath the surface. Resistance takes many forms which are concealed from those in power, especially since openly political and rebellious acts by subordinate classes are often quickly crushed by ruling authorities. Scott reminds us that "peasant rebellions, let alone peasant 'revolutions,' are few and far between," because they "are nearly always crushed unceremoniously."[73] Nevertheless, there are what Scott calls "everyday forms" of resistance which provide a gamut of "weapons" for those with little or no power. Acts such as foot dragging, pilfering, false

---

71. For more information, see Horsley, *Jesus and Empire*, 35-54.

72. Recall that Moore does not believe the Fourth Gospel contains any anticipation of the end of the Roman Empire at all (*Empire and Apocalypse*, 73-74). Carter, however, contests this perspective (*John and Empire*, 337-42). I argue below that the Gospel does anticipate the end of the Roman Empire. See pp. 133-34 below.

73. Scott, *Weapons of the Weak*, 29.

compliance, feigned ignorance, slander, and sabotage, for example, provide small opportunities for resistance and disrupt (however slightly) the constant endeavor of elites to extract wealth, labor, taxes, food, rent, and tribute from the lower classes. These small acts of resistance also sustain the dignity and autonomy of oppressed peoples.

Let us turn, then, to Scott's model of hidden transcripts and how it might inform a reading of the Fourth Gospel. Scott's overriding concern in his book *Domination and the Arts of Resistance: Hidden Transcripts* is to understand the effect of domination on subordinate people, and how they negotiate and resist that domination. In the process, he illustrates the difference between what he calls "public" and "hidden transcripts."

Scott classifies the sum total of all open, overt interactions that take place between subordinate people and those who exercise control as the "public transcript." Scott describes this as the "onstage" interactions between the two groups. These interactions may include, among other things, parades, festivals, speeches, and public rituals and punishments, in which members of both the subordinate and the dominant class are present. Public transcripts are "shaped to appeal to the expectations of the powerful" and are thus the "official" and "appropriate" engagements between the two groups.[74] For example, subjects bow as a ruler passes by and they use appropriate honorifics when addressing him. Subordinate individuals clap at the end of a speech from the governor even though they might detest the man himself, because that is the "appropriate" response to the speech.

However, Scott argues that subordinate groups also cultivate "hidden transcripts" out of the view and influence of the dominant. These hidden transcripts comprise both speech and actions that challenge, resist, inflect, and even confirm aspects of the public transcripts. While subject persons might wear a mask of acquiescence when in the presence of the dominant elite, they often have the capacity to develop and express their own perspectives, worldviews, and practices "off-stage," within a social space sequestered from the dominant.

Scott gives an example of the disparity between the content of public and hidden transcripts by drawing on an example from the antebellum US South. In the account, Aggy, a black cook, looks on helplessly and does not intervene as her daughter is unjustly beaten. However, when the master is out of earshot, Aggy says to a trusted friend:

---

74. Scott, *Domination*, 2.

> "Thar's a day a-comin'! Thar's a day a-comin'! ... I hear the rumblin ob de chariots! I see de flashin ob de guns! White folks blood is a runnin on the ground like a ribber, and de dead's heaped up dat high! ... Oh Lor! Hasten de day when de blows, an de bruises, and de aches an de pains, shall come to de white folks, an de buzzards shall eat dem as dey's dead in de streets."

Aggy's response in the presence of the master represents the "appropriate conduct" of slaves according to the unspoken public transcripts between white power-holders and subordinate black slaves in the South. However, her comments to her friend reveal her true feelings and represent part of a "hidden transcript" that resists the public transcripts of deference and envisions divine vengeance on her master in the near future.

1. Four Modes of Political Discourse

In light of the distinction between public and hidden transcripts, Scott identifies four modes of political discourse available to subordinate groups. The first intersects with the public transcript itself: subordinates can openly appeal to the self-image of elites, using flattery or ideological justification to harness political leverage for their own benefit. This is the safest and most overt means of political discourse available to subordinates. For example, slaves might appeal to a master for certain concessions by prefacing their request with a flattering statement such as, "Because you are such a generous master." The master, who likely perceives himself as generous, may be more likely to grant such concessions.

Scott's second mode of political discourse is the "hidden transcript" itself. In contrast to the public transcript, this discourse takes place "offstage" among subject people, out of sight of the dominant elite. Here, without fear of repercussion or retaliation, subordinates are free and safe to speak and act as they wish. Thus, the hidden transcript often contains angry, vengeful words that reject the content of the public transcripts, as well as "offstage parody, dreams of violent revenge, millennial visions of a world turned upside down."[75] Scott says that hidden transcripts contain all "speeches, gestures, and practices that confirm, contradict, or inflect what appears in the public transcript."[76]

Scott discusses a third mode of political discourse "that lies strategically between the first two," which he calls the "politics of disguise and

---

75. Scott, *Domination*, 9.
76. Scott, *Domination*, 4–5.

anonymity."[77] In this mode, "the hidden transcript is typically expressed openly—albeit in disguised form."[78] This expression of the hidden transcript takes place in the public sphere, but is characterized by obscurity. Words and actions often take on a double meaning, or the speaker or actor is anonymous.[79] Scott groups rumors, gossip, folktales, jokes, songs, rituals, codes, and euphemisms under this category. He says that this subdued, ambiguous version of the hidden transcript is always present in the public discourse between subordinate groups and power holders. Scott uses the stories of Brer Rabbit to illustrate his point: "At one level these are nothing but innocent stories about animals; at another level they appear to celebrate the cunning wiles and vengeful spirit of the weak as they triumph over the strong."[80]

The final mode of political discourse that Scott describes is the "rupture" of the hidden transcript onto the stage of the public transcripts. Scott calls this "the most explosive realm," where subordinates engage in open, overt defiance of their superiors.[81] The hidden transcript essentially becomes public, and typically leads to conflict and some form of violent repression on the part of the dominant. In the example given above, if Aggy repeated her diatribe in front of her master, it would likely lead to either some swift punishment, or, if unanswered, further words and acts of resistance by Aggy in the future. Josephus records an outburst of aggression by Jews that also illustrates this mode of discourse. Jewish discontent against the Roman imperial presence in Jerusalem "ruptured" into the public realm when a group of men destroyed—in broad daylight—a golden eagle statue that Herod had placed over the gate to the temple. This openly defiant act was met with a swift response: Herod's soldiers quickly attacked and arrested the large group of dissidents (*J.W.* 17.152–57).

---

77. Scott, *Domination*, 19.

78. Scott, *Domination*, xii–xiii.

79. For example, the epigraph in Scott's book is an ancient saying, "When the great lord passes the wise peasant bows deeply and silently farts." The peasant appears to be following the public transcripts of deference and respect while anonymously objecting to the proceedings (Scott, *Domination*, v).

80. Scott, *Domination*, 19.

81. Scott, *Domination*, 19.

2. Applicability of Scott's Model to the Fourth Gospel

A number of scholars have begun to discuss various texts and aspects of the New Testament in relation to Scott's model of hidden transcripts. Horsley declares, "According to scholarly consensus, the Gospel of Mark and the speeches of Jesus paralleled in Matthew and Luke ('Q') arose from and addressed communities of Jesus-followers who were opposed to and opposed by the rulers," and thus it is suitable to talk about them with respect to hidden transcripts.[82] Aside from Mark and Q, however, some of these same scholars have been more reticent to speak of hidden transcripts in relation to other texts of the New Testament. Speaking of the "later" New Testament writings, Horsley argues that "[t]he later literate leadership and literary products of what had become 'early Christianity,' such as Luke (Luke–Acts) and those who claimed to be writing in Paul's name (the Pastoral Epistles) still addressed communities of subordinate people, although they have clearly acquiesced in various ways to the dominant order."[83] However, not all of the later writings of the New Testament recommend accommodation to Roman rule as the most appropriate response to the empire. Revelation, for example, which was most likely written during the late first century, clearly resists many aspects of Roman imperialism and is highly critical of the empire. Recently, some scholars have also begun to speak of the way in which the Fourth Gospel is illuminated by Scott's notion of hidden transcripts.[84]

To what extent is Scott's model helpful for understanding the Fourth Gospel, and more specifically, John 18–19? Scott argues that every group that experiences some form of domination or oppression exhibits a hidden transcript of resistance in the face of that domination.[85] Horsley agrees: "Domination evokes resentment and resentment evokes resistance."[86] Scott's understanding of "hidden transcripts" does not demand that a group or community be poor or enslaved, but only that they be subordinate in some fashion.[87] Domination in all forms exacts a toll.

---

82. Horsley, "Introduction," 14.

83. Horsley, "Introduction," 14. This has by no means been a consensus, however.

84. Notably, Carter, *John and Empire*; and Thatcher, *Greater Than Caesar*.

85. Scott, *Domination*, xii.

86. Horsley, "Introduction," 8.

87. Even today, it is possible to detect hidden transcripts in many varied circumstances of "domination." In workplaces, employees frequently whisper about their manager behind his or her back, and the forced deference that professors receive in

It deprives persons of some measure of autonomy and dignity, and also engenders feelings such as inferiority, discontent, and anger. Domination also comes in different forms. Among the forms that are relevant to this study are material, status, and ideological domination.[88]

In the first century, material domination manifested itself in the way that taxes (grain, etc.) and other appropriations were funneled from rural areas to local cities, and then from those cities to Rome itself. Peter Garnsey and Richard Saller aptly describe Rome as a "parasite city," which appropriated the wealth of the provinces.[89] Nearly every person in the empire would have felt some degree of this form of domination. It is harder to determine to what degree the Johannine evangelist or community might have experienced status domination, because it is difficult to determine the social status of the majority of community members. Status domination includes the "rituals of hierarchy, deference, speech, punishment, and humiliation" that were routine in the Roman world.[90] Status domination is evident, however, in Jesus' appearance before Pilate, when a person of relatively low status (Jesus) is interrogated by the Roman governor, who stood near the top of the social status pyramid. Pilate presides over the proceedings which are intended to punish and humiliate: Jesus is tortured (19:1), taunted and slapped (19:3), paraded about (19:13), and finally executed (19:18). Finally, the surest and clearest form of domination experienced by Johannine Christians would have been ideological domination. Scott argues that "resistance to ideological domination requires a counter-ideology."[91] Such a counter-ideology is indeed evident in the Fourth Gospel. The Roman worldview, in which Caesar was the one true "Lord" and "Savior" and was god-ordained to rule, stood in stark contrast to the worldview evident in the Fourth Gospel. We will see Johannine negotiation of, and resistance to, this ideological domination in the arrest, interrogation, and crucifixion scenes.

---

the classroom often dissipates into rumors and gossip the moment students leave the class. Hidden transcripts represent the offstage discourse of the subordinate in which they dialogue, restore dignity, and stand in solidarity with others, no matter what form their oppression takes.

88. Scott, *Domination*, 111.

89. Garnsey and Saller, *Roman Empire*, 8. A more recent study, however, has contested the strict "parasitic" view by demonstrating that the city of Rome did provide some benefits to the surrounding region, such as promoting agricultural development, at the very least. See Morley, *Metropolis and Hinterland*.

90. Scott, *Domination*, 111.

91. Scott, *Domination*, 118.

Thus, it is appropriate to speak of hidden transcripts as they relate to the Fourth Gospel, since the community to which it was first addressed would have experienced some forms of domination living under Roman imperial rule. The Fourth Gospel itself, however, is not a—or the—"hidden transcript" of the Johannine community. It is only part of the Johannine hidden transcript. The Fourth Gospel gives us a glimpse into the hidden transcript of that community, or at the very least, of the person or persons responsible for producing the Gospel. Richard Horsley, discussing Paul's letters, asserts that "the hidden transcripts . . . are not Paul's letters themselves, but [rather] the evolving discourses of the communities . . . Paul's letters are a window into that process."[92] The hidden transcript of the Johannine community is the full measure of political discourse that took place outside the observation of the dominant elite, within the safety of the community, and the Fourth Gospel provides a window into this political discourse.

The Fourth Gospel might also offer a glimpse into the politics of anonymity and disguise that characterize the community's negotiation of life within the Roman Empire. The Fourth Gospel was most likely not written for elite consumption, and thus does not represent a direct form of disguised resistance in the public sphere. Nevertheless, it showcases a strategy for expressing the Johannine hidden transcript in an open, yet disguised, fashion: irony. Because irony has multiple levels of meaning that are only understood by "insiders" with the knowledge required to interpret it, this device presents an ideal tool for the Johannine community to insinuate its hidden transcript into the public sphere without fear of retaliation.[93]

Overview of Irony as a Literary Device

The Fourth Evangelist has been described as a "master of irony."[94] I will argue that one of the major expressions of the Johannine hidden

---

92. Horsley, "Introduction," 19.

93. It is possible that the Johannine community already employed irony in their negotiation of life within the empire. There is no way of knowing for sure, but that might help account for the prominent use of irony in the Gospel. If the community does not already employ irony to express its hidden transcript, then the Gospel's use of irony certainly offers it as a possible strategy for the community to employ in the future.

94. See, for example, Culpepper, *Anatomy*, 166; and Meeks, "Divine Agent," 59.

transcript in the Pilate scenes is the literary device of irony, which shows up frequently in the Gospel. The pervasive use of this literary device in John 18–19 demands that we give it careful attention in order to understand its meaning and implications. Three major literary studies in the mid-1980s by R. Alan Culpepper, Paul D. Duke, and Gail R. O'Day critically examined the presence of irony in the Fourth Gospel. However, none of them attended to the impact of irony on an understanding of the relationship between the Gospel and the Roman imperial world.[95] Here, I will lay out briefly my understanding of the device—what it is and what it does—and point to the way in which it will inform my understanding of the texts in question.

1. Definition

While definitions of irony vary from scholar to scholar, they nevertheless have much in common.[96] At its basic level, irony might be called "the mode of the unsaid, the unheard, the unseen."[97] Irony happens in the relationship between what is said and the meaning that is conveyed in the "unsaid." However, this alone is not enough to distinguish irony from other literary devices, such as metaphor. Irony often entails an antithetical or nearly opposite meaning to what one says, although this is not always the case.[98] It also involves real or imagined "victims" of the irony, who are unaware of the deeper meanings.

Duke, writing specifically about irony in the Fourth Gospel, offers the following definition: "Irony as a literary device is a double-leveled literary phenomenon in which two tiers of meaning stand in some opposition to each other and in which some degree of unawareness is expressed or implied."[99] Culpepper describes irony by saying that the "narrator

---

95. Culpepper, *Anatomy*; Duke, *Irony in the Fourth Gospel*; and O'Day, *Revelation in the Fourth Gospel*.

96. Scholars often point out the extent to which irony resists a conclusive definition. See, for example, Sharp, *Irony and Meaning*, 20.

97. Hutcheon, *Irony's Edge*, 9.

98. Wayne C. Booth argues that irony rejects the meaning that is plainly stated (*Rhetoric of Irony*, 10). This is often the case, but not always. I agree with Hutcheon who says that "the 'ironic' meaning is not, then, simply the unsaid meaning, and the unsaid is not always a simple inversion or opposite of the said: it is always different—*other than* and more than the said" (*Irony's Edge*, 12–13).

99. Duke, *Irony in the Fourth Gospel*, 17. While irony is not limited to literature, the concern in this project is to understand irony in a particular text. Thus, a thorough discussion of nonliterary manifestations of irony is not needed.

means more than he says and ... the characters do not understand what is happening or what they are saying" and that "the implied author smiles, winks, and raises his eyebrows as the story is told."[100] Carolyn J. Sharp observes that "[i]rony is a performance of misdirection that generates aporetic interactions between an unreliable 'said' and a truer 'unsaid' so as to persuade us of something that is subtler, more complex, or more profound than the apparent meaning."[101] And O'Day asserts, "There is always some kind of opposition between the two levels of meaning in irony—either contradiction, incongruity, or incompatibility," which distinguishes it from other literary devices, such as allegory and metaphor.[102]

While these definitions and perspectives differ, there are points of commonality. Irony operates on at least two levels of meaning: the meaning that is expressly stated, and the additional meaning that is communicated to an aware reader or listener. This meaning may or may not be directly opposed to the plainly stated meaning, but some form of opposition is conveyed. And irony carries with it an implication that some readers or listeners will be aware of and recognize it, while others will not.

2. Types of Irony

The term "irony" itself encapsulates many forms of communication in literature, in other forms of media, and in reality itself. "Irony" encompasses verbal, dramatic, and situational ironies, although it is not strictly limited to these types. Each of these three types—verbal, dramatic, and situational—may also be broken down further into subcategories. The discussion here will provide a brief overview of the different types of irony. Further details will be noted as specific cases are discussed in later chapters.

Verbal irony is a "statement in which the implied meaning intended by the speaker differs from that which he ostensibly asserts."[103] For example, Jesus' comment to his opponents in John 10:32 may be understood sarcastically: "I have shown you many good works from the Father. For which of these are you going to stone me?" On the surface level, Jesus asks them to identify the works for which they intend to kill him. However, Jesus—and presumably the opponents as well—know that there is

---

100. Culpepper, *Anatomy*, 165–66.
101. Sharp, *Irony and Meaning*, 24.
102. O'Day, *Revelation in the Fourth Gospel*, 23.
103. Abrams, *Glossary*, 80.

no work they can name that would justify killing him. In addition to sarcasm, verbal irony includes understatement, overstatement, litotes, and rhetorical questions, among other things.[104]

Dramatic irony is, in some ways, the reverse of verbal irony. Duke notes that "while verbal irony is achieved by an intentional speaker who knows more than may be apparent, dramatic irony employs a speaker (or actant) who knows less than is apparent and whose involvement in the irony is quite unintentional."[105] Sedgewick observes that "[d]ramatic irony, in brief, is the sense of contradiction felt by the spectators of a drama who see a character acting in ignorance of his condition."[106] The steward's final comment at the wedding at Cana may be understood as an example of dramatic irony: "Everyone serves the good wine first, and then the inferior wine after the guests have become drunk. But you have kept the good wine until now" (2:10). The author and audience know the true source of this "good wine," while the steward is left in the dark, an unwitting participant in the irony. The Pharisees' statement in John 12:19 may also be considered dramatic irony: "You see, you can do nothing. Look, the world has gone after him!" The Pharisees surely intend hyperbole, but unwittingly speak truth in this exchange. They inadvertently say more than they know in their statement. The audience possesses more knowledge than the Pharisees in the story, and thus is capable of grasping the deeper meaning expressed by the text.

Situational irony describes events in which an actual outcome is incongruous with the expected outcome. The events may include sharp contradictions, or the narrative may take a distinct turn away from what the audience ought to have anticipated. Duke suggests that the prophet Amos's image of fleeing a lion only to be met by a bear constitutes situational irony.[107] The means of escape—fleeing the lion—instead leads to one's demise at the hands of another threat. I will argue in chapter 3 below that Jesus' confrontation with the Roman army and Jewish police in John 18 involves situational irony. Though he is unarmed and vastly out-

---

104. Duke observes that verbal irony also includes "ambiguity, analogy, parody, insinuation, incongruity, pretended error, pretended doubt, and other dissimulating devices" (*Irony in the Fourth Gospel*, 23). While some expressions of verbal irony conceal the author or speaker's intent, some such as sarcasm hardly conceal the deeper meaning at all.

105. Duke, *Irony in the Fourth Gospel*, 23.

106. Sedgewick, *Of Irony*, 52.

107. See Duke, *Irony in the Fourth Gospel*, 26; and Amos 5:19.

numbered, Jesus is able to overpower his opponents by simply declaring his divine identity.

3. Purpose of Irony

Like its definition, irony and its various forms resist the attempts to identify one universal purpose or function. The power of the unsaid allows irony to communicate many things with various results. D. C. Muecke attributes three uses to irony, while Linda Hutcheon identifies nine functions, compiled from her survey of other theorists.[108] For example, irony may reinforce established beliefs, or merely underline a point an author wishes to make. It has the ability to playfully tease or the capacity to deliver critical judgments. It can engender and reinforce new community, or create an "in-group" while excluding others.[109] Sharp says that within sacred texts, irony has the "power for deconstruction and for building, for affirmation and subversion, for liberation and for scathing indictment."[110] In view of the variety of purposes and effects of irony, it is helpful to divide its many functions into two broad categories, as Duke proposes. Duke delineates a positive and a negative function for irony, saying that it can be used both as an *appeal* and as a *weapon*.[111]

When it functions as an *appeal*, irony invites a reader to reject the surface-level meaning of a given statement or situation, and "to leap to the higher level and share the perspective of the implied author."[112] Irony is appealing in this sense as readers become aware of the higher meaning of dialogue or events that are transpiring in the story. As a result of this awareness, they feel superior to characters in the story, or to an imagined audience, all of whom fail to grasp that meaning.

In the same vein, G. B. Caird says that irony creates "a double audience, the first understanding nothing beyond the face value of the words, the second seeing both the deeper meaning and the incomprehension of the first."[113] This second audience—readers who grasp the ironic mean-

---

108. Muecke, *Compass of Irony*, 46–56.

109. Hutcheon highlights the often opposing functions of irony by saying that it has the power "to ingratiate and to intimidate, to underline and to undermine; it brings people together and drives them apart" (*Irony's Edge*, 56).

110. Sharp, *Irony and Meaning*, 34.

111. Duke, *Irony in the Fourth Gospel*, 36–42.

112. Culpepper, *Anatomy*, 167.

113. Caird, *Language and Imagery*, 104.

ing—will often imagine an audience that fails to understand the ironic communication (the first audience). Whether or not there is an actual audience that misses the irony depends on the nature of the text. Nevertheless, this sense of superiority is one of the reasons that irony is appealing to readers.

Sharp maintains that this "persuasive force of irony works through its construction of community."[114] Irony seeks to unite readers who "get it," creating a group of "insiders" who share—at least in part—the perspective of the author. Muecke says that irony is appealing because it is "more than a riddle or a message in code; it is something to be savoured, not merely solved."[115] Ironic communication is sophisticated and stimulating, and it is enjoyable and appealing to the reader who grasps its deeper meaning.

The crucifixion scene in the Fourth Gospel serves as one example where irony functions as an appeal to readers to share the author's perspective. In it, Pilate has an inscription affixed to Jesus' cross that declares him "The King of the Jews" (19:19). While Pilate does not believe the statement on the inscription is true—it no doubt functions as mockery and serves to antagonize the Jewish authorities—it is ironic in the sense that Pilate has truthfully and unwittingly declared the identity of Jesus. Readers are able to grasp the truth in the inscription, even as the characters in the story miss its full meaning. This "aha moment" leads readers to share the perspective of the evangelist, that Jesus is in fact King, and reinforces the belief of those who already share that perspective.[116]

All of the above constitute "positive" uses of irony as an appeal. However, irony's negative use comes into view when it functions as a *weapon*. While irony invites readers to make an intellectual jump to a higher level of meaning to share the perspective of the author, it creates "a strong sense of rejecting a whole structure of meanings, a kind of world that the author himself obviously rejects."[117] Because of this, irony has the capacity to exhibit a judgmental attitude or offer a negative evaluation of people or ideologies. As Duke observes, "while Irony has her allurements

---

114. Sharp, *Irony and Meaning*, 12.

115. Muecke, "Irony Markers," 366.

116. Hutcheon says that irony is also often "used to reinforce . . . established attitudes" (*Irony's Edge*, 10).

117. Booth, *Rhetoric of Irony*, 36.

and richly rewards those who dance with her, she can be positively cruel to her enemies."[118]

Irony as a weapon targets its "victims," both unaware characters within the story as well as real-life persons and ideologies. Irony creates "victims" who fail to grasp its meaning, and targets "enemies" with its biting sting. Irony often has a "mocking intent," and has the power to deride various "persons, attitudes, beliefs, social customs, philosophical systems, or even life itself."[119] This weapon is indirect, of course—the victim of irony is usually unaware of the attack.[120] As Duke points out, irony's "aim is not so much to vanquish as to expose."[121] Irony can serve as a means of resistance, but not aggressive, violent resistance.

Irony functions both as *appeal* and as *weapon* throughout the Fourth Gospel. Irony's functions often overlap or occur simultaneously.[122] In the example given above, when Pilate places the inscription on Jesus' cross, the irony not only appeals to readers, but it also mocks Pilate, who unwittingly speaks truth but does not accept it. In the chapters to come, I will argue that through the use of irony in the Pilate scenes, the Johannine evangelist both appeals to readers to adopt a perspective in opposition to Roman imperial ideology and "attacks" the Roman Empire and the values of the dominant members of its society.

4. Audience Shared Knowledge

For irony to fulfill its purpose and convey its meaning effectively, it requires two things. First, the audience must possess relevant knowledge in common with the speaker of the ironic communication. Second, the speaker must provide some sort of "markers" to identify the presence of irony. Without shared knowledge, the meaning of the irony would be lost on the reader, who would grasp one level of meaning, but miss the multi-layered meaning and the "unsaid" communication intended by the speaker. However, a properly informed reader would be able to grasp the meaning. Hutcheon says that irony relies "on the presence of a common memory shared by addresser and addressee," as well as "mutually shared

---

118. Duke, *Irony in the Fourth Gospel*, 39.

119. Hutcheon, *Irony's Edge*, 26; and Duke, *Irony in the Fourth Gospel*, 40.

120. This fact sits well with the idea that irony is a component of the Johannine hidden transcript and the politics of anonymity and disguise.

121. Duke, *Irony in the Fourth Gospel*, 41.

122. Duke suggests this as well (*Irony in the Fourth Gospel*, 36).

background knowledge."[123] For example, in John 11:48, the chief priests and Pharisees discuss the trouble that Jesus is causing for them, and they declare, "If we let him go on like this, everyone will believe in him, and the Romans will come and destroy both our holy place and our nation." The obvious meaning is not so difficult, even if it is not explicitly stated why the Romans would destroy the nation due to widespread belief in Jesus.[124] However, the audience of the Fourth Gospel presumably would have known that the Romans *did* destroy the Jewish holy place and their nation in 70 CE. This added knowledge is necessary to understand the communication as ironic: it conveys more than the surface-level meaning. Even though Jesus was crucified, the Romans still came to destroy the temple and Jerusalem, although presumably not because of Jesus.

The shared knowledge between the author and the audience may be a result of shared experience or culture, or it may be the result of previous communication in the text. In the example just cited, the audience must have shared cultural/historical information, which exists outside the text. In the Fourth Gospel, much of the irony that suffuses the arrest and interrogation scene depends on the reader's engagement with the preceding seventeen chapters. Culpepper points out that the prologue is especially significant in setting up much of the Johannine irony.[125] It elevates the audience above the characters in the story by giving them special information about Jesus' identity that will inform a reading of the rest of the Gospel.[126]

5. Markers of Irony

In addition to shared knowledge between the author and audience, the ironist must also provide clues to the presence of irony in a text. Admittedly, these markers of irony are not always obvious. By its nature, irony is both allusive and elusive, and "the ironist's challenge is to be clear

---

123. Hutcheon, *Irony's Edge*, 98.

124. Given that Jesus is described as a "king," especially one unsanctioned by imperial rule, it becomes clear why rampant belief in Jesus is perceived as a threat to Roman hegemony.

125. Culpepper, *Anatomy*, 168.

126. Duke says that the omniscient prologue gives readers "essential information about Jesus' origin, identity, and destiny," thus elevating the audience to "a 'godlike' perspective, granting knowledge that the groping characters below cannot have, and making us heirs of irony" (*Irony*, 140).

without being evident, to say something without really saying it."[127] To signal irony, there are often contextual and textual signals that help the interpreter to identify some communication as ironic.[128]

In nontextual forms of communications, such as speeches or theater, the options for signaling irony are more diverse than in written communications. A politician giving a speech might wink or smirk, clear her throat, change her tone of voice, stress certain words, or even make "air quotation marks" with her hands to signal the presence of irony in what she is saying.[129] While an author of an ironic text does not have these options, a number of other markers may still signal irony: hyperbole, understatement, contradictions, incongruities, over-simplification, repetition, and mimicry.[130] Booth says that irony is marked by an "absurdity or impossibility in what is said," so that the informed reader can only continue by looking for an alternate meaning to what is expressly stated.[131]

Nevertheless, irony is often difficult to pin down in writing. Duke concedes that it is "slippery" to identify and challenging to explain why we sense that a particular statement or text is ironic.[132] There is a certain art to identifying and interpreting irony that resists absolute certainty. Sharp admits that "the interpretation of irony may not be able to avoid charges of being mercurial in its practice, of relying at crucial points on idiosyncrasies of reader perception or on special pleading in particular contexts."[133] Most expressions of irony will exhibit some sort of contradiction or incongruity, but different readers and audiences may not agree on irony's presence.

6. Overview of Irony in the Fourth Gospel

Previous interpreters have called attention to some of the major themes and effects of the irony in the Fourth Gospel. Culpepper highlights several major themes in John's irony, including the rejection of Jesus by his own people and the failure of people to understand the origin and identity of

---

127. O'Day, *Revelation in the Fourth Gospel*, 25.
128. Hutcheon, *Irony's Edge*, 142.
129. Hutcheon, *Irony's Edge*, 155–56.
130. Hutcheon, *Irony's Edge*, 156–58; and Sharp, *Irony and Meaning*, 26–28.
131. Booth, *Rhetoric of Irony*, 24.
132. Duke, *Irony in the Fourth Gospel*, 32.
133. Sharp, *Irony and Meaning*, 27.

Jesus.¹³⁴ Duke also calls attention to the major irony in Jesus' death: that it represents not defeat but rather Jesus' moment of exaltation.¹³⁵ The evangelist states from the beginning the fact that most of the Jewish people rejected Jesus: "He came to what was his own, and his own people did not accept him" (1:11). The primary thrust of this irony is directed at the Jewish authorities as the Gospel progresses, and culminates when the chief priests reject not only Jesus, but the God who sent him: "We have no king but the emperor" (19:15).

Much of the irony that permeates the theme of rejection also points back to Jesus' origin and identity. The audience of the Fourth Gospel knows of Jesus' true origin from the Father because of the prologue. Characters in the Gospel, however, repeatedly wrestle with and question where Jesus comes from, and fail repeatedly to grasp that he is sent from God.¹³⁶

Irony is also pervasive in the Fourth Gospel's presentation of Jesus' death as his exaltation and glorification. The Johannine Jesus speaks of his crucifixion in positive terms as being "lifted up" or "exalted" (3:14; 8:28; 12:32).¹³⁷ During his appearance before Pilate, Jesus is dressed in royal attire, and in contrast to the Synoptic Gospels, he is never stripped of it before he is crucified: Jesus is executed as a king. Ironically, this is not a tragic death, but rather Jesus' moment of triumphal return to his Father.

These are but three major, much-discussed themes that display Johannine irony. However, there has been very little discussion of the way in which irony intersects with the Gospel's relationship to the Roman Empire. My proposal is that irony informs an understanding of the Johannine community's engagement with, and negotiation of, life within the Roman Empire in significant ways. The evangelist's use of irony affects the way in which Johannine believers perceive and relate to the empire, and assists them in their negotiation of life under imperial domination. This irony is also a part of the Johannine community's hidden transcript.

---

134. Culpepper, *Anatomy*, 169–75.
135. Duke, *Irony in the Fourth Gospel*, 113–14.
136. See, for example, 1:46; 6:41–42; 7:26–30, 52; and 19:9.
137. The Greek verb is ὑψόω and it can take either of these meanings.

Hidden Transcripts and Irony

Irony is often political because it has the power to support or subvert perspectives and opinions. M. M. J. Fischer suggests that irony presents "a means of exposing or subverting oppressive hegemonic ideologies."[138] Hutcheon writes, "Irony can and does function tactically in the service of a wide range of political positions, legitimating or undercutting a wide variety of interests."[139]

The political use of irony has a legacy in the Hebrew Bible. Sharp describes how "irony in these texts about foreign rulers works as a distancing mechanism by means of which biblical authors could satirize dangerous systems of power."[140] She goes on to explain that "foreign rulers are figured in the Hebrew Bible as sources of considerable threat, not only militarily but culturally . . . . Concern about the threat posed to those who refuse assimilation suffuses the dramatic stories about Daniel in the Persian court. Concern about the lure of the foreign and its implications for Israelite constructions of power can be read in the deeply ambivalent ironies of Esther."[141] Irony has the capacity to make readers wary of political—especially imperial—powers. If readers are already wary of particular political powers, irony reinforces the distance. For example, in the Fourth Gospel's "trial" scene, the Johannine irony mocks and undercuts Pilate's—and therefore Rome's—authority and power. But it also undergirds the conviction of Johannine readers that Jesus is the true king, strengthening their Christian faith within the Roman imperial context.

Irony does not present a direct attack, however. By its nature it is subtle in its approach. This is why it makes sense to speak of irony as part of the Johannine hidden transcript. It does not represent overt resistance to the Roman Empire and its ideology, but is rather a manifestation of the hidden transcript. If members of the Johannine community do oppose facets of Rome's imperial ideology and values, then irony is one means of discourse by which they can safely challenge the norms. Irony can conceal dissent, allowing a speaker to appear as though she or he is following accepted public transcripts. Meanwhile, members of the speaker's own community, having a shared knowledge, can grasp the ironic meaning of the discourse or text. Hutcheon observes, "In a totalitarian regime . . . to

---

138. Fischer, "Ethnicity," 224.
139. Hutcheon, *Irony's Edge*, 10.
140. Sharp, *Irony and Meaning*, 49.
141. Sharp, *Irony and Meaning*, 50.

use or attribute irony in order to undermine-from-within is relatively straightforward, if dangerous: the rules or norms are known and adhered to in the letter, though not in the spirit, of the ironizing utterance. The dangers only materialize if the authorities also attribute irony and the protective cover of indirection is blown."[142] Irony functions as part of the hidden transcript and quite possibly as part of the community's politics of anonymity and disguise.

Thesis

In the passion narrative of the Fourth Gospel, there is evidence of a hidden transcript of the Johannine community. This hidden transcript is part of the political discourse of the Johannine community that assists them in negotiating life under Roman imperial power. The Johannine community was probably not homogenous. Its members did not necessarily share the same beliefs, opinions, and perspectives on what it meant to live as a Christian within the Roman Empire. Thus, the Fourth Gospel does not represent the monolithic perspective of the Johannine community, but rather the perspectives of the person or persons responsible for its creation. It is therefore not the sum total of the political dialogue within the Johannine community, but part of the community's ongoing discourse and evolving perspective on the Roman Empire.

This facet of the hidden transcript that is evident in the Fourth Gospel critiques and subverts imperial dominance, authority, and power while promoting the Johannine worldview. The expression of the Johannine hidden transcript in the arrest, "trial," and crucifixion scenes (18:1–11; 18:28—19:37) serves to mock the Roman governor, effectively eroding confidence in the Roman Empire and its agents, while bolstering faith in the power and authority of Jesus and God. To borrow Carter's terminology, it creates a "rhetoric of distance" that "tries to create lines between the empire and faithful followers of Jesus, urging Jesus-believers to a less-accommodated and to a more-distinctive way of life as an antisociety or alternate community."[143] The Fourth Gospel has the capacity to appeal to Johannine Christians in a number of circumstances. For those who might be too comfortable within the Roman imperial world, the Gospel challenges them to reevaluate the empire in light of the person and

142. Hutcheon, *Irony's Edge*, 16.
143. Carter, *John and Empire*, 82.

message of Jesus. For those who might feel marginalized or persecuted, the Gospel has the capacity to inspire perseverance and ongoing faithfulness to Jesus.

This project will explore the features in the arrest, interrogation, and crucifixion scenes that bear witness to that hidden transcript, giving special attention to the literary device of irony. I will argue that the irony present in the scenes is a particularly effective expression of the Johannine hidden transcript that both criticizes the Roman Empire and appeals to readers to adopt the Johannine evangelist's own perspectives.

CHAPTER 2

The Gospel of John and the Roman Imperial World

Models of Empire

It is difficult to imagine how much life in the United States a century ago differed from life in the United States in the twenty-first century. Social structures, economics, politics, culture, religion, and legal systems have all changed significantly in the last one hundred years. The realities of life in the New Testament period are even more foreign to readers today, owing to the separation of geography, culture, and two thousand years' time. Because we are far removed from such realities of day-to-day life in the Roman Empire, this chapter will attempt to illumine facets of the historical context of the Fourth Gospel. Specifically, this chapter will lay out an understanding of many of the social, economic, and political realities of life within the Roman imperial world toward the end of the first century that are relevant to a reading of John 18–19. The chapter will begin by engaging two sociological models, and then move to more specific details, based on extant sources of historical information. These details are essential for an informed understanding of the Fourth Gospel texts to be examined in the chapters to come. Realities of the first-century Roman world are important for understanding all of the texts of the New Testament, but especially so in these chapters within the Gospel of John, as they depict Jesus' direct engagement with Roman power and authority.

Sociological models flesh out the social, economic, and political realities of the Roman Empire. We are constrained in our historical understanding of the period because of our distance from it, in both space and time, and because of insufficient extant sources.[1] The models help us to fill in the gaps and better understand the structures of the empire, and the sources that we do have from the period support the perspective developed by the sociological models.

Dennis Duling contends that "[t]heories and models of empire are implicit in any utterance about empire, ancient or modern."[2] For the interpretation of John 18–19, sociological models are especially helpful in that they help clarify the social stratification within the Roman Empire. They delineate the sharp rift between the elite and the non-elite. The elite were those few within the empire who possessed most of the wealth, power, and status, and they included Pilate and the Jewish authorities. The non-elite, which included Jesus, his followers and the vast majority of the population, were those who had few assets, little power, and marginal status.[3]

For the purposes of this study, the sociological models of Gerhard E. Lenski and John H. Kautsky provide a framework for understanding the Roman Empire in the first century.[4] The Roman Empire was both

---

1. Not only are the historical sources from the period limited, but as Carter says, "such sources [that do survive] privilege elite rather than nonelite experience" (*John and Empire*, 53). Those with power and wealth had occasion to leave behind far more writings and records than those without the means to do so.

2. Duling, "Empire: Theories, Methods, Models," 74.

3. It is difficult to define the term "elite" with absolute precision. Gerhard Lenski admits that a decisive definition is somewhat elusive, and settles for saying that the term "elite" suggests "the highest ranking segment of any given social unit, whether a class or total society, ranked by whatever criterion one chooses" (*Power and Privilege*, 78–79). The criterion that Lenski selects for his use of the term is *power*. However, the boundaries of the "elite" will always be imprecise. Dealing specifically with the Roman Empire and the Fourth Gospel, Carter classifies the emperor, members of the provincial and local governing classes, priests, Pharisees, and retainers of the governing class as "elites." Artisans, peasants, slaves, and expendables constitute the non-elite segment of the population (Carter, *John and Empire*, 65–67). There are variances within each of these populations—e.g., a slave of the emperor might wield considerable power and thus be considered an "elite"—but they can serve as approximate divisions for this study.

4. Lenski, *Power and Privilege*, esp. 189–296; and Kautsky, *Politics of Aristocratic Empires*.

an *agrarian* empire and an *aristocratic* empire. Lenski's study of agrarian societies helps sketch out the socioeconomic stratification of the different classes of persons within the empire. Kautsky's study then deals with aristocratic politics and is helpful for understanding the dynamics and power relationships between elites and non-elites.

The chief contribution of Lenski's model is that it brings attention to social stratification and the huge gap between the elite and the non-elite within agrarian societies. Lenski defines agrarian societies by the presence of specific technological developments, namely the plow, the harnessing of animal energy, and the invention of metallurgy. These technological advances allowed for the production of an agricultural surplus that was not available in more primitive horticultural societies. The new technology allowed farmers to produce larger fields and crops, and thus more food.[5] This economic surplus and its uneven distribution among the populace is a primary focus of Lenski's study.[6]

Agrarian societies were characterized by pronounced social inequalities: the economic surplus flowed toward the top, to the powerful elite members of society. Of the five types of societies that Lenski's study examines, he suggests that agrarian societies typically had the highest degree of social inequality, and government was a primary cause of this: the elite members of the government extracted the economic surplus created by the non-elites.[7]

Lenski identifies several social classes in his model of agrarian societies that are helpful for understanding the context of the Fourth Gospel: the ruler and governing class, retainers, artisans, peasants, the unclean and degraded, and finally expendables. Lenski is careful to point out that these "levels" or strata are not always clearly separated and distinct from one another in a neatly layered, pyramidal scheme. "On the contrary," he says, "each covers a range of the distributive spectrum, and what is more, each overlaps certain others to some degree."[8] A trusted retainer of the emperor, for example, would probably have more power and wealth than many members of the governing class.[9]

5. Lenski, *Power and Privilege*, 190.

6. Lenski emphasizes a classic sociological question: "Who gets what and why?" (*Power and Privilege*, 3).

7. Lenski, *Power and Privilege*, 437.

8. Lenski, *Power and Privilege*, 285.

9. Steven J. Friesen's "poverty scale" is useful in this sense, because it largely ignores social status and focuses instead on a spectrum of wealth and poverty within

Lenski begins his discussion of the strata at the top, with the ruler. The ruler of an agrarian society stood high above all others in terms of power, privilege, and wealth. Wealth was derived primarily from land, and "all agrarian rulers enjoyed significant proprietary rights in virtually all of the land in their domains."[10] Because of these rights, the rulers, Roman emperors included, could exact enormous wealth through taxes and tribute from the land. It is difficult to overemphasize the vast gap in power and wealth enjoyed by the emperor vis-à-vis all others in agrarian societies. Rome's Caesar, lauded by the Jewish authorities in John 19:15, was the most powerful and wealthy person—by far—in the empire at that time.

Beneath the emperor was a small governing class that assisted him in ruling. To be a member of the governing class meant that one controlled the land, and had the right and means to a share of the economic surplus produced by the lower classes. Officials in the governing class enjoyed the benefit of political appointments to various public and bureaucratic offices. Between the ruler and the governing class, these elites controlled most of the land and the labor supply, both of which were the primary sources of wealth in agrarian societies and in the Roman Empire. According to Lenski's data, "the governing classes of agrarian societies probably received at least a quarter of the national income of most agrarian states, and . . . the governing class and ruler together usually received not less than half."[11] Pilate, one of the central figures in John 18–19, would have had tremendous wealth, power, and influence as the governor of Judea. Likewise, the Jewish chief priests and authorities who conspire to kill Jesus fall into this category. Josephus describes them as the rulers of the nation, who, although not equal to the governor in power, nevertheless collaborated with him to exercise dominion over the country (*Ant.* 20.251).

---

the first-century Roman Empire ("Poverty in Pauline Studies," 323–61). Friesen establishes seven tiers of financial resources. The top three tiers ("imperial elites," "regional or provincial elites," and "municipal elites"), who constitute less than 3 percent of the population, can be described as "super-wealthy" ("Poverty in Pauline Studies," 340–41). The vast majority of the population (approximately 90 percent) falls within the bottom three tiers ("stable near subsistence," "at subsistence," and "below subsistence") and hovers around subsistence level ("Poverty in Pauline Studies," 343–45). A small percentage of the population had modest financial resources ("moderate surplus") and fall in the middle of Friesen's seven tiers ("Poverty in Pauline Studies," 346–47).

10. Lenski, *Power and Privilege*, 215–16.
11. Lenski, *Power and Privilege*, 228.

The retainer class consisted of those persons who aided the ruler and governing class and were in some way dependent on them. According to Lenski, this class, which may have accounted for as much as 5 percent of the population, included "officials, professional soldiers, household servants, and personal retainers, all of whom served them in a variety of more or less specialized capacities."[12] This class was significant in that it performed most of the actual work of transferring economic surplus from producers to the ruler and governing class. Lenski stresses that, because of their relationship with and dependence on the political elite, retainers could enjoy considerable power and wealth themselves. The police and soldiers in John 18–19, who aid the ruling elite in maintaining order, fall appropriately into this class.

The power, privilege, and wealth enjoyed by members of these elite classes and their retainers far surpassed that of those at the bottom of the social ladder: the merchant, peasant, artisan, laboring, unclean, degradable, and expendable classes. The socioeconomic disparity between the elite and non-elite classes was so great that John Dominic Crossan speaks of an "abysmal gulf" between these groups.[13] While the non-elite classes of the Roman Empire constituted the vast majority of the population, they possessed only a tiny portion of the total wealth and power within the empire. Of course, even within these strata, there were considerable gradations of poverty and economic instability.

The merchant class was comprised of those who engaged in the business of buying, trading, and selling goods. Lenski contends that merchants "stood in a *market* relationship with the governing class, not an *authority* relationship," and thus had better opportunities to deal favorably with the elite classes and gain some wealth.[14] On this account, a few amassed sizable fortunes. Others were able to accumulate modest resources by means of buying and selling. The majority remained relatively poor, however, falling at or just above the subsistence level.[15]

Of all the classes within agrarian societies such as the Roman Empire, the peasant class is the largest of Lenski's strata. The peasant class consisted of those who were engaged in actual agricultural production, including the farmers who worked the land. To them fell the burden of

---

12. Lenski, *Power and Privilege*, 243.
13. Crossan, *Historical Jesus*, 45.
14. Lenski, *Power and Privilege*, 250.
15. Friesen, "Poverty in Pauline Studies," 341.

producing the food that sustained the rest of the society. The government imposed heavy taxes on the peasant class, extracting from them the surplus produce made possible by the advances in farming technology mentioned above. In some agrarian societies, estimates for taxes ranged upwards of 50 percent of the peasants' production. Peasants were also "taxed" by the elite through *corvée*—forced labor for elite members of the society. According to Lenski, "the great majority of the political elite sought to use the energies of the peasantry to the full, while depriving them of all but the basic necessities of life."[16] Therefore, peasants typically lived at or around subsistence level, with just enough to survive. They could easily fall below the minimum needed to sustain life and they often did.

The artisan class was closely related to the peasant class and included workers who were skilled in particular trades, such as carpentry and the production of textiles. In agrarian societies, many artisans began life as peasants, and later joined the artisan ranks for various reasons.[17] The median wealth and income of artisans was typically lower than that of peasants; yet again, however, there were significant gradations within the class.[18] Members of this class often worked for merchants, selling them goods from which the merchants, in turn, profited.

Because peasants and artisans had to work hard to survive and sustain their way of life, the elite classes in many agrarian societies looked upon them as something like a different breed of person altogether, wholly lacking in any of the qualities and values of the elites.[19] Many of Jesus' followers in the Fourth Gospel could accurately be described as artisans or peasants. Jesus' disciples who go fishing at the end of the Gospel are artisans (21:1–14). Many of the crowds that follow him around the countryside would have been composed of members of the peasant class (e.g., chapters 6 and 7). Jesus is difficult to classify conclusively, but he does

---

16. Lenski, *Power and Privilege*, 270.

17. For example, younger male sons who did not inherit their family farmlands, and thus did not have a way to provide for themselves, may have entered the artisan class.

18. Friesen proposes that, while most artisans lived near or at subsistence level, some were able to gain a modest surplus ("Poverty in Pauline Studies," 341).

19. See, for example, Ramsay MacMullen's "lexicon of snobbery," in which he lists words and phrases employed by elite authors that "indicate the range of prejudice felt by the literate upper classes for the lower" (*Roman Social Relations*, 138–41). MacMullen also notes how members of the elite classes arrogantly displayed their superiority by means of conspicuous consumption of wealth (*Roman Social Relations*, 110).

identify himself with these classes. He calls himself a "shepherd" and a "gatekeeper" for his sheep, both of which involve agricultural production (10:3, 14). His status as a teacher, a specialized trade, also associates him with the artisan class.

Members of Lenski's unclean and degradable class occupied "a position in society that was clearly inferior to that of the masses of common people."[20] Such persons were treated with contempt or disregarded altogether by the vast majority of the population. The so-called "untouchables" in Hindu society, who historically were severely ostracized, provide a good example of this class. Tanners, whose profession involved offensive, foul-smelling processes, would be included in this stratum as well. Lenski also assigns to this class those "who had only their bodies and animal energies to sell and who were forced to accept occupations which quickly destroyed them."[21] Prostitutes, miners, and others—all whose degrading work dramatically shortened their life expectancy—fit this class. It is hard to identify specific characters within the Fourth Gospel who fall into this category.

Finally, at the bottom of the social hierarchy of agrarian societies was the expendable class. Such a class, according to Lenski, was inevitable in any society where the total number of persons exceeded the number of people necessary to satisfy labor needs. This class, therefore, was composed of persons for whom society had little or no need: they were quite literally "expendable." The expendables of an agrarian society may have constituted a significant portion of the population, as much as 5 to 10 percent, and encompassed beggars, criminals, outlaws, underemployed itinerant workers, and others who had to survive by using their wits or by relying on the charity of others.[22] Several characters within the Fourth Gospel fall within this class, including the blind, lame, and paralyzed, the woefully diseased, and Barabbas, the bandit.

Lenski's sociological model of classes within agrarian empires is helpful for understanding the socioeconomic world of the first-century Roman Empire. It also enables us to better understand the various

20. Lenski, *Power and Privilege*, 281.

21. Lenski, *Power and Privilege*, 281.

22. Such persons would certainly fall within Friesen's "below subsistence" level on his poverty scale. Of such persons, Friesen says that "[h]uman bodies can survive for some time at the low end of this scale, but the lives of people living below the subsistence level are usually shortened by chronic malnutrition and disease" ("Poverty in Pauline Studies," 343).

characters within the narrative of the Fourth Gospel and within the passion narrative, specifically. Nowhere in the Gospel is the gulf between elite, imperial power and that of non-elites more clearly on display. The Roman governor Pilate, who stands near the very top of the socioeconomic pyramid and enjoys vast power and privilege, and the Jewish authorities, who are local elites allied with Roman imperial power, clash with Jesus, a lowly provincial, a non-elite member of society, whom they certainly view as vastly inferior. In contrast to them, he has virtually no ostensible power or privilege in his social class. Nevertheless, the narrative conveys a tremendous incongruity between expectations and reality by depicting Jesus as king, with supernatural power and authority. The evangelist disrupts the socioeconomic pyramid by portraying Jesus in terms more appropriate to the one at the very top in first-century Rome: Caesar.

Kautsky's study of aristocratic empires also illumines the world of the Roman Empire, and significantly informs a reading of John 18–19. His sociological model, like Lenski's, is not specific to the Roman Empire, although he does frequently cite examples from it. Kautsky explicitly notes that his model of aristocratic empires overlaps with Lenski's model of agrarian societies.[23] Like Lenski's model, Kautsky's sheds light on the relationships between the various characters within the Fourth Gospel, and also on the world in which the Fourth Gospel was written. He also clarifies the function of aristocrats within society and government.[24] Their governmental functions were limited, and primarily entailed the collection of taxes and conduct of warfare.

To understand taxation in Rome and other aristocratic empires, one must put aside contemporary understandings of government, which entail the collection of taxes in order to provide services beneficial to the majority of the population. To be sure, aristocratic empires were not entirely without such benefits. For example, tax revenue afforded the presence of an army for protection, the creation of roads, sanitation systems in some cities, and other services. However, the aristocracy primarily imposed taxes for its own benefit, and government in aristocratic empires is best understood as an "extractive enterprise."[25] For the most part, peasants were allowed to keep enough of their agricultural produc-

---

23. Kautsky, *Politics of Aristocratic Empires*, 20.

24. Kautsky's "aristocrats" overlap roughly with Lenski's ruler, governing class, and retainers. Within John 18–19, Pilate and the Jewish authorities fall into this category.

25. Kautsky, *Politics of Aristocratic Empires*, 118.

tion in order to survive, but the aristocrats were entitled to the surplus, and extracted it through taxes or rent. Thus, aristocrats lived off of the labor and efforts of the peasants. Lenski says, "In one way or another, peasants always work for the aristocrat, whether they work on his land as agricultural laborers or rent it from him or own their own land and pay taxes to him."[26] This exploitative reality is a key facet of the relationship between aristocrats and nonaristocrats. Thus, taxation, which served to create and to maintain the wealth of the elite, was one of the primary concerns of government.

Warfare, the other primary governmental function of aristocrats, was a means of expanding the territory of the empire, which in turn expanded the potential for income by creating a larger source of tax revenue.[27] Warfare also served to protect those within the empire from hostile foes both outside and within its boundaries. Finally, the threat of violent retaliation served as a deterrent to potentially rebellious segments of the population within the empire. If an uprising did occur, warfare was employed to dispense consequences to those who participated in it. Warfare provided many benefits for elite members of society, and was thus a frequent reality of life in the ancient world. Kautsky claims that it was "virtually continuous in traditional [aristocratic] empires."[28]

All other government functions were subordinate to taxation and warfare and included such tasks as the maintenance of peace and order, the construction of roads and buildings, minting coins, and the administration of civil and religious affairs. Aristocrats fulfilled a number of necessary occupations within the government by serving as administrators, judges, military leaders, and priests. There was often considerable overlap between these roles. For example, Pontius Pilate, a Roman governor of Judea in the first century, commanded troops, oversaw administrative affairs, directed building projects, and also served in a judicial capacity.

Kautsky devotes considerable attention to the "politics" of the aristocracy, by which he means primarily politics *within* the aristocracy. This largely involved competition with fellow aristocrats for wealth, power, and property rights.[29] Aristocrats stood to gain or lose based on their position

26. Kautsky, *Politics of Aristocratic Empires*, 100.
27. Warfare also allowed elites to procure new wealth by seizing spoils of war.
28. Kautsky, *Politics of Aristocratic Empires*, 145.
29. Property rights were significant because wealth and power in aristocratic empires were centered on control of the land. The ownership of more land meant the potential for more wealth and power.

within the hierarchy of the aristocracy. All aristocrats were members of the elite segment of the population, but there were still large degrees of variation in wealth, power, and status amongst them.[30] Because of this, "intra-aristocratic politics, then, produces a high degree of instability . . . territories changed hands, military leaders, bureaucrats, and priests are transferred, promoted, demoted, and killed."[31] Many aristocrats desired to achieve greater wealth, power, and status through promotions and greater land ownership.

The social network of the aristocratic elites entailed a hierarchy of patron-client relationships. Patronage involved relationships between elites of unequal status in which both parties benefitted by providing one another with goods and services. By associating with wealthier, highly-esteemed aristocrats, one would not only gain the benefit of their loyalty and services, but also increased prestige by mere relation to them. In turn, a wealthy elite gained even more honor and prestige by having a broad client base which he served with favors and recognition.[32]

Display and conspicuous consumption of aristocratic wealth was typical. Wealth, created through taxes and the productive labors of the lower classes, was not saved or invested, but devoted primarily to enjoyment and public exhibition, which increased the honor and prestige of the aristocrat. Aristocrats wore expensive clothes, created ostentatious dwellings for themselves, employed servants, commissioned artwork, and held private parties and public festivals and feasts. They also engaged in works of euergetism, which entailed generous public philanthropy. Such beneficence might include funding building projects such as aqueducts or baths, and providing humanitarian relief during food shortages.[33] Such works increased the honor and prestige of the elite benefactors who sponsored them.

However, peasants and the lower classes were hardly involved in aristocratic politics at all.[34] In Kautsky's view, they were largely incapable of engaging in or influencing that sphere. He does note, however, that

---

30. Kautsky, *Politics of Aristocratic Empires*, 212.

31. Kautsky, *Politics of Aristocratic Empires*, 247.

32. For more information, see Agosto, "Patronage and Commendation," 103–9; Carter, *John and Empire*, 57; and Garnsey and Saller, *Roman Empire*, 152–54.

33. Garnsey and Saller, *Roman Empire*, 33–34, 101.

34. Kautsky says that "nonaristocrats play no role in the politics of the aristocracy or are at least unable to change their relationship to the aristocracy" (*Politics of Aristocratic Empires*, 269).

peasants often tried to withhold part of their production from taxation, but this was "clearly ineffective." As Kautsky notes, it did not stop the practice of exploitation and "can hardly be thought of as participation in aristocratic politics."[35] He is right, as far as his study is concerned. But this notion is countered by Scott's concept of hidden transcripts, which presumes that significant activity and discourse did take place out of sight of the ruling aristocrats. These small acts of resistance may not have caused concern among the aristocrats themselves, but they were nevertheless important for the peasants and other non-elites.

The Roman Imperial World

Now that I have established some basic parameters and understandings of the Roman Empire as an agrarian-aristocratic empire, I will consider some of the specific realities of the Roman imperial world to flesh out Lenski and Kautsky's models. Much of the discussion above will be confirmed and reinforced through specific details and examples from the Roman Empire itself. These realities will inform our interpretation of the Johannine arrest and "trial" scenes, especially our understanding of the Roman governor Pilate, the Jewish authorities, the relationship between the two groups, and their roles within the Roman imperial system.

1. Roman Economy

Garnsey and Saller describe the economy of the Roman Empire as "underdeveloped," meaning that "the mass of the population lived at or near subsistence level."[36] The principal source of wealth and investment, as in other agrarian-aristocratic empires, was agriculture. Land was "the basis of personal fortunes of the rich and of the wealth of the empire" because the more land one possessed, the more agricultural products one could produce.[37] The wealth that farmers produced, whether they were tenants, slaves, or owners, was transferred to landowners and local elites, and ultimately to Rome, through taxes and tributes. Thus, the small elite majority benefitted from the agricultural surplus and wealth generated from it, while the majority experienced scarcity of resources and food.[38]

---

35. Kautsky, *Politics of Aristocratic Empires*, 275.
36. Garnsey and Saller, *Roman Empire*, 43.
37. Garnsey and Saller, *Roman Empire*, 64.
38. For more information on matters related to food availability and scarcity, see

2. Administration of Empire

The Roman Empire, like most agrarian-aristocratic empires, had an exceedingly small bureaucracy.[39] Very few officials were needed to carry out the main tasks of governance, which, as noted above, primarily entailed the collection of taxes and the maintenance of order. Garnsey and Saller suggest that, in part, "the secret of government without bureaucracy was the Roman system of cities which were self-governing and could provide for the needs of empire."[40] The cities served as the governmental centers of the provinces, and played an instrumental role in extracting the surplus wealth from the provinces. In contrast to modern cities, Roman cities are best understood as centers of consumption rather than production. They relied on taxes and rents from the surrounding agricultural areas. Much of this wealth was then funneled to Rome. Garnsey and Saller refer to Rome as a "parasite city," because it siphoned off the wealth and surplus of the provinces.

3. Alliances with Local Elites

Roman alliances with local elites in the provinces provided another means by which Rome maintained order and imposed taxes without a large, cumbersome bureaucratic system. Wealthy men who dwelled in cities and earned income from their agricultural estates often served in various civic positions, as members of the council or as magistrates, for example. These men would have handled many local matters, such as providing a police force, maintaining public buildings and services, supervising the grain supply, and sending the annual tribute to Rome. Local elites also commonly performed acts of euergetism, spending their own wealth to fund building projects and festivals, and in return received honor and recognition for their generosity. Libraries, arches, baths, markets, and temples were among the many things that local elites financed for their cities. Inscriptions on extant buildings such as these dot the landscape of the former Roman Empire and testify to the desire of these elites to garner fame and prestige for themselves and their families, in

---

Carter, *John and Empire*, 221–26.

39. In fact, Garnsey and Saller's chapter on Roman administration is entitled "Government without Bureaucracy" (Garnsey and Saller, *Roman Empire*, 20–40).

40. Garnsey and Saller, *Roman Empire*, 26. Rome's ability to govern their vast empire without extensive bureaucracy was also enabled by the maintenance of alliances with local elites, to be discussed below.

return for providing valuable services and public spaces for the residents of their cities.

Much of the governance in the provinces and their cities was conducted without heavy interference from Rome and its governors. However, as an account from Dio Chrysostom makes clear, improper governance by local elites could lead to Roman intervention. In response to mob complaints about the rising price of bread, he asserted, "Nothing which happens in the cities goes unnoticed by the governors; on the contrary, just as the families of children who have been naughty at home report them to their teachers, so the misbehavior of the assembly is reported to them" (*Tumult.* 14).[41] Local elites were not exempt from discipline from their superiors.

Both Rome and its allies ultimately benefitted from these local alliances. Roman rule could be maintained without the expense of extensive bureaucracy or frequent involvement of the Roman army. Collusion with Rome strengthened the status and power of allied elites, and also played to their own interests. For example, those who took on the responsibility of collecting the annual tribute were best positioned to pay lower taxes on their own properties. Some stood to gain further benefits as well, such as Roman citizenship.

4. Jewish Authorities

The Jewish authorities who appear throughout the narrative of the Fourth Gospel—and who are instrumental in Jesus' arrest and "trial" in chapters 18 and 19—are among the local elites allied with Rome. It is tempting, in many present-day contexts, which presume the separation of religion and politics, to think of these "religious" leaders of Jewish society as strictly spiritual figures, and to ignore the political dimensions of their leadership. However, as we will see, they are certainly also political figures.[42]

Carter argues that the chief priests and the Pharisees were part of "the ruling aristocracy who in alliance with Rome [had] immense political, social, and economic power."[43] Tom Thatcher agrees, noting that the

---

41. Quoted from Kelly, *Roman Empire*, 47.

42. Warren Carter identifies these religious officials as part of the retainer class: "Religious officials are part of the retainer class within the ruling elite as those who maintain and advance the interests of the ruling elite." See *Matthew and Empire*, 148. Carter cites Lenski, *Power and Privilege*, 256–66; Kautsky, *Politics of Aristocratic Empires*, 81–83; and Saldarini, *Pharisees, Scribes and Sadducees*, 35–49.

43. Carter, *Pontius Pilate*, 39; see also 47–49.

priests and Pharisees in the Fourth Gospel are "essentially auxiliaries of Rome" and "agents of imperial power," and he even contends that "John viewed the priests and the Pharisees as puppets on Caesar's string."[44] While Thatcher may go a bit too far in this last claim, his basic premise is accurate. The Jewish authorities were certainly part of the network of Roman imperial power relations and did assist the Romans in maintaining order. The Romans had incorporated the aristocratic Judean elite into their own power structure when Pompey had conquered Jerusalem in 63 BCE, and continued to rely on them for assistance in governance following the imposition of direct Roman rule in 6 CE.[45] Yet the Jewish authorities were not strictly "puppets" because they had their own motives and were involved in their own ongoing, tensive negotiation of Roman imperial power.[46] Nevertheless, both the historical evidence and the narrative of the Fourth Gospel support the claim that the Jewish authorities were agents of imperial power, local allies who collaborated with Rome and worked toward common purposes.

For a lengthy period of time, the Romans controlled the priestly leadership of the Jews, and could elect and depose the high priests at will, according to their own political agenda.[47] Bond notes that "only men who could be relied on to pursue an actively pro-Roman policy would be chosen [as high priest]."[48] Thatcher highlights the political relationship between Rome and the Jewish authorities by pointing out that "the most durable high priest, Caiaphas . . . lasted eighteen years, a remarkable tribute to his political savvy."[49] His tenure as high priest continued even when Pontius Pilate took over as governor of Judea, presumably because he was "a man who could be relied on to support Roman interests and who could command some respect amongst the people."[50]

---

44. Thatcher, *Greater Than Caesar*, 46.

45. For an overview of the history and relationship between the Roman and Jewish elite, see Goodman, *Ruling Class of Judea*, 29–50.

46. Horsley surmises that "certain tensions" were likely "built into the very structure of their role in the Roman imperial system, tensions between 'the groups which enjoy the profits'" (Horsley, "High Priests," 24).

47. Goodman observes that, from the period of 6 CE until 66 CE, the ability of the high priests "to lead the Jewish nation rested . . . entirely on the whim of the Romans, or in later cases Herodian princes, who appointed them" (*Ruling Class of Judea*, 44).

48. Bond, *Pontius Pilate*, 18.

49. Thatcher, *Greater Than Caesar*, 51.

50. Bond, *Pontius Pilate*, 19.

A couple of brief accounts from Josephus further illustrate how thoroughly enmeshed Jewish politics were in Roman politics. In one example, Josephus recounts how the Roman governor Valerius Gratus appointed and deposed a quick succession of Jewish high priests during his reign (*Ant.* 18.33–35). These high priests were expected to support Roman interests and were replaced if they did not suit the needs of the Roman governor. E. Mary Smallwood observes that "the religious leaders of the Jews were appointed by the representatives [of Rome], and they could retain their position only by keeping in their good books."[51]

Another episode also illustrates the close relationship between the Romans and the Jerusalem priesthood. During the Jewish revolt in the late 60s CE, a group of insurgent Jews took it upon themselves to appoint their own high priest (*J.W.* 4.147). Josephus, himself a Roman sympathizer, denigrates this group, whom he says cast lots to choose the high priest. The historian mocks them, speaking of the elected priest, Phannias, son of Samuel, as "such a mere rustic" (*J.W.* 4.155). In Josephus's view, Phannias is not worthy to serve as high priest because he does not come from one of the traditional aristocratic families. Instead, Phannias is "unknown and ignoble" (*J.W.* 4.148). Most likely, the aim of the insurgent Jews was to install their high priest by lot to avoid the disgrace of having a high priest chosen by Rome.

Both of these incidents illustrate the close relationship between the Jewish elite and the Roman Empire. The narrative of the Fourth Gospel also portrays the Jewish authorities as local elites allied with imperial power. For example, the narrative suggests that the motive for arresting and killing Jesus was political rather than theological in nature. The Jewish authorities fear that if they do not stop Jesus' activity, "everyone will believe in him, and the Romans will come and destroy both our holy place and our nation" (11:48). Howard-Brook observes that "their plea has nothing to do with God, but is simply a matter of holding on to the puppet power delegated by empire."[52]

John 18 provides another example of how the Fourth Gospel portrays the Jewish elite in alliance with Rome: Roman soldiers collaborate with a Jewish police force from the chief priests and the Pharisees in order to arrest Jesus. The arresting party takes Jesus first to Annas, the father-in-law of the high priest, then to the high priest Caiaphas, and

---

51. Smallwood, "High Priests and Politics," 22.
52. Howard-Brook, *Come Out*, 438.

then finally to the Roman governor. The entire proceeding progresses as an interaction and negotiation between the two parties, Jewish and Roman, as they seek to maintain control and eliminate a perceived threat to the imperial status quo. Furthermore, the Jewish authorities themselves confess their allegiance to Rome and their status as imperial agents when they declare at the end of the proceedings, "We have no king but the emperor" (19:15).

5. Roman Military Power

Lenski says that "the great agrarian states of the past were all *conquest states*, or social units formed through the forcible subjugation of one group by another."[53] The Romans formed their empire through the conquest and occupation of other people and realms. Writing around 25 BCE, Livy records an account of Romulus, the mythological founder of Rome, instilling this ideology: "Go . . . and tell the Romans Heaven's will that my Rome shall be the capital of the world; so let them love the art of war, and let them know and teach their children that no human strength can resist Roman arms" (*History of Rome* 1.16.7).[54] Roman military power, in the form of its legions and its smaller auxiliary units of force, was a principal means by which Rome both extended its boundaries and maintained its control over the broad expanse of its empire.

Throughout the early period of the Roman Empire, the concept of the *Pax Romana*—Augustus's golden age of peace—prevailed. Aelius Aristides, writing in the early second century CE, observes that "since [the Romans'] appearance confusion and revolt have come to an end. Order has returned everywhere and in everyday life and in state there is clear light of day. Laws have come into being, and faith has been found at the altars of the gods" (*Oration* 26).[55] However, this so-called "peace" was established and maintained through considerable warfare and bloodshed. As Wengst notes, "the *Pax Romana* is a peace which is the political goal of the Roman emperor and his most senior officials and is brought about and secured by military action through the success of his legions."[56] In many respects, the *Pax Romana* was a "peace" in name only, sustained

---

53. Lenski, *Power and Privilege*, 195.
54. Quoted in Champion, *Roman Imperialism*, 204.
55. Quoted in Wengst, *Pax Romana*, 8.
56. Wengst, *Pax Romana*, 11.

by the threat of violence or punishment by the Roman military and for the benefit of Roman elites.

Roman military might was acknowledged and feared throughout the provinces. Josephus, writing about the provinces of the Gauls, explains how the Romans kept them subjugated with so few troops stationed there: "But if there is one people above all others which should be tempted ... to raise the standard of revolt, it is surely the Gauls.... [But] the Gauls are yet content to be treated as a source of revenue to the Romans ... because they are overawed at once by the power of Rome and by her fortune ... they submit to the orders of twelve hundred soldiers, they who have cities enough almost to outmatch that number" (*J.W.* 2.372–73). Rome's military could intimidate and curb potential uprisings by mere presence in a turbulent province such as Judea, and could decisively end revolts when needed, as they did in 70 CE, by destroying Jerusalem and crushing the Jewish revolt. The Roman soldiers who are part of the arresting party in John 18 would thus have been seen as potent instruments of Roman imperialism and domination. Their involvement in the arrest of Jesus—missing in the Synoptic Gospels, which only indicate the presence of representatives of the Jewish elite (Matt 26:47; Mark 14:43; Luke 22:47–52)—establishes the dominating presence and fearsome strength of the Roman military from the very beginning of the passion narrative.

6. Imperial Theology and Ideology

Imperial theology and ideology were tightly enmeshed in the politics and public life of the first-century Roman Empire. Poets, historians, statues, temples, cultic festivals, inscriptions, and coins testified to a pervasive belief that Rome was destined to rule the entire world at the will of the gods.[57] Cicero described the Romans as the people whom "the immortal gods wanted to rule over all peoples" (*Phil.* 6.19).[58] In the Aeneid, an epic poem popular among elites in Roman society, Virgil has Jupiter declare, "For these [Romans] I place neither physical bounds nor temporal limits;

---

57. These same media also no doubt reinforced belief in the legitimacy of Roman rule. Howard-Brook and Gwyther say, "The Roman media included temples, monuments, inscriptions, festivals, orations, coinage, games, and so forth. Taken together, these media communicated powerfully the message that Rome was a beneficent and well-ordered society, and that its emperor was the guarantor of peace and harmony" (Howard-Brook and Gwyther, *Unveiling Empire*, 88).

58. Quoted in Champion, *Roman Imperialism*, 203.

I have given empire without end" (*Aen.* 1.278–79).[59] Even Josephus, a pro-Roman Jew, argued that Jerusalem should surrender to Rome during the Jewish war, saying "that God was on the Roman side," and he reasoned that "without God's aid so vast an empire could never have been built up" (*J.W.* 5.368 and 2.390–91). That Rome ruled by the divine will lent some justification to their dominion and territorial expansion. Some authors, writing hyperbolically, spoke as if Rome had already succeeded in conquering the entire world.[60]

In addition to divine justification for Roman rule, imperial theology promoted the belief that the Roman emperor served on earth as the agent of the gods. Seneca writes these dramatic words of the emperor Nero:

> Have I of all mortals found favour with heaven and been chosen to serve on earth as vicar of the gods? I am the arbiter of life and death for the nations; it rests in my power what each man's lot and state shall be: by my lips fortune proclaims what gift she would bestow on each human being: from my utterance peoples and cities gather reasons for rejoicing; without my favor and grace no part of the whole world can prosper; all those many thousands of swords which my peace restrains will be drawn at my nod, what nations shall be utterly destroyed, which banished, which shall receive the gift of liberty, which have it taken from them, what kings shall become slave and whose heads shall be crowned with royal honour, what cities shall fall and which shall rise—this is mine to decree. (*Clem.* 1.1.2)[61]

The quote illustrates that the Roman emperor was viewed as utterly powerful, and it highlights the perceived relationship between the emperor and the gods. Many poets also referred to emperors as "fathers" over the inhabitants of the empire. The poet Martial calls Domitian the "parent" or "father of the world" (*Epigrams* 7.7.5; 9.6.1; Latin: *parens orbis*). The Roman Empire is imagined as a household, with its inhabitants obedient children to their symbolic father, the emperor. Carter writes that the audience of the Fourth Gospel would have been familiar with the epithet accorded to the emperor, "Father of the Fatherland," from

---

59. Quoted in Champion, *Roman Imperialism*, 202.

60. E.g., see Cicero, *De or.* 1.14. P. A. Brunt also discusses this idea in "*Laus Imperii*," 26–28. This brings to mind the Pharisees' observation that "[t]he whole world has gone after [Jesus]" (John 12:19).

61. Quoted in Wengst, *Pax Romana*, 47.

inscriptions, coins, and writings.[62] The title "Father" certainly would have resonated with the audience of the Fourth Gospel, as it refers to God as "Father" well over one hundred times.

The emperors were not only considered agents of the gods on earth, but they were also granted divine honors. Philo observed, "The whole inhabited world voted him honors usually accorded the Olympian gods. These are so well attested by temples, gateways, vestibules, and colonnades that every city which contains magnificent works new and old is surpassed in these by the beauty and magnitude of those appropriated to Caesar" (*Legatio ad Gaium* 149–50).[63] The following quotation from a Greek inscription is representative in its estimation of the divinity of Caesar: "The people of Karthaia dedicate [this statue of] the god and imperator and savior of the inhabited world, Gaius Julius Caesar."[64] Virgil says this about Augustus, articulating both his high assessment of the emperor and also the expectation of prosperity because of Caesar's rule: "Here is Caesar . . . this in truth is he whom you so often hear promised you, Augustus Caesar, son of a god, who will again establish a golden age in [Rome] . . . he will advance his empire beyond the Garamants and Indians to a land which lies beyond our stars, beyond the paths of year and sun" (*Aen.* 6.788–97).[65]

The imperial cults were one means of promoting and reinforcing an exalted, deified view of the Roman emperors. These cults were widespread throughout the provinces in the first century, so much so that they "provided the principal means by which disparate cities and provinces were held together and social order produced."[66] Their presence was not isolated to religious sanctuaries, either. Much of public life was suffused with the emperor cults. Festivals, temples, rituals, statues, calendar dates, and games were all connected to the veneration of the emperor and his family. Public spaces such as council houses, theaters, stadia, gymnasia, and baths often contained imperial imagery, as well.[67]

---

62. Carter, *John and Empire*, 236–38.
63. Quoted in Horsley, *Paul and Empire*, 10.
64. *Inscriptiones Graecae*, 12.5.557, quoted in Champion, *Roman Imperialism*, 265.
65. Quoted in Richey, *Roman Imperial Ideology*, 43.
66. Horsley, *Paul and Empire*, 20. Some scholars refer to the imperial cults in the plural, rather than singular, recognizing that there was diversity in the phenomenon. See, for example, Rives, "Religion in the Roman World," 265–68.
67. Price, *Rituals and Power*, 109–10.

As part of their participation in the imperial cults, inhabitants of the empire would pray to the emperor, and also to the gods for the health of the emperor. As the agent of the gods, the emperor ensured that divine benefits extended to subjects across the empire. Wengst observes, "The gods protect and sustain [the Roman Empire] in the person of the emperor, who stands surety" for "peace, concord, security, riches and honour, all aspects of the *Pax Romana* which this empire provides."[68] Steven J. Friesen writes, "the twofold prayer accurately reflected imperial theology: the gods looked after the emperors, who in turn looked after the concerns of the gods on earth to the benefit of humanity. Imperial authority ordered human society, and divine authority protected the emperors."[69]

Such an understanding of theology and ideology within the Roman Empire reinforced the social hierarchy, with the emperor at the top, as the focal point of its worldview.[70] Rome and the emperor ruled at the will of the gods, and the emperor, viewed as divine, mediated benefits to all of humanity.[71] This worldview would have proved challenging for the author of the Fourth Gospel, who views Jesus, not the emperor, as the agent of the divine will, the one who mediates the Father's love and blessing to the world.

7. Governors in the Roman Empire

Pontius Pilate looms large in John 18–19. In one sense, he is even more prominent than Jesus, since the narrative follows his movements back and forth during the proceedings in 18:28—19:16, alternating between his interactions with Jesus and with the Jewish authorities. Pilate was the most powerful Roman figure in the province of Judea during his rule, and this encounter therefore represents a particularly significant interaction between Jesus and Roman imperial power.[72] In order to grasp the dynamics of these scenes, it is important to establish the historical context of governorship within the Roman Empire broadly, and within Judea in particular.

---

68. Wengst, *Pax Romana*, 47.

69. Friesen, *Twice Neokoros*, 152.

70. Richey, *Roman Imperial Ideology*, 28.

71. In practice, of course, the elite few enjoyed the majority of the benefits.

72. The boundaries of the Judean province were not fixed over time. It roughly included Judea proper, Samaria, and Idumea. See Malamat and Ben-Sasson, *History of the Jewish People*, 246.

Appointed by the Emperor, Roman governors served as the chief officials of provinces within the empire. As the highest ranking representatives of imperial power within their provinces, they were responsible for managing various administrative, military, and legal matters, all in the interest of maintaining order and a steady stream of tax revenue. A few brief examples will suffice as illustrations of their administrative and military responsibilities. It will then be important to consider legal matters at some length as they are pertinent to a reading of John's narrative of Jesus' appearance before Pilate.

Roman governors fulfilled various administrative roles within their provinces. They were responsible for the collection of taxes, and also minted coins as necessary for the operation of the economy (e.g., *J.W.* 2.273). Pilate himself minted at least three series of coins during his reign, and several other Judean governors did likewise.[73] Governors also frequently engaged in building projects. For example, Josephus recounts an episode in which Pilate built an aqueduct using money from the Jewish temple treasury, evoking public anger. There are also many extant letters from Pliny the Younger, a Roman governor, to the emperor Trajan regarding several building projects. In them, Pliny, the governor of Bithynia and Pontus, a province to the north of Asia, consults with the emperor regarding problems he must address in connection with the construction of aqueducts, theaters, gymnasiums, and baths (*Ep.* 10.37-44).

Governors were also responsible for managing Rome's military presence when there was a need to subdue troublesome provincials. Josephus describes at length the actions—and eventual defeat—of the Syrian governor Cestius's military forces against feisty provincials in Galilee and Judea at the beginning of the Jewish revolt (*J.W.* 2.499-555). Josephus also recounts how Pilate, during his reign, moved Roman troops from Caesarea to Jerusalem because he was anticipating public protest from the Jewish population over images he had brought into the city (*Ant.* 18.55-59). Josephus records yet another military intervention by Varro, governor of Syria, to eradicate a vexing band of robbers from the province (*J.W.* 1.398-99). As these examples illustrate, Roman governors were responsible for utilizing the military forces at their disposal for the maintenance of order in their territories.

While managing these aspects of life in the provinces, many Roman governors perpetrated various abuses during their rule. Tacitus describes

---

73. Bond, *Pontius Pilate*, 20.

how one Judean governor, Felix, "practiced every kind of cruelty and lust, wielding the power of king with all the instincts of a slave" (*Historiae* 5.9). Josephus also rails against the Judean governors Albinus and Florus, whose reigns immediately preceded the Jewish War. Josephus says that Albinus engaged in the theft of property, raised taxes to excessive levels, accepted bribes, and allowed robbers to plunder at will (*J.W.* 2.273–76). Though Albinus's offenses were grievous, Josephus says that "his successor, Gessius Florus, made him appear by comparison a paragon of virtue" (*J.W.* 2.277). Josephus also explains why the emperor Tiberius allowed many governors to reign for long periods of time, noting that it was "out of consideration for the feelings of the subject peoples. For it was a law of nature that governors are prone to engage in extortion. When appointments were not permanent, but were for short terms, or liable to be cancelled without notice, the spur to peculation was even greater. If, on the contrary, those appointed kept their posts longer, they would be gorged with their robberies and would by the very bulk of them be more sluggish in pursuit of further gain" (*Ant.* 18.172–73).[74] The rationale was that governors who reigned briefly would more quickly and brutally exploit their provinces for their own benefit than governors who were allowed to rule for a greater length of time. Governors, as part of the ruling elite, were part of the extractive process in an aristocratic-agrarian empire. As such, they were prone to exploit their power for their own benefit.

Governorship in Judea is especially relevant for a reading of John 18–19. Pontius Pilate served under Emperor Tiberius as the fifth governor of the province, from roughly 26 CE until 37 CE (*Ant.* 18.32–35, 89).[75] Judea itself had become an imperial province in 6 CE, at the will of

---

74. To illustrate this point, Josephus relates the story of a wounded man who was covered in flies. When a well-meaning passerby attempted to shoo the flies away, the wounded man begged him to stop. He explained that the flies that were already covering his wounds were sated, but if if they were to leave and others come, the new flies would have a "fresh appetite" for his blood (*Ant.* 18.174–76). Josephus' story illustrates the strong resemblance he sees between governors and "bloodsucking flies" (Carter, *John and Empire*, 296).

75. The Roman governors took the title "prefect," a military title, until the 40s CE, when it was changed to "procurator" under the reign of Emperor Claudius. Perhaps because of this change, there is some inconsistency in the manner in which Philo, Josephus, and New Testament texts refer to the Roman governors. They are variously called ἔπαρχος (prefect), ἐπίτροπος (procurator), and ἡγεμών (governor). See Bond, *Pontius Pilate*, 12; and Lémonon, *Pilate et le gouvernement*, 45–48. In the New Testament, ἡγεμών (or a participial form of the verb ἡγεμονεύω) is the preferred term for Roman governors (e.g., Matt 27:2; Acts 23:24), although none of these terms appear

Emperor Augustus, which meant that it came under direct Roman rule, direct taxation was established, and a succession of Roman governors began their administration of the territory.[76]

The Roman governors of Judea were drawn from the equestrian order, and thus had considerable status and wealth. As procurators of a minor imperial province, however, they only had a small auxiliary force of Roman troops at their command.[77] Although he lacked legions of his own, the Judean governor could call for military support upon the province of Syria, just to the north, where four legions were stationed during Pilate's reign.[78] During the beginning of Pilate's reign, however, there was no Syrian legate in place, which may have presented the governor of Judea with difficulties. The absence of the Syrian legate meant that Pilate would not have been able to rely on the help of the Syrian legions in case of unrest. Until 32 CE, Pilate would have been dependent on his own small military force and would likely have tried to put down any potential uprising quickly before it could escalate. Thus he, perhaps more than other Roman governors of Judea, may have been especially anxious about revolts.[79]

The Roman prefect resided in Caesarea, instead of Jerusalem, Judea's religious and cultural center, and would occasionally move to Jerusalem during significant festivals when the population of the city swelled and rioting was likely.[80] This fact makes sense of Pilate's presence in Jerusalem for the Passover festival as reported in the Fourth Gospel. As noted above, Pilate and the other Roman governors of the province had small staffs, and were primarily concerned with maintaining order and with taxation. To maintain order, the governor had auxiliary troops at his command,

---

in the Gospel of John.

76. Up until this time, Judea and its surrounding regions were ruled by members of the Herodian dynasty, who served as vassal kings for Rome. In 6 CE, Archelaus the ethnarch was removed from his rule, and his property was confiscated for the imperial treasury. See Josephus, *J.W.* 2.11; *Ant.* 17.342-44; and Dio Cassius, *Roman History* 55.27. Tacitus writes in 17 CE, regarding taxation, that "Syria and Judea were tired of the burden of taxes and requested their reduction" (*Ann.* 2.42, quoted in Malamat and Ben-Sasson, *History of the Jewish People*, 248).

77. Bond, *Pontius Pilate*, 5. See also Hanson and Oakman, *Palestine*, 61-62.

78. Lémonon, *Pilate*, 62.

79. Bond, *Pontius Pilate*, 14-15.

80. E.g., see Josephus, *Ant.* 18.55-59; and *J.W.* 2.169-74, 280, which describe the governor Florus arriving at Jerusalem for the Passover festival. See also Acts 23:23-24 and 25:1-13, which describe the Roman governors Felix and Festus.

which included several cohorts of five hundred to one thousand troops stationed in Judea, with two cohorts posted in Jerusalem. According to the Fourth Gospel's presentation of Jesus' arrest, one of these cohorts, composed of several hundred soldiers, was involved in taking Jesus into custody (18:3, 12).[81]

Because of minimal staffing, the Judean governors, like other Roman governors, would have relied, to a large degree, on alliances with the local authorities. Because they had the power to appoint the Jewish high priests, Judean governors held sway over the political loyalties of the priests. Pilate's predecessor, Valerius Gratus, during the course of his eleven-year tenure, removed a number of high priests and installed others, apparently as it suited his own agenda.[82] When Pilate assumed office, he allowed the incumbent Jewish high priest, Caiaphas, to remain in that position until Pilate himself was removed from office ten years later. As noted above, we may presume that a high priest such as Caiaphas was allowed to remain in his position under the Roman governor for so long because he was "a man who could be relied on to support Roman interests."[83]

The Fourth Gospel reflects an awareness of many of these realities of Roman governorship in the "trial" scene. An accused provincial of low social status appears before the most powerful Roman official in the Judean province, who is responsible for overseeing administrative, economic, military, and legal matters, and whose goal is to preserve Roman interests. Let us now turn to consider several aspects of Roman justice and the ways in which governors were involved in the legal system.

8. Governors, Roman Justice, and "Trials"

As Kautsky points out, the separation between military, governmental, administrative, judicial, and priestly functions is largely a modern phenomenon.[84] In the Roman Empire, there would have been no separate oc-

---

81. One of the cohorts stationed in Jerusalem is mentioned in Acts 21:31–35. An "Italian cohort" stationed at Caesarea is also mentioned in Acts 10:1.

82. Josephus, *Ant.* 18:33–35.

83. Bond, *Pontius Pilate*, 19. It should be noted that after Pilate was deposed, the Roman governor of Syria, Vitellius, returned control of the high priestly garments to the Jewish priests. However, this does not mean that the priests no longer collaborated with the Romans, especially insofar as collaboration benefited them. See, for example, Carter, *Matthew and Empire*, 149.

84. Kautsky, *Politics of Aristocratic Empires*, 161.

cupation for "judges." Instead, this governmental function was exercised by the rulers. Thus, Pilate and other local ruling elites exercised judicial power. In the Fourth Gospel, the Jewish authorities and the Roman governor interact and negotiate with one another in order to establish "justice" while Jesus is in their custody. Yet the historical context and the narrative of the Fourth Gospel suggest that justice is not their principal concern.

Our knowledge of Roman legal codes and judicial procedures is limited, given the scarcity of sources from the period describing legal proceedings in Roman provinces.[85] Nevertheless, general observations can be made about the nature of Roman justice and the governor's role in its implementation.

Roman laws and justice were a means of maintaining order and preserving the power, control, and tax revenue of the ruling elite. According to O. F. Robinson, "For the Romans 'crime' meant actions which threatened social well-being and stability; the repression of crime aimed to protect society more than its individual members, who were traditionally expected to be responsible for their own safety."[86] Therefore, order was likely of greater concern than a question of law or justice for any one person involved in a criminal trial. As Matthew Skinner observes, "The foundational question beneath a governor's ruling in criminal cases, then, was not necessarily 'Has this person broken a law?' (although that could be a relevant, secondary question). The inquiry was more along the lines of 'Has this person done anything that endangers social welfare or threatens Roman values?'"[87] Pilate's concern as he questioned Jesus would have been primarily to maintain order and protect Roman interests, rather than to ascertain Jesus' innocence or guilt.

In discussing the historical trial of Jesus, William R. Herzog argues that it is anachronistic to even speak of a "trial," so much so that he claims that there "never was a 'trial of Jesus.'"[88] The word "trial" itself evokes a number of ideas not present in Jesus' appearance before Pilate; to call legal proceedings such as Jesus' interrogation by Pilate a "trial" fails to understand the realities and politics of such so-called trials in the first-century Roman Empire. Herzog claims that a "trial" implies "bringing

---

85. Skinner, *Trial Narratives*, 14.
86. Robinson, *Penal Practice*, 3.
87. Skinner, *Trial Narratives*, 15.
88. Herzog, *Jesus, Justice, and the Reign of God*, 240.

charges, providing for a prosecutor and defense attorney, introducing evidence and weighing its relevance, impaneling a jury of peers, adhering to a code of law, following court procedures designed to protect the rights of all involved, determining innocence or guilt only as the outcome of the legal process, allowing appeals, and regarding the accused innocent until proven guilty," none of which apply in the case of Jesus' "trial."[89] Herzog thus contends that Jesus' appearance before Pilate was merely a political show trial, in which the system conformed to the power, inclinations, and benefit of the elite, not to laws and legal precedents. They were a means by which elites sought to bolster their own interests and remove threats. The purpose of such show trials was not a fair hearing or "justice," but rather "the public degradation and humiliation of an enemy of the state before his foreordained execution."[90] Show trials and subsequent executions also aimed to dissuade others from adopting the same behavior as the condemned, and thus they provided Roman governors with a powerful political tool.

For these reasons, with respect to the Fourth Gospel, it is neither suitable nor advantageous to call Jesus' appearance before Pilate a trial. It is more precise to call it a show trial, in which matters of guilt, innocence, and fairness are of marginal importance while political concerns are paramount. Jesus' fate is largely determined from the outset of the "trial": he has predicted his death (e.g., 2:19–22); both the Jewish authorities and Pilate perceive him as a threat because they collaborate in arresting him (18:1–12); and Pilate has little reason within the narrative to release the non-elite Jesus anyway. The interactions between Pilate and the Jewish authorities develop as a tensive negotiation between the Roman governor and local allied elites, in which both sides vie for political gain.

A number of other factors inform an interpretation of the Roman show trial in the Fourth Gospel. To assist in the maintenance of order and undergird judicial proceedings, the Roman governors possessed the power of *imperium*, which meant that they had "supreme administrative power in the province including both military and judicial authority."[91] *Imperium* meant that governors had the ability to exercise control over virtually every element of judicial proceedings, including the hearing of evidence and testimony and the determination of the verdict and sen-

---

89. Herzog, *Jesus, Justice, and the Reign of God*, 240.
90. Herzog, *Jesus, Justice, and the Reign of God*, 241.
91. Bond, *Pontius Pilate*, 13.

tencing.⁹² This supreme judicial authority also entailed the authority to execute provincials within their jurisdiction, effectively removing from society those groups and individuals who were perceived threats to order.

Governors had considerable latitude in their exercise of judicial authority, but an observable and acute legal bias was usually at play. Legal proceedings favored members of the elite, and non-elites could expect more severe trials and harsher sentences. Peter Garnsey has written at length about the legal advantage of elites, observing that "[i]n general it can be said that judges and juries were suspicious of, if not resentful towards, low-status plaintiffs who attacked their 'betters' in court, and were prepared to believe the worst of low-status defendants, while the pleas of high-status plaintiffs or defendants . . . were given more credence."⁹³ For example, the legal bias against lower-status persons is evident in a story by Apuleius which recounts the trial of a wealthy woman who is merely condemned to exile following her attempt to commit murder, while the lower-status slave whom she employed is executed for the same crime.⁹⁴ Another example from Josephus also illustrates this bias. The historian displays great surprise at the actions of the Roman governor Florus when the governor did "what none had ever done before": he had equestrian members of the Jewish elite whipped and then crucified (*J.W.* 2.308). Such penalties were normally reserved for lower-status defendants.⁹⁵

While governors did have considerable flexibility in making their judicial decisions, this does not mean that they could do whatever they wanted. Practicalities constrained their judgments. First, they had to keep members of the local elites reasonably appeased. Skinner echoes this idea, noting that in legal decisions, "the governor's work often had to benefit a province's local elites."⁹⁶ Local elites did have recourse to appeal to higher authorities if they disapproved of a governor's actions. Pilate himself was deposed because local elites decried his response to a Samaritan uprising. He was removed from his post in 37 CE and was sent to Rome when a group of local Samaritan elites complained to the

---

92. Aubert, "Double Standard," 99. See also Skinner, *Trial Narratives*, 15.

93. Garnsey, *Social Status and Legal Privilege*, 100. See further 65–100, 103–52, and 221–80.

94. Apuleius, *Metam.* 10.12. For the original text with English translation, see Apuleius, *Golden Ass*, 495.

95. In addition to a legal bias against low-status individuals, there is also evidence that there was a bias against provincials. See Brunt, "*Laus Imperii*," 29.

96. Skinner, *Trial Narratives*, 16.

governor of Syria, objecting to Pilate's violent retaliation (Josephus, *Ant.* 18.85–89). While being mindful of how their actions affected the local elites, governors also had to consider the opinions of the non-elite masses to some degree, in order to maintain order and control.

These realities of Roman justice are in play in the Fourth Gospel's "trial" scene, and inform a reading of it in significant ways. For example, we can surmise that Pilate's primary concern in John 18–19 is not to implement "justice" but rather to maintain order and control in his province, while negotiating his political relationship with the Jewish authorities. It is also apparent that Jesus stands before Pilate as a low-status, non-elite provincial. Carter soberly observes that "[a] provincial of lower status, no political power, and little wealth has no chance of any other outcome [aside from death]."[97] Therefore, the first-century audience of the Fourth Gospel would not necessarily have been surprised at the harsh treatment Jesus receives, and would not expect that Jesus would receive what we consider a fair trial. The text of the Gospel hints at this as well. When Pilate proposes that the Jewish authorities take Jesus and judge him themselves, they reply, "We are not permitted to put anyone to death" (18:31). Their response suggests that Jesus' fate is sealed from the beginning of the Roman show trial; they leave no possibility in their response that Jesus might be declared innocent. They also admit their subservience to and dependence on imperial Rome and its representative, Pilate, who alone possesses the power of the death penalty.

9. The Function of Trials in Greco-Roman Literature

At this juncture it seems appropriate to comment on the function of trial scenes in Greco-Roman literature, as this can shed light on expectations a first-century audience might have brought to bear on their reception of this text. I am not suggesting that the author or audience of the Fourth Gospel would have had access to other writings of the period that contained trial scenes. However, at the very least, this inquiry provides us with a sense of the cultural undercurrents and associated audience expectations relating to trial narratives at that time.

Throughout history, trial narratives in literature have captivated audiences. When such stories portray an accused protagonist who is forced to face the judicial system, they often "heighten critical awareness of the legal system as a whole" and serve as "vehicles for discussions of

---

97. Carter, *Matthew and Empire*, 151.

larger social issues rather than rehashings of judicial procedure."[98] Trials also reveal much about the characters caught up in them, even as they explore issues of justice within the legal system itself. They also tend to "draw readers in as courtroom observers who also await an outcome or verdict, nearly urging readers to react to claims made in the trials and their outcomes."[99] Trials in literature provide opportunities to influence readers and to contribute to the impact of the larger narrative.

Saundra Schwartz has examined the trial scenes in several Greek novels that circulated during the first three centuries of the Common Era and identified several useful points that inform a reading of Jesus' show trial in the Fourth Gospel. She suggests that the trial scene formula in ancient Greek novels "is ideally suited to the illumination of opposing social values," and that they involved issues that "were important to the novelists and their reading public."[100] The show trial in the Fourth Gospel revolves around theological issues that were significant to its author and audience, contrasting Pilate, the representative of Roman imperial power, with Jesus, who represents God.

Schwartz notes that trial scenes also typically involved irony. This is certainly the case in the Fourth Gospel's show trial scene. Protagonists were often innocent defendants in such trial scenes, and while the reader would be aware of the truth, it was typically obscured from the judge and the court. Schwartz writes,

> The moral universe of the novels tends to be painted in black and white, and the reader is rarely in doubt as to the guilt or innocence of the parties involved in the trial scenes. Despite this, trials often result in verdicts which are contrary to what the reader knows is right. Indeed, they often confound or subvert justice, and thereby perpetuate the dramatic conflict. The novelists make great use of the dramatic device of irony in order to heighten the pathos of the wrongly accused defendant.[101]

While the Johannine Jesus may not be "innocent" with respect to Roman imperial power—he is described as an unsanctioned king with an alternative empire who demands the loyalty of his followers—there is a sharp contrast drawn between the prisoner Jesus and the elite

98. Fludernik and Olson, "Introduction," xx.
99. Skinner, *Trial Narratives*, 25.
100. Schwartz, "Courtroom Scenes," 386.
101. Schwartz, "Courtroom Scenes," 28.

representatives of imperial power. Readers are expected to side with Jesus. The audience of the Fourth Gospel, having followed the prior seventeen chapters, knows who Jesus is, even while the imperial agents cannot fathom his true identity. Skinner further describes the function of irony: "Trial scenes can employ dramatic irony to great effect by allowing that irony to persist and even to leverage a trial's outcome, such as when characters prove themselves unable to grasp information that readers see clearly, or when they remain blind to the fact that the truth is the complete opposite of what they think it is."[102] Again, in the Fourth Gospel's show trial scene, these observations ring true. While readers have the information necessary to interpret the events as they transpire, Pilate and the Jewish authorities are unable to understand Jesus' identity and God's purposes.

Furthermore, the irony in trial scenes often provides commentary. It has the ability to criticize those in authority for their incapacity to discern the truth, and therefore it "denigrates their qualifications to regulate social well-being and offer judgments on truth or justice."[103] This polemical function of irony is also manifest in the Fourth Gospel's show trial scene.

While Skinner examines trial scenes in ancient Greek novels, he also examines trials in other ancient writings, including the short story of Susanna in the Apocrypha, the *Acts of the Pagan Martyrs*, and Plato's *Apology*.[104] All offer a critique of those in power. In Susanna, the two elders who falsely accuse Susanna find themselves as the defendants when Daniel intervenes and interrogates them. The *Acts of the Pagan Martyrs* reflects "a persecuted group's attempt to engage in polemic by using literary accounts of trials as a mode of resistance," according to Skinner.[105] Finally, although Socrates was condemned by an Athenian jury, Skinner says that later authors, writing about the deaths of other popular teachers under Roman power, used Socrates' death as a backdrop to juxtapose "the irresistible power of Rome against the wisdom, self-control, and the virtues of the ostensibly overwhelmed defendants," as a means of voicing "resistance, rebuke, and vindication."[106] Thus there is precedent for the

---

102. Skinner, *Trial Narratives*, 27.

103. Skinner, *Trial Narratives*, 28.

104. To clarify, I am referring to the short story "Susanna" found in the Greek edition of the book of Daniel.

105. Skinner, *Trial Narratives*, 31.

106. Skinner, *Trial Narratives*, 31.

show trial in the Fourth Gospel functioning as a means of critique or resistance against imperial power and authority.

Conclusion

The world of the Roman Empire in the first century was the primary setting of both the events narrated in the show trial scene in the Fourth Gospel, as well as the life of the Johannine community and evangelist. Yet the bearing of imperial realities on a reading of the Gospel narrative has received insufficient attention. This chapter has attempted to lay out some of the realities of life within the first-century Roman Empire, so that they might inform an interpretation of the show trial scene in the Fourth Gospel in the following chapters. In John 18–19, Jesus directly engages Roman power and authority, and to interpret these scenes it is essential to understand the social structures and power dynamics at work.

CHAPTER 3

The Arrest Scene

INTRODUCTION

THE ARREST SCENE (18:1–12) is one of the most dramatic moments in the Fourth Gospel, pitting Jesus and his followers against a massive, hostile arresting party sent to protect both Jewish and Roman elite interests. In the Synoptic Gospels, a Jewish police force carries out the arrest. John's arrest scene is unique in that an entire cohort of Roman soldiers—several hundred strong—accompany the police on this mission. The scene begins as Jesus concludes his lengthy Farewell Discourse, in which he has prepared his disciples for his departure and prayed to the Father on their behalf (13:1—17:26). Jesus and the disciples have also finished their last meal together and Judas has left them with the intent to betray Jesus (13:30). After Jesus has finished speaking, he goes out from the city with his disciples and crosses the Kidron valley, where they enter an unnamed garden. Judas, knowing that they would be there, brings a massive, armed force to arrest him. Taking the initiative, Jesus comes out to meet them and begins a brief exchange in which he identifies himself as the one whom they are seeking. The force of his self-disclosure, in which he invokes the power of the divine name ("I am"), knocks all of his captors to the ground. Jesus initiates another brief exchange to secure his disciples' freedom and security, but Peter strikes a member of the arresting party with his sword. After Jesus admonishes him and declares his intention to fulfill the Father's will, he is finally placed under arrest, and the Roman soldiers and Jewish police haul him off to face the Jewish authorities, his first stop on the way to the cross.

Readers will have anticipated the arrival of the passion narrative for some time. As early as John 11:53, members of the Sanhedrin formally resolved to have Jesus killed. Even before that, the evangelist noted malicious intentions against Jesus on a number of occasions (5:18; 7:1, 19, 25; 8:37, 40). Thus, as his captors arrive at the garden where Jesus and his disciples are located, they are acting on intentions and plans that have been percolating for some time. Tensions have escalated throughout the Gospel and now the Jewish authorities finally send their police force, in concert with Roman forces, to apprehend Jesus. The moment of arrest fulfills the plans of Jesus' antagonists, but also signals the beginning of the fulfillment of God's eschatological plans. Jesus himself has repeatedly anticipated his coming "hour," which symbolically represents his glorification through death (7:30; 8:20; 12:23, 27; 13:1; 16:32; 17:1; cf. 2:4). He has also predicted that he would lay down his life of his own accord (10:17–18). With the arrival of the arresting party, Jesus' eschatological hour of glorification begins in earnest.

In this chapter, I will argue that the irony that pervades the Johannine arrest scene mocks the agents of Roman imperialism while promoting belief in Jesus. The irony is part of a Johannine hidden transcript that negates aspects of the dominant public transcripts of Rome. Yet it also mimics imperial power by its emphasis on Jesus' overwhelming power and his ability to secure victory over his opponents. I will begin by providing an overview of the irony in the scene and will argue that both the Roman cohort and the Jewish police represent agents of Roman imperialism. The rest of the chapter will follow an outline of the Johannine arrest scene, which breaks neatly into five subsections.

The opening verses (18:1–3) set the scene as both Jesus' entourage and his captors arrive at the garden. The narrator provides a thorough description of the composition of the arresting party, including the items they carry to assist in the arrest. Jesus takes the initiative in vv. 4–6, confronting the arresting party and knocking them to the ground with divine power. A second exchange between Jesus and the antagonists follows in vv. 7–9, in which Jesus secures the safety and freedom of his disciples. In vv. 10–11, Peter reacts violently to the possibility of Jesus' arrest and then is reprimanded by Jesus. Finally, Jesus is arrested and bound in v. 12.

Irony and the Arrest

Ironies abound in the arrest scene in the Fourth Gospel, and a number of incongruities in the narrative draw attention to them. Two closely related ironies run throughout the scene. First, in spite of all appearances to the contrary, Jesus is fully in control of the events as they unfold. This ironic theme surfaces throughout the passion narrative. Jesus knows what is going to happen and proceeds to his death on his own initiative, in full obedience to the will of the Father. In contrast to the Synoptic Gospels, he never seems to doubt or waver. For example, John presents no moment of agony and indecision for Jesus. Nor does Jesus lie prostrate in the dust of Gethsemane, praying for God to "remove this cup from me" (e.g., Mark 14:36).[1] In the Fourth Gospel, Jesus seizes the initiative in his own arrest. And in the face of the overwhelming armed opposition that arrives to arrest him, as many as six hundred Roman troops, he is able to overpower them with a divine word. Ultimately, he is taken into custody because he intends and allows it. This pervasive irony mocks the efforts of the arresting party and undercuts public transcripts of Roman domination, but it also displays mimicry by asserting Jesus' domination and the overwhelming power that he possesses.

The second major irony underlying the scene is what Duke calls an "irony of identity." Duke says that "irony of identity" is present when "one character or group of characters fails to recognize the true identity of another . . . and consequently acts or speaks in ways either grossly inappropriate or accidentally appropriate."[2] The effect of this use of irony in John 18–19 is to mock the arresting party and promote belief in Jesus. The Jewish police and Roman soldiers do not understand who Jesus is, and their misguided efforts to arrest him reveal their ignorance. They prove that they are aligned with darkness—not the "light of the world" (8:12).[3] Yet, in spite of their overwhelming numbers and force, they are utterly inadequate to the task of arresting Jesus and are able to take him into custody only because he allows it.

Meanwhile, readers of the Fourth Gospel have inside information that the characters in the narrative lack; they know who Jesus is.

---

1. In John, the members of the arresting party will, in fact, be the ones lying prostrate on the ground!

2. Duke, *Irony in the Fourth Gospel*, 100.

3. For the symbolic value of light and darkness in the Fourth Gospel and the ironic contrast between light and darkness in this scene, see pp. 85–89 below.

Beginning with the prologue (1:1–18), the evangelist has given the audience enough information to realize the full significance of Jesus' identity: he is the divine, preexistent *logos*, the Son of God. The members of the arresting party essentially serve as "foils" while readers are "invited to the 'upper room'" to share the perspective of the author.[4] Readers are inclined to believe that Jesus is who the evangelist says he is, while noting the foolishness of the Jewish police and Roman soldiers, who act in vain because of their ignorance.

Other ironies in the arrest support these two central ones. For example, the arresting party brings weapons to apprehend Jesus, which further proves that they do not understand who it is that they intend to take into custody. They will not need to resort to violent force to arrest Jesus, who has displayed little propensity to perpetrate violence himself (with the exception of 2:15–16), and who fully intends to give himself up into their custody in accordance with God's purposes (10:17–18). Weapons and violent intent cannot interfere with the divine plan as Jesus proceeds toward the cross. Their ignorance is also highlighted by their bearing of lanterns and torches—artificial sources of light—to assist them in arresting the one who is the "light of the world" (e.g., 8:12). These ironic moments support and emphasize the two major ironies that run throughout the scene.

The Jewish Police and the Roman Cohort as Agents of Imperial Power

A major contention of this project is that the Fourth Gospel represents part of a Johannine hidden transcript of resistance against Roman imperialism. But in the arrest scene, both Jewish police and Roman soldiers arrive to arrest Jesus and seem to have equal responsibility in taking Jesus into custody. How does this cooperation between Jewish and Roman interests figure in the argument that the Fourth Gospel assists readers in negotiating Roman imperial realities? The cohort from the Roman army is certainly an instrument of imperial domination and order in the province. I have already argued above that the Jewish authorities are not strictly spiritual leaders, but allies with and agents of Roman imperialism as well.[5] Here, I will extend that argument by demonstrating that as Jew-

---

4. Culpepper, *Anatomy*, 168.
5. See pp. 55–58 above.

ish and Roman forces fulfill their roles in Jesus' arrest, both are allied in representing the interests of elite members of society who are committed to maintaining the imperial status quo.

First, although Jewish and Roman forces collaborate throughout the passion narrative to execute Jesus, and receive fairly equal attention during the arrest scene, Roman representatives receive far more attention throughout the remainder of the passion narrative—especially in Jesus' interrogation by Pilate and the crucifixion scene. If, as Duke has argued, the irony in the Fourth Gospel primarily functions as polemic against Jews, then why is the Roman presence so significant in the passion narrative?[6] One might reasonably conclude, from a cursory reading of the arrest, the Roman show trial, and the crucifixion accounts, that the evangelist was far more interested in polemic against Rome.[7]

Second, the police forces (Greek: ὑπηρέτης) who have been sent "from the chief priests and the Pharisees" are retainers of the Jewish elite (18:3).[8] They are most likely agents of the Sanhedrin, the same council (συνέδριον) composed of chief priests and Pharisees that met at 11:47 in response to Jesus' raising of Lazarus.[9] As representatives of the Jerusalem Sanhedrin, a council composed of members of the Jewish aristocracy, these police sent from the chief priests and the Pharisees are agents of elite Jewish interests.[10] As noted in chapter 2, these Jewish aristocratic elites were allied with Rome and assisted in maintaining imperial order.[11] Thus, they also represent imperial interests.

---

6. See Duke, *Irony in the Fourth Gospel*, 149–50. Duke also suggests a positive effect of irony: to inspire faith in Jesus (151–56).

7. Of course, it is possible that both are in view. My concern here is to note that Duke has overlooked a significant effect of the Johannine irony.

8. The Greek word ὑπηρέτης generally describes "one who functions as a helper" or an assistant (BDAG 1035). The Fourth Gospel will also use this word to describe Jesus' followers (18:36).

9. Howard-Brook agrees that these Jewish representatives in the arrest are "Sanhedrin officers" (*Becoming Children of God*, 374). Josef Blinzler identifies another option: they may be Levites who had jurisdiction within the temple area itself who were occasionally called upon to assist in crisis situations (*Trial of Jesus*, 62–68). Blinzler also (in my opinion mistakenly) assumes that the cohort represents a division of the Jewish military, and thus believes that only Jewish forces are involved in the Johannine arrest.

10. Horsley, "High Priests," 30.

11. See pp. 55–58 above.

Many commentators fail to note the significance of these Jewish authorities in the political sphere, assuming that they were solely religious leaders. For example, in his discussion of the arrest scene, Senior draws a false dichotomy by claiming that the Roman soldiers and police from the Jewish authorities are "Gentile and Jew, secular power and religious leader."[12] This statement by Senior suggests a distinct separation between politics and religion in the first century. The Jewish authorities and their agents, however, are by no means solely focused on religion; they certainly have political interests in mind. The political and religious spheres were intertwined in the Roman Empire.[13] For example, Jews offered sacrifices on behalf of Caesar in the Jewish temple (*J.W.* 2.197). Roman procurators also had the power to depose high priests at will; high priests who served imperial interests could expect a longer tenure in office.[14] The text of the Fourth Gospel itself also suggests that the Jewish authorities had political motivations and interests. In the aftermath of the raising of Lazarus, the chief priests and Pharisees, the same groups that send "police" in the arrest scene, worry together that if Jesus continues to perform many signs, "everyone will believe in him, and the Romans will come and destroy both our holy place and our nation" (11:48). Their desires to placate Caesar, to keep order, and to preserve their land motivate them to seek Jesus' death.

Furthermore, during the Roman show trial, the Jewish authorities ironically and tragically declare that they "have no king but the emperor" (19:15), even while they are prepared to celebrate God's sovereignty through their observance of the Passover festival. Throughout the arrest, interrogation, and crucifixion scenes, representatives of the Jewish authorities negotiate and collaborate with representatives of Rome to secure their own interests, to eliminate a potential threat, and to maintain the status quo. The Jewish authorities undoubtedly had some autonomy, but ultimately they had to collaborate with imperial power to maintain control of the province.[15] The Fourth Gospel certainly presents these Jewish authorities as agents of the imperial order.

Thus, when police from the Jewish authorities arrive with an entire cohort of Roman soldiers to arrest Jesus, the Johannine audience would

---

12. Senior, *Passion of Jesus*, 55.
13. Carter gives a number of examples that indicate this (*John and Empire*, 21).
14. Cf. Brown, *Gospel According to John*, 2:798.
15. Historically, when they were not able to do so, Rome would intervene.

not have assumed that the two groups are collaborating begrudgingly, one with religious interests and the other with political interests. Rather, both groups have vested interests in protecting and maintaining the imperial status quo and they work together to achieve this goal. Both parties represent elite agents of imperial control in the province.

THE ARRIVAL OF THE ARRESTING PARTY (18:1–3)

After the Farewell Discourse concludes, the Fourth Evangelist sets the stage for Jesus' arrest by having Jesus and his disciples move out from Jerusalem across the Kidron valley to an unnamed garden. The narrative includes a description of Jesus' captors as they arrive, including the items that they bear with them for the purpose of apprehending Jesus: lanterns, torches, and weapons. The evangelist's presentation of both the composition of the arresting party and the items they bring contributes to the irony of the scene.

1. THE ROMAN COHORT

As the Johannine passion narrative begins, Roman soldiers arrive at the garden with Judas and the Jewish police force to arrest Jesus (18:3). The Greek word that the evangelist uses to describe the Romans, σπεῖρα, suggests the military unit is a cohort, a tenth of a Roman legion, composed of approximately six hundred soldiers.[16] Although he is not mentioned until the end of the scene, their officer, a tribune (Greek: χιλίαρχος) who would have commanded as many as a thousand troops, arrives with them (18:12).[17] Among the Gospels, John alone explicitly notes this Roman presence at Jesus' arrest. And John does so in indelible fashion, flooding the garden with an overwhelming show of Roman military power.

Historically speaking, it is hard to imagine that a massive force of hundreds of troops would be deployed for the simple task of arresting Jesus; after all, Crossan claims that a cohort would have been "the

---

16. BDAG 936. The Greek word σπεῖρα is used to translate the Latin *cohors*. In a passage describing the military forces under the command of Titus, Josephus says that "[o]f the twenty-three cohorts, ten numbered each a thousand infantry, the remaining thirteen had each a strength of six hundred infantry and a hundred and twenty cavalry" (*J.W.* 3.67–68).

17. Literally, "leader of a thousand" (BDAG 1084).

complete body of Roman troops permanently garrisoned in Jerusalem."[18] This complaint shows up often in discussion of this text, and a number of scholars contend that the scene is historically implausible. These arguments influence how interpreters understand this scene: for example, if the involvement of Roman troops in Jesus' arrest is historically implausible, is it not more likely that the σπεῖρα indicates a Jewish force rather than a Roman one in the narrative world of the Fourth Gospel? If it is historically unlikely that the Romans would deploy six hundred troops to arrest one man, surely we should interpret the σπεῖρα as a smaller force. However, I will argue that while it is historically improbable that six hundred troops arrived to arrest Jesus, Roman military involvement in his historical arrest is not unlikely. Furthermore, in the narrative world of the Fourth Gospel, Roman troops are certainly involved in the arrest, and the evangelist does include an overwhelming number of them in the scene for rhetorical force.

Many scholars argue that, historically, Romans soldiers would not—or could not—have been involved in Jesus' arrest.[19] They find it improbable that the Roman governor would have made his troops available to the Jewish authorities for such a purpose of arresting Jesus. Some commentators, following this line of reasoning, have assumed that, in the Fourth Gospel, the term σπεῖρα must refer to a Jewish force, not a Roman one.[20] To be sure, there are instances in the Septuagint and in Josephus's writings in which the Greek term is used to describe non-Roman forces.[21] However, when the Greek term σπεῖρα is used in the New Testament, it always refers to a contingent of Roman soldiers.[22] In addition, the presence of the Roman commander in 18:12 favors the interpretation that the troops in the arrest scene are, in fact, Roman soldiers. Furthermore, the evangelist clearly states that Judas brings a second group in addition to the σπεῖρα: police from the chief priests and the Pharisees. Because this second group is specifically described as Jewish, in all likelihood the σπεῖρα is not.

18. Crossan, *Who Killed Jesus*, 80–81.

19. E.g., Schnackenburg, *Gospel According to St. John*, 3:222; Barrett, *Gospel According to St. John*, 518.

20. E.g., Blinzler, *Trial of Jesus*, 64–70; Benoit, *Passion and Resurrection of Jesus Christ*, 46.

21. E.g., Judith 14:11; 2 Macc 8:23; Josephus, *J.W.* 2.11; and Josephus, *Ant.* 17.215. See further Brown, *Death of the Messiah*, 1:248.

22. See Matt 27:27; Mark 15:16; John 18:3, 12; Acts 10:1; 21:31; 27:1.

Even if the Fourth Evangelist presents Roman soldiers in Jesus' arrest, would such a detail not have strained the credibility of the scene for readers? Probably not. There are good reasons, historically speaking, to believe that Roman soldiers might well have been involved in the arrest. Both the Roman and Jewish elites had an interest in maintaining order in Jerusalem, especially during the potentially volatile festival of Passover, which swelled the population of Jerusalem (11:55). Roman troops were stationed in the Antonia fortress, overlooking the temple; they surely would have acted swiftly to quell any potential disturbances related to the festival or Jesus' arrest.[23] Roman agents respond in a similar situation in Acts, for example, when a Roman tribune and his cohort arrest Paul because a riotous mob poses a threat to the stability of Jerusalem (Acts 21:27–36). It is not difficult to imagine that Roman troops would have been involved at Jesus' arrest out of a concern to avoid civic unrest; it is entirely possible that Roman troops and the Jewish police forces would have collaborated for the sake of maintaining order in the city. Such cooperation would have served both Jewish and Roman elite interests. Given these considerations, it is entirely possible, historically speaking, that Roman soldiers were present at Jesus' arrest and in any case that John's audience would not have found their participation in the scene implausible.

Haenchen takes issue with another aspect of John's presentation of the Roman cohort in the scene. When the evangelist says that "Judas brought a detachment of soldiers" (18:3), Haenchen doubts that Judas could command a cohort of Roman soldiers himself, adding sarcastically: "as though the Roman garrison in Jerusalem, together with its tribunes, were subordinate to a Jewish civilian."[24] Haenchen assumes that Judas is not merely leading the soldiers, but is in command of them. However, the Greek verb λαμβάνω surely does not imply that Judas has any sort of jurisdiction over these troops. Indeed, the evangelist explicitly mentions the presence of the officer who has command over the Roman cohort (18:12). The more logical implication of the verb λαμβάνω is that Judas *led* them to the garden.[25] Judas's role in the scene is merely to direct the arresting party to Jesus' location.

---

23. See further O'Day, "Gospel of John: Introduction," 801–2.
24. Haenchen, *John 2*, 164.
25. See BDAG 583–85.

Many scholars also object to the vast number of Roman troops present in the Fourth Gospel's arrest scene. Does the Fourth Evangelist really indicate that an entire cohort of soldiers arrived to arrest Jesus? Is not the use of six hundred troops to arrest one Galilean clearly overkill on the part of the Jewish authorities and Romans? Dodd deals with this difficulty by suggesting that the evangelist may have a maniple, a smaller division within a Roman cohort, in mind when using the term σπεῖρα.[26] Still, Dodd admits that "even a maniple ... would seem a very ample provision" of soldiers for the arrest.[27] Stibbe contends that the evangelist does have a maniple in mind, and argues that this is probably a historical detail that the Fourth Gospel alone has preserved.[28] Whether the evangelist indicates that a cohort or a maniple is present, however, an excessive number of soldiers is involved for the arrest of one man.

Speaking in terms of historical probabilities, Winter believes that Roman troops were likely involved in Jesus' arrest, but proposes a much smaller force as more plausible: perhaps ten soldiers commanded by a *decurio*.[29] Winter goes on to argue that the presence of Roman troops in the Fourth Gospel is strong evidence of the historical involvement of Rome in the arrest of Jesus. In his view, it is unlikely that the evangelist would have invented Roman involvement in the arrest.[30] His suggestion that a much smaller force of Roman troops was present at Jesus' arrest is reasonable. To bring an entire cohort would have left Jerusalem's defenses dangerously undermanned.[31] Further, it is unlikely that the Romans would have thought that such a large force would be needed to arrest Jesus. More likely, the Fourth Evangelist has exaggerated the size of the arresting force for rhetorical purposes. The evangelist's primary concern

---

26. Dodd, *Historical Tradition*, 73–74. Brown indicates that there are instances in Greco-Roman literature where the Greek term σπεῖρα is used to translate the Latin *manipulus*, which designates a unit of two hundred troops. He does not, however, provide supporting references (*Death of the Messiah*, 1:248).

27. Dodd, *Historical Tradition*, 74.

28. Stibbe, *John As Storyteller*, 170.

29. Winter, *Trial of Jesus*, 42.

30. Winter, *Trial of Jesus*, 61–63. Winter suggests that, because of John's "conciliatory attitude towards Pilate and Rome," it is unlikely that the inclusion of Roman troops in this scene would have been an invention of the Fourth Evangelist because it paints Rome in an antagonistic light. My project, of course, adopts the perspective that John is not conciliatory towards Rome. Regarding the historicity of Roman troops at Jesus' arrest, Stibbe makes a similar argument (*John As Storyteller*, 170).

31. Barrett, *Gospel According to St. John*, 433.

is to make theological—not historical—claims about Jesus. The hyperbolic presentation of the size of the Roman army's arresting party sets up a grand confrontation between Jesus and a seemingly overwhelming military force.

The exaggerated size of Jesus' opposition in the arrest scene suits the Johannine style: it is one of numerous examples of hyperbole in the Gospel: Jesus turns over one hundred gallons of water into wine (2:1–11); he feeds five thousand people with five loaves of bread and two fish with ample leftovers to spare (6:2–13); Mary lavishes an extraordinarily expensive perfume on Jesus' feet (12:1–8); Joseph of Arimathaea and Nicodemus seek to preserve Jesus' body with approximately seventy-five pounds of spices (19:38–40); and Peter and the other disciples catch one hundred and fifty-three fish (21:6, 11). Hyperbole appears frequently in the Fourth Gospel and serves both theological and rhetorical interests.[32] As we shall see, the hyperbolic description of Rome's military presence sets the stage for irony in the arrest scene. The evangelist has placed hundreds of Roman soldiers and Jewish police opposite Jesus' entourage in the narrative, only to knock them down with a single statement from Jesus (18:6).

The explicit reference to the commanding officer with the σπεῖρα in 18:12 lends further credence to the likelihood that the evangelist intends such a large number of troops in the narrative. The Greek word for the officer, χιλίαρχος, is the typical rendering of the Latin *tribunus militum*, an officer who commanded a cohort of soldiers, and means "ruler" or "leader of a thousand."[33] Given that σπεῖρα commonly refers to a cohort, and the officer mentioned in 18:12 would have commanded a cohort, the evangelist clearly had a sizable force of Roman troops in mind. Thus, whatever the historical probabilities may have been, in the narrative world of the Fourth Gospel the evangelist does indeed flood the garden with Roman soldiers, as many as six hundred, who stand shoulder-to-shoulder with their commander and police sent from the Jewish authorities, as they prepare to arrest Jesus.

The inclusion of such a large force of Roman soldiers in this scene has a number of rhetorical effects. First, in contrast to the Synoptic Gospels, Rome's presence is felt directly and is emphasized from the very beginning of the Johannine passion narrative. As Moore says, "From the

---

32. See Michaels, *Gospel of John*, 887.
33. Brown, *Death of the Messiah*, 1:248. See also BDAG 1084.

outset ... and to a degree entirely unmatched by its Synoptic counterparts, the Johannine passion narrative represents its towering protagonist as engaged in a toe-to-toe contest with Roman imperial might—and with Rome hitting the canvas hard early in the first round."[34] The cohort and their commander function as agents of Roman imperial power. As a Roman military presence takes Jesus into custody, John's audience would certainly assume that Pilate is involved in the arrest as well. Bond says that "John's readers would surely know that these Roman troops could only have been placed at the disposal of the Jewish leadership by the prefect himself."[35] Pilate must have authorized the deployment of his troops for this purpose. Second, the presence of Roman soldiers acting under Pilate's authority and in collaboration with a Jewish police force reinforces the idea that Jewish and Roman elites are allied and collaborate to maintain control for their mutual benefit. Third, Jesus is perceived as a tremendous political threat by the Jewish and Roman authorities given that such a sizable military force is deployed to arrest him. Howard-Brook calls this the "most political of arrests," and maintains that there is no sense that Jesus is "a purely 'religious' concern" in the narrative.[36] Finally, the excessively large detachment of soldiers sets up irony in the scene, which will be discussed further below. The tremendous incongruity between Jesus' small, peaceful band of followers and a massive, armed police and military force emphasizes to readers that irony is present.

2. Lanterns and Torches

After describing the composition of the arresting party, with its Roman and Jewish representatives, the Fourth Evangelist specifically lists the equipment they bring in order to arrest Jesus: "[T]hey came there with lanterns and torches and weapons" (18:3).[37] Only John among the

---

34. Moore, *Empire and Apocalypse*, 53.

35. Bond, *Pontius Pilate*, 167. Haenchen draws similar conclusions (*John 2*, 165).

36. Howard-Brook, *Becoming Children of God*, 374.

37. In Greek, they come bearing φανῶν, λαμπάδων, and ὅπλων. It is difficult to say with certainty what exactly the evangelist has in mind for each of these terms, beyond that they are light sources. Louw and Nida describe a φανός (related to the verb φαίνω) as "a small fire which was carried about for the sake of its light and which had some type of protection from wind and weather," and suggest that "by NT times it appears to have been used primarily to identify a type of lamp used outdoors" (L&N 66); hence, its translation as "lantern" by the NRSV. A λαμπάς, from the verb λάμπω, meaning "to shine" or "to give light," is also an item for creating light at night, and its use in Matt 25:1–8 suggests that it also requires oil to use. In this story, five bridesmaids lack oil for

evangelists mentions that the captors arrive bearing two types of light sources, both lanterns and torches. The Synoptic Gospels only indicate that they carry weapons. The mention of lanterns and torches alerts readers, who have just completed the lengthy farewell discourse, that it is still nighttime (cf. 13:30).[38] It also creates a clever dramatic irony that mocks the soldiers and Jewish police, who are figuratively "in the dark" as they arrest Jesus, the light of the world (1:4, 5, 9; 3:19–21; 5:35; 8:12; 9:5; 11:9; 12:35–36, 46).

Light is one of the most widely recognized symbols across all cultures. Philip Wheelwright says that "of all archetypal symbols there is probably none more widespread and more immediately understandable than light."[39] Light conveys life, goodness, knowledge, clarity, and divinity. In contrast, darkness typically represents death, fear, ignorance, and evil powers. The dualistic symbolism of light and darkness pervades the Fourth Gospel and is significant in the arrest scene as well.

The Fourth Gospel is filled with light imagery, so much so that Culpepper identifies it as one of the three core symbols of the Gospel, along with water and bread, all of which are essential to life.[40] From the very beginning, the Johannine prologue symbolically equates the divine *logos* with light (φῶς), announcing that "the light shines in the darkness" and "the true light, which enlightens everyone, was coming into the world" (1:5, 9). Later Jesus identifies himself with the *logos* and the light, declaring that he is the "light of the world" (8:12; 9:5). The Gospel also establishes dualistic conflict between light and darkness early on. Characters within the narrative are aligned with either one or the other. Followers of Jesus "will never walk in darkness but will have the light of

---

their lamps (λαμπάς), while the other five have an ample supply of oil. Other occurrences in the New Testament, however, are ambiguous, and could describe a torch-like object composed of sticks bound together. See Acts 20:8; Rev 4:5; 8:10.

38. Haenchen suggests that the night of the arrest would have been a full moon, since it was Passover, and wonders if they would have needed artificial lights at all to see (*John 2*, 164). While this is an interesting notion, it strains credibility to believe that all readers would have realized this unspoken detail, if the evangelist intended it at all. Brown disagrees with Haenchen's assessment, pointing out that "common sense indicates that an olive grove would have had dark corners in which a man might hide" (*Gospel According to John*, 2:809). It is perfectly reasonable to conclude that the arresting force would have needed artificial lights as they approached the garden to seize Jesus.

39. Wheelwright, *Metaphor and Reality*, 116.

40. Culpepper, *Anatomy*, 189–97.

life" (8:12). In contrast, "those who walk at night stumble, because the light is not in them" (11:10). Those who fail to believe in Jesus reveal that they are aligned with darkness. Light also reveals goodness: "[T]hose who do what is true come to the light, so that it may be clearly seen that their deeds have been done in God" (3:21). But light also exposes: "[F]or all who do evil hate the light and do not come to the light, so that their deeds may not be exposed" (3:20).

Day and night are also theologically significant settings in the Fourth Gospel. Nicodemus, who seems skeptical at first and utterly misunderstands Jesus, comes "by night" (3:2), under the cover of darkness. In marked contrast, in the very next chapter the Samaritan woman meets Jesus in the full light of day, arriving at the well at "about noon" (4:6). She engages in a theological discussion with Jesus and her testimony to her encounter with him leads many other Samaritans to confess Jesus as "Savior of the World" (4:42). The timing of these two meetings, one at night and the other at high noon, suggests something important about the receptivity of Jesus' conversation partners to him. The Samaritan woman, associated with the light, becomes a paradigmatic public witness to Jesus, drawing others to faith in him. Nicodemus, associated with darkness, is her antithesis. However, Nicodemus's character does appear to evolve throughout the course of the Gospel. Later he defends Jesus' right to a hearing before the chief priests and Pharisees (7:45–52) and is involved in Jesus' burial (19:38–42). When Nicodemus brings spices to prepare Jesus' body for burial, the evangelist reminds readers that he had originally come "by night." We do not know whether he has come, at last, to full faith in Jesus, but at least he has become more receptive (19:39).[41]

Time of day is also significant in another key text: when Judas leaves the last supper in order to betray Jesus, the narrator provides a brief comment insinuating the deeper theological significance of Judas's departure: "So, after receiving the piece of bread, he immediately went out. And it was night" (13:30). In leaving to betray Jesus, Judas aligns himself with darkness rather than light (13:27).

In the Fourth Gospel, daytime also conveys Jesus' presence and the power associated with it, while night indicates his absence. Before healing the man born blind, Jesus declares, "We must work the works of him who sent me while it is day; night is coming when no one can work"

---

41. Culpepper says that Nicodemus represents "those who believe but refuse to confess" Jesus (*Anatomy*, 136). According to Michaels, Nicodemus has a "secret allegiance to Jesus" (*Gospel of John*, 981).

(9:4). In chapter 21, the narrator uses day and night symbolism to convey the abundance his disciples find in his presence. In Jesus' absence, Peter and the disciples are unsuccessful in their nighttime fishing endeavor: "[T]hey caught nothing at night" (21:3). But when the resurrected Jesus appears to them "just after daybreak," they are able to catch an abundance of fish (21:4–6).

Culpepper observes that "the conflict of light and darkness evokes a universal and primordial response. The symbols are used universally in religious discourse and had deep roots both in Hellenism and in Judaism."[42] Having read or heard the preceding seventeen chapters of John, the audience of the Fourth Gospel is well-informed and equipped to grasp the symbolism of light and darkness by the time they arrive at the arrest scene. They have been prepared from the very beginning of the Gospel to appreciate this symbolism and to understand its meaning. They know that Jesus is the "light of the world" (8:12) while the arresting party lacks this knowledge.

The image of Roman soldiers and Jewish police arriving with lanterns and torches is an example of dramatic irony. Duke says that "ironic imagery is the author's implied commentary whispering to the reader: all is not as it appears."[43] The Roman soldiers and Jewish police arrive at night with Judas, who the audience already knows is aligned with darkness (13:30). In spite of their lights, the soldiers and police cannot grasp Jesus' identity; Brown observes that "these forces need illumination because they cannot see the light of the world (3:19; 8:12; 9:5)."[44] The characters fail to perceive the incongruity between their artificial light sources and Jesus' identity as "the light of the world," and they fail to understand the full significance of their actions. The irony implicates both the Roman soldiers and the Jewish police and reveals that they all are aligned with darkness. Their effort to arrest Jesus proves that they do not walk in the light; rather, they "walk in the darkness" (12:35). They are synonymous with "those who walk at night" and they stumble "because the light is not in them" (11:10). They are opposed to Jesus in the dualistic conflict between light and darkness that runs throughout the narrative of the Gospel. Their association with darkness demonstrates that they are ignorant of Jesus' true identity and antagonistic toward God's pur-

---

42. Culpepper, *Anatomy*, 191.
43. Duke, *Irony in the Fourth Gospel*, 108.
44. Brown, *Death of the Messiah*, 1:250.

poses. The irony also prompts readers to recall that Jesus is the light of the world and reinforces their belief in him, even in moments when they face opposition.

3. Weapons and Irony

The weapons the arresting party bears are also ironic. A striking incongruity here signals the irony: the Roman soldiers and Jewish police come armed and prepared to use brute force to arrest Jesus, who will not resist arrest with violence (18:11). Their weapons are entirely unnecessary. And even though they bear weapons, they are ultimately rendered powerless in their showdown with Jesus.

The Synoptic Gospels and the Fourth Gospel present different descriptions of the weapons that the arresting party wields. Matthew, Mark, and Luke note that the party arrives carrying "swords and clubs" (μαχαιρῶν καὶ ξύλων).[45] John, however, is less specific, mentioning only that they are bearing "weapons" (ὅπλων) in addition to their lanterns and torches. John does not mention a "sword" specifically until Peter draws one in 18:10. The Greek term ὅπλον implies "any type of tool or instrument" in general, and can more specifically denote "an instrument used in fighting."[46] According to BDAG the term ὅπλον means "any instrument one uses to prepare or make ready" for something, or more specifically, "an instrument designed to make ready for military engagement."[47] It is related to the verb ὁπλίζω, which means "to get ready, especially by equipping."[48] The use of the word thus indicates that the soldiers are prepared to make use of violent force to arrest Jesus. Explicit mention of weapons of any type would also indicate violent intent, but the use of this verb implies that they are prepared to fight if need be. In John, the specific weapons of the arresting party are not noteworthy, but the violent capability and intent that they evince is significant.

That the arresting party bears weapons and is prepared for violence highlights their fundamental misperception of Jesus and strikes an ironic note. Their instruments of warfare serve no purpose in arresting Jesus,

---

45. See Matt 26:47; Mark 14:43; Luke 22:52. Presumably, Matthew and Luke are following their Markan source.

46. See L&N 54, 57.

47. BDAG 716. This can be a weapon, but can also indicate a shield that is necessary to prepare for battle.

48. BDAG 716.

whose identity and power they do not grasp. They come prepared for a fight, but Jesus will go willingly to his death. The audience recalls that Jesus himself said, "No one takes [my life] from me, but I lay it down of my own accord" (10:18). Thus dramatic irony is clearly in view: there is a sharp contradiction between Jesus' plan to lay down his life willingly and the arresting party's misperceptions about the necessity of violence and force to seize him. Irony surrounding Jesus' identity is also in play. If the arresting party knew the true identity of Jesus—as the audience does—then they would know that their weapons are neither necessary nor sufficient to arrest him. Their misperception signals that they do not grasp the identity of the man they have come to arrest. The irony mocks their misguided plans and casts judgment on those who would use violence to maintain the imperial status quo. Weapons and violence cannot disrupt God's plans. But even the disciples demonstrate that they fail to understand this: Peter attacks the high priest's slave in a misguided effort to defend Jesus (18:10).[49] Both the arresting party and Peter serve as foils to Jesus, who models faithful obedience to the will of the Father.

As Jesus, his disciples, and his captors arrive at the garden, the details that the evangelist includes are significant. The size and composition of the arresting party, a massive cohort of Roman soldiers with Jewish police, sets up irony that will come to fruition in 18:6 when the entire group falls to the ground. The light sources and weapons that the captors bring signals irony as well: they would need no lanterns and torches to light their way if only they would believe in Jesus, who is himself the "light of the world" (8:12) and "the way" (14:6). Yet by bringing this equipment, they prove they walk in darkness. Their bearing of weapons also creates irony; they prove that the agents of Roman imperial power have no understanding of Jesus' identity and the nature of the true power that he will shortly display in 18:4–6.

Jesus and the Arresting Party (18:4–6)

The first exchange between Jesus and his captors in the Fourth Gospel occurs as Jesus steps forward to meet them. Jesus identifies himself to the Jewish police and Roman soldiers and the force of this self-identification knocks them to the ground (18:6). This exchange between Jesus and his

---

49. Peter's violent response to Jesus' captors will be dealt with at length on pp. 103–5 below.

captors emphasizes Jesus' initiative and control of the events leading up to his death. It also represents an ironic jab at his opponents: the police and soldiers stand in the divine presence and have no capacity to realize it. They seek Jesus for the wrong reasons, not that they might gain life from him, but that they might end his life. However, they are overwhelmed momentarily by his divine power, proving that imperial might cannot conquer God's Son, even as it takes him into custody and eventually takes his life. Yet in Jesus' display of immense power and the certainty of victory over his opponents, mimicry of imperial power is also evident.

1. Jesus' Initiative and Omniscience

Upon the arrival of the Roman soldiers and Jewish police at the garden, the narrator says, "Then Jesus, knowing all that was to happen to him, came forward and asked them, 'Whom are you looking for?'" (18:4). The Greek text suggests that the garden is somehow enclosed or encircled by a wall.[50] The scene opened with Jesus and his disciples "entering" (εἰσέρχομαι) the garden, and now Jesus "comes forward" or "exits" (ἐξέρχομαι) the garden to meet his captors. Jesus' action of coming forward and exiting the garden conveys his initiative in the arrest. Only in the Fourth Gospel does Jesus step forward to meet his captors, an action that conveys his control of the events of his passion from the beginning.

The narrative aside in 18:4, that Jesus knows all that is about to happen, further strengthens the perception that Jesus is in command. It also signals a major irony in the arrest scene, reminding readers of Jesus' many allusions to and predictions of the events of his passion (e.g., 2:19; 3:14; 7:33; 8:21, 28; 10:17–18; 12:32; 13:3, 21, 27, 33, 38; 14:4, 19, 28; 16:16, 32). Readers are thus "in the know" when the arresting party arrives, while the Roman soldiers and Jewish police act in ignorance of the underlying reality of the situation as well as of their role in it.

The evangelist has repeatedly drawn attention to Jesus' divine foresight and knowledge. Readers should not be surprised that Jesus knows what is coming. Early in the Gospel, Jesus shocks Nathanael when he reveals that he knows more about Nathanael than Nathanael would have thought (1:47–49). The narrator later declares that Jesus "knew all people and needed no one to testify about anyone; for he himself knew what was in everyone" (2:24–25). Jesus knows that the Samaritan woman has had five husbands (4:17–18), and he knows who does not believe and

---

50. O'Day calls it a "walled garden" ("Gospel of John: Introduction," 802).

who will betray him (6:64). He later explicitly predicts that Judas will betray him (13:21), that Simon Peter will deny him (13:38), and that his disciples will scatter (16:32). Time and time again, the Johannine Jesus has proven his supernatural awareness and predictive powers.

In addition to his general divine foresight and knowledge, the narrator has also repeatedly stressed Jesus' awareness of his impending death and return to the Father. Early in the Gospel Jesus alludes to his death, saying, "Destroy this temple, and in three days I will raise it up" (2:19). The narrator clarifies for readers that "he was speaking of the temple of his body," so that readers have early access to the knowledge that Jesus will die (2:21). Jesus also predicts early in the Gospel that one of his disciples will betray him—"[O]ne of you is a devil"—and the narrator clarifies the meaning of this prediction: Judas will betray him (6:70–71). Jesus frequently says that he is "going away" and returning to the one who sent him (e.g., 7:33; 8:21; 13:3, 33; 14:4, 28) and refers to the time when he will be "lifted up" on the cross (3:14; 8:28; 12:32). Finally, when the time comes, he knows that "his hour [has] come to depart from the world" (13:1), and he alludes to his death several times in the Farewell Discourse that follows (13:21, 27, 33; 14:19, 28; 16:16). The narrator's comment in 18:4, that Jesus knew all that was about to happen to him, brings to mind all these allusions and predictions. Jesus is aware of all that is to come and he is in full command of all the events leading to his death.

2. Seeking Jesus

Astute readers will find the question Jesus addresses to the arresting party when he exits the garden enclosure patently ironic: "Whom are you looking for?" (18:4). The Greek word ζητέω has already appeared twenty-nine times in the Fourth Gospel and bears theological significance. Brown comments, "The language of seeking, drawn from the sapiential literature of Israel, is very strong in John, where Jesus is incarnate divine wisdom."[51] Notably, Jesus' question here in the arrest scene clearly echoes his very first words in the Gospel: "What are you looking for?" (1:38).[52] And at the end of the Gospel, among the first words the resurrected Jesus directs to Mary Magdalene are these: "Whom are you looking for?" (20:15). The answer to all three of these inquiries, of course, is "Jesus." Jesus also tells

---

51. Brown, *Death of the Messiah*, 1:260.

52. In 1:38, Jesus asks two followers τί ζητεῖτε, while in 18:4 he asks his captors τίνα ζητεῖτε.

his followers that after he is gone, they will seek him but will not find him (7:34-36; 8:21; 13:33). In the Fourth Gospel, it is appropriate and wise to seek Jesus. After all, he has the words of eternal life (6:68) and those who believe in him will not perish (3:16). More often, however, people seek Jesus in the Fourth Gospel in order to imprison or kill him (5:18; 7:1, 11, 19, 25, 30; 8:37, 40; 10:39; 11:8, 56).

By the time readers arrive at the arrest scene in John, they know that the soldiers and police ought to seek him in order that they might have life, but instead, they seek his death. This incongruity signals the irony in Jesus' question to them. There is an evocative similarity between this question and the one the man born blind directs to the Pharisees in 9:27: "Do you also want to be his disciples?" Neither the Pharisees in chapter 9 nor the arresting party in chapter 18 want to follow Jesus, but readers of the Fourth Gospel know that they should. Instead, their "search" for Jesus will end in his death. Fortunately, as Brown says, "the hostile seeking in the arrest scene is not the final word."[53] Mary Magdalene provides the perfect antithesis to the arresting party: she will seek Jesus and find him resurrected after the Roman and Jewish collaborators have put him to death. She will then declare to Jesus' other followers, "I have seen the Lord" (20:18). Mary Magdalene is a model disciple in her search for Jesus. Meanwhile, Jesus' question to the Roman soldiers and the Jewish police, "Whom are you looking for?" (18:4), delivers an ironic jab at his opponents.

Another incongruity surfaces in Jesus' question to his opponents. Jesus has no need to ask "Whom do you seek?" The narrator has just told us that Jesus knows all that is about to happen to him. Jesus already knows whom they seek, yet he asks the question anyway. The evangelist neatly creates the incongruity in v. 4 by having Jesus ask a question to which he and the audience already know the answer. Haenchen suggests that two things are achieved by this: "[F]irst, the demonstration of his power described in verses 5f. thus becomes possible; and, second, the request of Jesus narrated in verse 8, that they let the disciples go, is prepared for."[54] Jesus' question sets up their response, which in turn sets up his overwhelmingly powerful self-identification in v. 5. Their response that they are just seeking Jesus—not his followers—gives him leverage in v. 8 to convince them to let his followers go. The question also conveys

---

53. Brown, *Death of the Messiah*, 1:260.
54. Haenchen, *John 2*, 165.

the ironic suggestion that they should be seeking Jesus in order to follow him, not to kill him. The incongruity also underlines one of the deep ironies that run throughout this entire scene: the captors are able to arrest Jesus only because he allows it. He has foreseen his death and willingly embraces it as he exercises control over the events of his passion.

Thus, the irony is thick in this moment in the arrest scene. Jesus' question "Whom are you looking for?" draws attention to the misguided intentions of the soldiers and police: they seek Jesus to kill him, not to have life. The Roman soldiers and Jewish police are thereby ridiculed, while the irony reinforces for readers who grasp it that they should seek—or continue to seek—Jesus in order to find life. The narrator's indication that Jesus knows all that is about to happen also injects irony into the scene. Jesus and the audience know something that the arresting party does not. The reality of the situation, in contrast to appearances, is that Jesus is intent on being arrested and killed. As O'Day observes, "verse 4 leaves no doubt as to who is in control of Jesus' arrest."[55] Jesus is.

3. Jesus' Self-Identification

Jesus' self-identification, "I am he" (ἐγώ εἰμι), further signals his control of the situation (18:5). Brown points out that in both the Synoptic Gospels and John, Jesus needs to be identified to the arresting party.[56] In both traditions, there are several logical reasons why this is so. For one thing, it is dark when they come to arrest him, making it harder to identify someone. Moreover, many members of the arresting party may not have seen Jesus before, and he is surrounded by a number of his followers. In the Synoptic Gospels, a significant aspect of Judas's role in the arrest is to identify Jesus by means of a prearranged kiss. In John, however, Judas leads the arresting party to the garden but does not kiss Jesus, for Jesus identifies himself. He takes the initiative himself by coming forward and asking the initial question, "Whom are you looking for?" (18:4). Because he knows what is about to happen, he can initiate the action of the scene and has no need for Judas to identify him. Jesus is in control of the events as they unfold according to the divine plan.[57] He has already declared, "I lay down my life . . . no one takes it from me, but I lay it down of my

---

55. O'Day, "Gospel of John: Introduction," 802.

56. Brown, *Death of the Messiah*, 1:252.

57. Brown says that the "principle of sovereignty" that governs the passion narrative is at play here (Brown, *Death of the Messiah*, 1:259).

own accord" (10:17-18). Jesus identifies himself in order to further his purpose and fulfill the events that he has already predicted. It is Jesus, rather than the representatives of the Jewish and Roman elite, who moves the action of the arrest scene along.

4. Jesus' Betrayer

After Jesus initiates the action by coming forward and asking his captors whom they are looking for, they respond, "Jesus of Nazareth" (18:5). When Jesus identifies himself by declaring "I am he," the evangelist interjects a seemingly out-of-place statement, "Judas, who betrayed him, was standing with them" (18:5). Judas has already fulfilled the only role he will have in this scene by leading the arresting party to the garden (18:2-3). There would seem to be no reason for the evangelist to mention him again at this point, since he has no new role to fulfill. For those who know of the Synoptic tradition in which Judas kisses Jesus to identify him, this comment draws attention to the fact that Jesus, not Judas, has taken the initiative here.[58] It is certainly possible that the evangelist removed the detail of the kiss from the source material, as Brown suggests, and that the reference to Judas that remains in 18:5 is an awkward remnant.[59] Whatever the case may be, the reference to Judas in 18:5 does contribute to the irony of the scene, especially through its inclusion of the comment that Judas was the one "who betrayed him" (ὁ παραδιδοὺς αὐτὸν). In the Johannine portrayal, Judas is primarily a passive agent while Jesus directs the events. Judas does "betray" Jesus, but only because Jesus intends for him to do so.

Irony also surrounds the use of the Greek verb παραδίδωμι in this scene, which appears twice, both times in connection to Judas (18:2, 5). The word παραδίδωμι is often translated "betray," but it more precisely means to "hand over," "give (over)," "deliver," or "entrust."[60] The verb is prominent throughout the upcoming interrogation and crucifixion scenes as well. It even serves as a subtle framing device for the entire Johannine passion narrative. Judas is introduced as "the one who handed

---

58. It is, of course, difficult to determine whether or not the Fourth Evangelist and the Johannine community would have known the Synoptic tradition. See further Smith, *John Among the Gospels*.

59. Brown, *Death of the Messiah*, 1:259.

60. BDAG 761-62. It is a compound form of the preposition παρά and the verb δίδωμι, meaning "to give from (one person to another)."

him over" in 18:2, at the beginning of the passion narrative, and when Jesus finally dies on the cross in 19:30, he "hands over the spirit."

In this scene, Judas is described twice using the participial form of this verb, and it takes on the qualities of a title for him: "Judas the betrayer" or "Judas the traitor" (18:2, 5). This most likely represents a common reference to him in the Johannine community and in the early church at large.[61] In the Johannine arrest scene, however, it highlights an even greater irony. As noted above, Jesus has repeatedly predicted that he will be "handed over." By the end of the arrest scene, however, readers have reason to question whether Jesus has been "handed over" at all. Judas is necessary in the scene because he brings the arresting party to the garden, but the events proceed in accordance with Jesus' predictions and with God's plans. After the arresting party arrives, Judas is entirely passive as Jesus steps forward to deliver himself into the hands of the authorities.

Thus, while Judas hands Jesus over to the authorities by leading their agents to him, readers know that Jesus willingly goes to his death, and even takes the initiative in his arrest. Jesus is "handed over" only at a superficial level of understanding of the events. Judas unwittingly helps to fulfill God's purposes. Even the Roman soldiers and Jewish police do very little "arresting" in the scene. In fact, they are unable to take Jesus into custody until 18:12, after he has secured safe passage for his disciples. Thus, both references to Judas's "handing over" of Jesus are instances of irony that serve to remind readers of Jesus' own active and catalyzing role in the events of the arrest and the passion narrative. Even at the culmination of the crucifixion, Jesus, who has supposedly been "handed over" to the authorities, actively "hands over" his own life when he gives up ($\pi\alpha\rho\alpha\delta\iota\delta\omega\mu\iota$) his spirit and dies on the cross (19:30). Jesus proves that he is in control to the very end.

5. The Overwhelming Force is Overwhelmed

After the brief comment about Judas's presence with the arresting party in 18:5, the narrator underlines Jesus' response ("I am he") by repeating it, thereby emphasizing that it prompts what happens next: "When Jesus said to them, 'I am he,' they stepped back and fell to the ground" (18:6). In dramatic fashion, the Jewish police and the entire assembled Roman

---

61. See also Matt 26:25, 48; 27:3; Mark 14:42, 44; Luke 22:21. See further Papias 1:5.

cohort—as many as six hundred troops—topple before Jesus' powerful self-revelation. Even with vastly superior numbers, the Roman army and Jewish police force are unable to match the power of Israel's God and Jesus. This remarkable moment is filled with verbal, dramatic, and situational irony, and undercuts public transcripts of Roman military might. Yet mimicry is also evident here, as Jesus responds to Rome's military might with his own overwhelming power and ability to dominate the scene.

When his captors state that they are seeking "Jesus of Nazareth," Jesus responds with ἐγώ εἰμι, simply "I am" in Greek, without any predicate nominative. The verb is preceded by the pronoun ἐγώ, and the construction is thus emphatic. Codex Vaticanus preserves the effort of at least one scribe to clarify Jesus' statement, by emending Jesus' response to read "I am *Jesus*," but the simple ἐγώ εἰμι is certainly the original version, as it is a formulaic saying used by Jesus throughout the Fourth Gospel to identify himself.[62] And throughout the Gospel, this construction clearly conveys Jesus' divine identity.

This important and theologically evocative construction appears numerous times in the Fourth Gospel. Early in the narrative, Jesus reveals that he is the Christ to the Samaritan woman at the well by declaring to her, ἐγώ εἰμι (4:26). Later, when Jesus approaches his disciples by walking on the sea, he uses ἐγώ εἰμι to identify himself and convey his divine power over creation (6:20). While in the midst of an antagonistic discussion with several Jews, Jesus uses ἐγώ εἰμι in a manner suggestive of a confession of faith: "[Y]ou will die in your sins unless you believe that *I am*" (8:24). Again, when predicting Judas's betrayal, Jesus says to his disciples, "I tell you this now, before it occurs, so that when it does occur, you may believe that *I am*" (13:19). In addition to these examples lacking an explicit predicate, there are seven "I am" expressions in the Fourth Gospel that do have explicit predicates, and they are also profoundly christological in character. Jesus declares that he is "the bread of life" (6:35, 51), "the light of the world" (8:12; 9:5), "the gate" (10:7, 9), "the good shepherd" (10:11, 14), "the resurrection and the life" (11:25-26), "the way, the truth, and the life" (14:6), and "the true vine" (15:1, 5). In each of these instances, the evangelist places the words ἐγώ εἰμι on Jesus' lips to convey his divine origin, identity, and the character of the life-bearing gifts that he provides.

---

62. Brown, *Gospel According to John*, 2:810.

Both Hellenistic and Jewish parallels to this particular Greek construction illumine its meaning within the Fourth Gospel. Kysar draws attention to several Hellenistic sources in which gods use the emphatic ἐγώ εἰμι followed by a predicate to reveal themselves.[63] In each of these instances, the expression is used as a means of divine revelation. For example, Kysar finds significant examples in inscriptions about Isis, in the Hermetic Corpus, and in the Mandaean literature.[64] Because these "I am" statements are a part of the cultural milieu of the Hellenistic world, it is probable that Johannine Christians would have heard echoes of these divine revelatory statements whenever Jesus utters similar phrases in the Fourth Gospel. Kysar even suggests that by co-opting this language, the evangelist is intentionally contrasting Jesus' divine claims with the claims of some Hellenistic gods.

The connections are even stronger to the Septuagint, the Greek version of the Jewish Scriptures. When Moses asks for God's name early in Exodus, God responds with this emphatic formula followed by a participle phrase: ἐγώ εἰμι ὁ ὤν, "I am the one who is" (Exod 3:14 LXX). This formula is part of the divine name that God declares to Moses as he prepares to liberate the Hebrew people from enslavement by Egypt, an oppressive foreign power. Furthermore, in several other places in the Septuagint, the Greek translators have used ἐγώ εἰμι to render the Hebrew phrase "I, Yahweh."[65]

Brown argues that ἐγώ εἰμι is used explicitly as a divine name for God in Deutero-Isaiah as well. The Greek text of Isa 43:25 reads ἐγώ εἰμι ἐγώ εἰμι, doubling the emphatic construction. While this might be translated with the ensuing phrase as "I am he, I am he who blots out your transgressions," it could also be rendered as "I am 'I AM,' the one who blots out your transgressions." In the latter translation, the phrase ἐγώ εἰμι becomes an explicit name for God.[66] Brown offers a similar interpretation of Isa 52:6, translating the Greek as follows: "My people shall know *my name;* in that day (they shall know) that I am He who speaks." He argues that the latter half of the sentence can be rendered "in that day

---

63. Kysar, *Maverick Gospel*, 58. See also Brown, *Gospel According to John*, 1:533–38.
64. Kysar, *Maverick Gospel*, 58.
65. For example, Isa 45:18–19 and Joel 2:27. See Kysar, *Maverick Gospel*, 59.
66. Brown, *Gospel According to John*, 1:536.

(they shall know) that *egō eimi* is the one who speaks."⁶⁷ Again, ἐγώ εἰμι becomes an explicit name for God.

These examples in the Septuagint suggest that when the Johannine Jesus uses the phrase ἐγώ εἰμι, readers familiar with the Old Greek of the Jewish scriptures would have heard explicit utterances of the divine name on Jesus' lips. Jesus' use of this construction thus reveals his divine origin, his oneness with the God of Israel, and his identity as the incarnate Word of God. Kysar agrees, insisting that the phrase amounts to a "theophany—the appearance and revelation of God."⁶⁸ By using these words, the evangelist affirms that Jesus represents the very presence of God.

Given that these texts in Deutero-Isaiah are found in the context of divine deliverance from an imperial power (Babylon), the use of the name by Jesus in the face of an imperial force is even more significant.⁶⁹ If ἐγώ εἰμι is the name that is known by God's people "in that day," when they are released from imperial domination, Jesus' use of the name hints that liberation from imperial Rome is at hand. Jesus' power over the arresting party confirms this possibility.

In the Fourth Gospel's arrest scene, the response of the Jewish police and the Roman soldiers to Jesus' utterance confirms this perspective. When Jesus says ἐγώ εἰμι, the entire assembled crowd falls to the ground. O'Day points out that, throughout the Bible, "to fall prostrate on the ground is a conventional response to a theophany (e.g., Ezek 1:28; Dan 10:9; Acts 9:3–4; Rev 1:17)."⁷⁰ Brown has a similar take on the incident, observing that "the adversaries of Jesus are prostrate on their face before his majesty."⁷¹ By using the divine name, Jesus reveals the fullness of his identity to the arresting party, but they prove that they are unable to grasp it when they proceed to arrest him in spite of this revelation.

This moment displays three different ways in which irony is functioning in the text: as verbal, dramatic, and situational irony. Jesus means more than he says with the expression, "I am," but only aware, informed readers can grasp the deeper meaning. The dramatic irony is what Duke calls "irony of identity." As we have noted, he describes this particular irony as a "situation of unknown or mistaken identity," in which "one

67. Brown, *Gospel According to John*, 1:536.

68. Kysar, *Maverick Gospel*, 59.

69. Isa 43 speaks of Israel's redemption from Babylonian captivity, and Isa 52 looks forward to the restoration of Jerusalem following the exile.

70. O'Day, "Gospel of John: Introduction," 802.

71. Brown, *Gospel According to John*, 2:818.

character or group of characters fails to recognize the true identity of another ... and consequently acts or speaks in ways either grossly inappropriate or accidentally appropriate."[72] The arresting party has the opportunity to recognize Jesus' true identity and divine origin, but fails to do so.

As we have noted, irony is a two-leveled phenomenon. The members of the arresting party, who are "outsiders," are not able to make the interpretive leap to the second level of understanding. They seek to arrest Jesus as a perceived threat to the elite status quo. When Jesus utters "I am," he identifies himself to them as the very presence of God, but they cannot grasp this reality. Jesus reveals his identity in spectacular fashion, and readers, who possess more knowledge than Jesus' captors, are equipped to recognize this. Meanwhile, the arresting party, in an oblivious state, proceeds to apprehend him and prove its ignorance. This dramatic irony mocks the Roman army and the Jewish police force, while reinforcing the audience's belief in Jesus as the agent and very presence of God.

This scene also displays situational irony because there is a sharp incongruity between the expected outcome and the actual results of an encounter. In this case, Rome's arrival with a cohort, an absurdly large military force, leads readers to expect a one-sided fight. The hyperbole of the scene tips off readers to the ironic—and humorous—aspects of the scene: six hundred Roman troops are not needed to arrest one man. The "fight" that ensues *is* one-sided, but in this case, the overwhelming force of Rome is itself overwhelmed and falls to the ground at the divine utterance of Jesus. Readers know, of course, that Jesus is the one through whom all things were created (1:3). There is a sharp contrast between the "appearance" of Rome's power and the "reality" of Jesus' power.[73] Rome is unable to overpower Jesus through sheer force, and the Fourth Gospel mocks—yet also mimics—the excess and the overkill of the Roman army by having Jesus topple them all with but a few words.

All these points highlight the underlying irony of identity in this scene: the soldiers and police who arrive to arrest Jesus have no idea who he is, while readers do. Throughout the Gospel of John, characters have failed to grasp Jesus' identity. The evangelist often employs irony at these moments to highlight misperceptions and ridicule Jesus' opponents. If the arresting party was aware of Jesus' true identity, they would have

---

72. Duke, *Irony in the Fourth Gospel*, 100.

73. Haakon Chevalier notes that "the basic feature of every irony is a contrast between a reality and an appearance" (*Ironic Temper*, 42).

known that the size of their military cohort and their bearing of weapons and torches would prove insufficient to overpower the "light of the world." This scene underscores Jesus' identity in a powerful way. It also exposes the might of the Roman imperial army as wholly inadequate to challenge the power of Israel's God.

The Second Exchange between Jesus and His Captors (18:7–9)

The first exchange between Jesus and his captors leaves the reader with the impression that Jesus could avoid arrest if he wished. He is much too powerful to succumb to the might of a Roman cohort and Jewish police force. It is only because he embraces the Father's will that he allows himself to be arrested. The second exchange between Jesus and the arresting party begins in a manner similar to the first, but in this instance, it demonstrates Jesus' divine protection of his followers and paves the way for him to be taken into custody.

With his captors apparently still prostrate on the ground, Jesus repeats his question: "Whom are you looking for?" Their second response is identical to their first: "Jesus of Nazareth" (18:7). Jesus, speaking down to them, taunts them with a reminder that he has already identified himself. He then uses their response, that they seek only him, as leverage to ensure that they release his followers (18:8). If the arresting party is seeking only him, they have no cause to detain his disciples. Jesus keeps his followers from harm.

The narrator uses this moment to declare the fulfillment of one of Jesus' earlier predictions, "I did not lose a single one of those whom you gave me" (18:9). This quotation is not a perfect match with any of Jesus' other statements in the Gospel, but it does have strong parallels with two of his earlier declarations: "And this is the will of him who sent me, that I should lose nothing of all that he has given me" (6:39) and "While I was with them, I protected them in your name that you have given me. I guarded them, and not one of them was lost except the one destined to be lost, so that the scripture might be fulfilled" (17:12). Jesus does protect his disciples from the arresting party, and the language of the scene evokes the shepherd imagery of 10:1–18.

Stibbe discusses at length the parallels between the arrest scene and Jesus' discourse on the good shepherd.[74] The settings are similar: the arrest takes place outside an enclosed garden, and the good shepherd cares for his sheep in an enclosed sheepfold (αὐλή). Judas, who is described earlier in the Gospel as a "thief" (12:6), approaches the garden with the arresting party just as the "thief" approaches the sheepfold in 10:1. Stibbe also observes that "Jesus' protective stance towards the disciples (he stands outside the walled garden whilst they huddle inside) imitates the protective conduct of the shepherd throughout John 10."[75] Finally, both passages anticipate Jesus' death as an act of willful obedience to the Father on behalf of his followers. Jesus, describing himself as the good shepherd, affirms that "[f]or this reason the Father loves me, because I lay down my life in order to take it up again. No one takes it up from me, but I lay it down of my own accord" (10:17–18). The echoes of John 10 in the arrest scene evoke and reinforce the emphasis on Jesus' initiative and willingness to die, as well as his command of the situation.

In the face of hostility and violent intent, Jesus, the good shepherd, demands that his disciples go free (18:8). There are indications within the Gospel that some members of the Johannine community may have experienced some form of suffering because of their identity as Christians. In his Farewell Discourse, Jesus tells his disciples that "an hour is coming when those who kill you think that by doing so they are offering worship to God" (16:2). At the very least, the Fourth Gospel constructs the expectation of persecution within the narrative, perhaps expecting that it will come as a result of distancing themselves from elements of Roman imperialism. If Johannine Christians were experiencing suffering as a result of their faith, or if expected persecution materialized in the future, 18:7–9 would offer comfort and remind them of Jesus' care and protection for them as well.

One further element of these verses serves to reinforce Jesus' command and foresight in this scene. The use of the word "fulfill" (πληρόω) lends considerable clout to Jesus' words. Senior says that this word is "a term reserved in other parts of the New Testament for the Hebrew Scriptures."[76] While the word has a mundane meaning, simply "to fill" an object with something else, its theologically loaded meaning, "to fulfill,"

---

74. Stibbe, *John As Storyteller*, 102–4.
75. Stibbe, *John As Storyteller*, 103.
76. Senior, *Passion of Jesus*, 53.

is used almost exclusively with quotations from the Jewish Scriptures.[77] Thus, to say that this happened "to fulfill" Jesus' words grants a significant degree of authority to his sayings, authority normally attributed only to the sacred Hebrew writings. This, too, underscores Jesus' authority and mastery of the situation.

Peter's Violent Resistance (18:10–11)

Once Jesus has secured the safety of his disciples, readers might expect that the arrest is at hand. However, perhaps sensing this, Simon Peter reacts violently to prevent Jesus' capture. The narrator says that Peter "had a sword, drew it, struck the high priest's slave, and cut off his right ear," and then relays the curious detail that the slave's name was Malchus (18:10). In response, Jesus reprimands Peter by ordering him to sheath his sword. Jesus then declares, through a rhetorical question, that his arrest and eventual death are part of God's plans: "Am I not to drink the cup that the Father has given me?" (18:11). In this brief incident, the Fourth Gospel draws a sharp distinction between those who employ violence to further their own purposes and those who follow the will of the Father. The scene also reinforces the motif that Jesus is arrested only because he allows it.

The disciples have been present throughout the arrest scene, and have even been the topic of Jesus' dialogue with his captors, but they have been standing quietly in the background until now. No longer content to observe the proceedings passively, Peter reacts by attacking a member of the arresting party.[78] Peter previously promised that he would follow Jesus to his death (13:36–37). Since the disciples are hopelessly outnumbered by the Roman soldiers and Jewish police, he might well fulfill this promise with this burst of violent resistance! More significantly, however, Peter's response reveals that he fundamentally misunderstands the meaning of the events as they develop. Peter becomes the object of

---

77. BDAG 827-29.

78. Curiously, while all four canonical Gospels include this scene (cf. Mark 14:47; Matt 26:51–52; Luke 22:50–51), only the Fourth Gospel identifies both the attacker (Peter) and the victim (Malchus) by name. The Fourth Gospel often casts Peter in an unfavorable light, and this may account for the assignment of his name to the violent disciple (e.g., 13:6–10, 36–38; 18:15–18, 25–27; 20:3–4), but it is difficult to account for the name Malchus. This may be an authentic historical memory that only the Fourth Gospel preserves, or it may even be the name of someone known to the Johannine community.

the Gospel's irony at this point in the narrative. Moloney points out that "Peter fails to understand the significance of what lies ahead and draws a sword in a violent attempt to change the course of events," even though the events are happening at Jesus' will.[79] Peter inadvertently attempts to thwart God's plans just as Judas has attempted to thwart God's plans. Jesus, however, unequivocally rejects Peter's violent interference.

Stibbe observes a significant contrast between Peter and Jesus here: "[T]he evangelist depicts Peter assaulting a servant of the high priest in v. 10, whilst Jesus is presented as being assaulted by an official of the same high priest in v. 22." Peter employs violence while Jesus willingly receives it later in the passion narrative. Ironically, Peter's use of violence resembles the violence that the elite agents of the empire (both Roman and Jewish) use to maintain order and control. Later, in the Roman show trial, Jesus will stress this point again when he tells Pilate, "If my kingdom were from this world, my followers would be fighting to keep me from being handed over to the Jews. But as it is, my kingdom is not from here" (18:36). Jesus explicitly states that those who participate in his kingdom will not resort to violence. Ironically, in the arrest scene, Peter does attempt to prevent Jesus from being handed over to the authorities by fighting, but he acts out of profound misunderstanding. As Senior notes, "John draws a sharp contrast between the exercise of power used by the enemies of Jesus who come with weapons (18:3), and the liberating power of Jesus' own life and death."[80] Even in the face of violent intent, followers of Jesus should not resort to brutal methods employed by Roman imperial agents.

The Greek verb that the evangelist chooses to describe Peter's removal of his sword from its sheath, ἕλκω ("to draw"), has interesting connections throughout the Gospel.[81] The Father draws people to himself (6:44), and Jesus says that he will draw people to himself when he is lifted up (12:32). Even Simon Peter will draw (NRSV: "haul") in a net full of one hundred and fifty-three large fish toward the end of the Gospel (21:6, 11). In each of these other occurrences the verb ἕλκω has life-giving implications. However, Simon Peter draws his sword in 18:10 with violent, deadly intent. The use of this verb heightens the contrast between Pe-

---

79. Moloney, *Gospel of John*, 484.

80. Senior, *Passion of Jesus*, 55.

81. While all four Gospels include this brief scene, this particular verb is only used by John to describe the action of drawing the sword. Mark uses σπάω, Matthew uses the compound form ἀποσπάω, and Luke does not include this action (Mark 14:47; Matt 26:51; Luke 22:50).

ter, who retaliates violently, and Jesus, whose acceptance of his pending death will culminate in liberation from death and draw people to himself (12:32).

Finally, Jesus reminds Peter and readers one more time that he goes to his death willingly: "Am I not to drink the cup that the Father has given me?" (18:11). The term "cup" (ποτήριον) symbolizes Jesus' death in all of the Gospels, although the context is different here. In the Synoptic Gospels, Jesus prays that the "cup" might pass from him, with the hope that there might be an alternative to death.[82] In the Fourth Gospel, however, Jesus shows no hesitation to drink from the figurative cup.[83] At the end of the last supper, Jesus declared to his disciples, "I do as the Father has commanded me, so that the world may know that I love the Father" (14:31). With his question in 18:11, Jesus reminds Peter and readers that he embraces death willingly in order to reveal his love and his obedience to the will of his Father. The violence and force that the Roman soldiers, the Jewish police, and even Peter display are antithetical to the values that Jesus represents.

The "Arrest" (18:12)

Jesus is finally arrested after asking rhetorically, "Am I not to drink the cup that the Father has given me?" It is not insignificant that the arrest immediately follows this statement.[84] The arresting party is able to take him into custody only because he allows it. Jesus has been in command of the entire arrest scene and in uttering the divine name has demonstrated

---

82. See Mark 14:36; Matt 26:39; and Luke 22:42.

83. John 12:27 may represent an exception to this, but it is not a strong one. Jesus says, "Now my soul is troubled. And what should I say—'Father, save me from this hour'? No, it is for this reason that I have come to this hour." If Jesus hesitates, it is a very brief hesitation. Of course, it is also possible to interpret this verse with an emphasis on Jesus' willingness and determination to proceed toward his death.

84. In Mark and Matthew, Jesus is explicitly arrested before his follower strikes at one of his captors. Luke is similar to John in that Jesus is explicitly arrested at the end of the scene. In Luke, however, Jesus only protests that they could have arrested him earlier had they wanted. It is not clear in Luke that Jesus is intent on being arrested. John seems to emphasize much more than the Synoptics that Jesus is arrested at his own will. Mark highlights the failure of the disciples. Matthew largely follows Mark, but also emphasizes the fulfillment of Scripture, while Luke emphasizes that the arrest is ordained as the "hour" for the "power of darkness." See Mark 14:43–50; Matt 26:47–56; and Luke 22:47–54.

his power. Even though he is bound by them, he is scarcely under their control.

The evangelist reiterates the entire composition of the arresting party as they take Jesus into custody, noting that it includes the enormous cohort of Roman soldiers, their officer, and the police from the Jewish authorities (18:12).[85] O'Day points out that "the exaggerated use of force by Jesus' opponents—all of the soldiers and their leader are depicted as being involved in the arrest—reinforces the theme of the enemies' misperception of the nature of Jesus' arrest."[86] Excessive force has been critiqued throughout the arrest scene, and this final moment further underscores this.

Curiously, of the four Gospels, only John mentions that Jesus is "bound" (δέω) at this point in the arrest story. It is possible that a subtle connection to Lazarus is intended, for Lazarus was described as having "his hands and feet bound with strips of cloth" as he emerged from the tomb, after being restored to life by Jesus (11:44). Jesus is "bound" by his captors, and his fate is effectively sealed as he goes willingly to his death. Moreover, after Jesus dies on the cross, Nicodemus and Joseph of Arimathea "wrap" (δέω) him in linen cloths and spices before sealing him in the tomb. However, astute readers know that Jesus, like Lazarus, will be resurrected. Thus, when the narrator notes that Jesus is "bound" by the arresting party, the text ironically points forward to his resurrection beyond his death.

Irony, Hidden Transcripts, and Negotiating Roman Rule

The Johannine arrest scene is filled with irony that mocks the Roman soldiers and the police sent from the Jewish authorities while promoting belief in Jesus. This irony functions as part of a Johannine hidden transcript of resistance to assist readers in negotiating life under Roman imperial domination in the first century. Terdiman observes that ironic communication is a means "to displace and annihilate a dominant

---

85. The Roman officer is described as a χιλίαρχος, literally "a leader of one thousand." Typically, this Greek word is used to translate the Latin *tribunus militum*, a commander of a cohort. The inclusion of this term serves to reinforce the size of the Roman arresting party. See Brown, *Gospel According to John*, 2:813.

86. O'Day, "Gospel of John: Introduction," 803.

depiction of the world."[87] It provides a means of resisting and negating the public transcripts of Rome's elite and expresses an alternative, "offstage" worldview of a dissident subculture living under imperial rule. It also has the capacity to strengthen the Johannine community and to inspire and restore dignity to Johannine believers who experience Roman domination.

While public transcripts in imperial Rome promoted *Pax Romana*, the idea that order, peace, and wellbeing were created and sustained by the empire, the arrest scene in the Fourth Gospel disrupts this notion. The ironic presentation of the arresting party reminds readers that Rome maintains control through the threat and implementation of violence. "Peace" is sustained by a military presence throughout the provinces, and force is used to suppress threats to the imperial status quo. This scene rejects the violence of Rome in favor of the life-giving reality of Jesus and exhorts readers to do likewise. The violent intent of the arresting party and Peter's violent outburst serve as foils to Jesus and to the Johannine audience. Rome requires violence to maintain its dominion and enforce its will upon the residents of the empire. Jesus' followers, however, ought to resist violence and live in obedience to the will of the Father.

This scene also negates the public transcripts of Roman domination and the view that Rome is destined to rule the entire world at the will of the gods. In contrast, it advances the perspective that God is sovereign, and that history is subject to the plans of Jesus' Father, not the plans of Rome. It also promotes belief in Jesus over the Roman imperial status quo. Jesus controls and directs the sequence of events in accordance with God's will, while Rome's representatives are virtually passive agents in the narrative. God is the true sovereign of the world and Jesus is the agent of the divine will on earth. Caesar and his representatives are not.

The Johannine arrest scene also has the capacity to inspire and restore the dignity of Johannine Christians experiencing imperial domination.[88] Domination in all its forms, whether material, status, or ideological, deprives persons of autonomy and dignity and evokes feelings of inferiority, discontent, and anger. It is not difficult to imagine that Johannine Christians living toward the end of the first century felt these

---

87. Terdiman, *Discourse/Counter-Discourse*, 12.

88. I argued in chapter 1 that Johannine Christians surely experienced ideological domination (see pp. 28–29). They may also have experienced forms of material and status domination, although in my estimation this is harder to discern with any certainty from the text of the Fourth Gospel.

things. After all, their messiah had been killed by crucifixion, a public ritual of punishment and execution designed to maximize humiliation and express Roman dominance.[89] Further, they regarded this humiliated and crucified one as "Lord," in stark contrast to a dominant Roman ideology that proclaimed Caesar as such.

From the perspective of the Fourth Gospel, Jesus—a person of low social status—proves to be in control of the proceedings as he faces an arresting party sent by elite members of imperial society. The Gospel rejects the imperial perspective that Jesus was merely a criminal who was arrested, publicly humiliated, and executed against his will. Instead, the Gospel ironically advances the perspective that Jesus chose to go to his death willingly and was in complete control of events as they occurred. This alternative perspective has the capacity to promote faith in Jesus and to inspire and restore dignity to Johannine believers who are experiencing domination themselves.

This Johannine perspective addresses a tricky problem for early Christians: if Jesus was of divine origin, why and how could he have been arrested and killed? Could he not have prevented it? Origen quotes objections circulating in his day regarding this issue: "How should we deem him to be a God.... He who was a God could neither flee nor be led away a prisoner; and least of all could he be deserted and delivered up by those who had been his associates" (*Cels.* 2.9). The Fourth Gospel provides an answer for this difficult question by asserting that it was part of God's plan, and thus Jesus' plan, from the beginning.

Scott argues that "resistance to ideological domination requires a counter-ideology."[90] Just such a counter-ideology is present in the arrest scene of the Fourth Gospel. The Fourth Gospel thus assists its audience in negotiating life within the empire by providing an alternative vision as part of the Johannine hidden transcript. Moreover, in addition to negating public transcripts out of sight of the dominant elite, the arrest scene in the Fourth Gospel could well have provided readers with a model of resistance in the public sphere as well. While it is impossible to know

---

89. While the comparison to the issue in view here is not perfect, Scott discusses how violence and public punishment inflicted upon a loved one affect one's dignity and cause one to suffer. He gives the example of a slave forced to watch as his or her child is punished, commenting, "The direct harm in this case is inflicted upon the child; what the parents suffer is a devastating public display of their powerlessness to keep their child from harm" (Scott, *Domination*, 113–14).

90. Scott, *Domination*, 118.

to what extent the Fourth Gospel would have informed the Johannine community's "politics of anonymity and disguise"—Scott's third mode of political discourse, in which the hidden transcript is expressed on the public stage in covert fashion—the Gospel does offer readers a tool or a strategy for this mode of indirect resistance to imperial domination. Specifically, it offers irony: discourse whose meaning lies beneath the surface. By means of irony, the Johannine community might insinuate its hidden transcript of resistance into the public sphere. As Scott contends, "the condition of [the public expression of the hidden transcript] is that it be sufficiently indirect and garbled that it is capable of two readings, one of which is innocuous."[91] Irony certainly fits the bill, especially if an outsider does not share the knowledge necessary to interpret the ironic meaning. Because the arrest scene is not flagrantly defiant of Roman imperialism, it provides a means of expressing the hidden transcript in the public sphere without the threat of retaliation.

A further connection in this passage to Scott's concept of hidden transcripts is worth noting, and is tied to the moment when the entire arresting party falls to the ground. Scott says that for subjugated persons in systems of domination, there is a "systemic frustration of reciprocal action," meaning that there are no reasonable opportunities to act out against the "routine harvest of insults and injury to human dignity."[92] Subordinate persons cannot respond in kind to insults, humiliations, abuse, and violence without inevitably suffering some sort of retaliation from the dominant. They can only respond as they wish when they are safely beyond the realm of elite observation. Thus, Scott writes, "at its most elementary level the hidden transcript represents an acting out in fantasy . . . of the anger and reciprocal aggression denied by the presence of domination."[93] The desired revenge, whether verbal or violent, is only safe when it takes place within the realm of the imagination. Thus its expression is also able to function as both a coping mechanism and an accommodating force, allowing dissent and compliance to coexist.

Beyond reinforcing Jesus' power and identity, the moment of Jesus' self-revelation in the arrest scene provides a "safety valve" by which the evangelist and the audience can express frustration and imagine revenge upon the Roman soldiers and the entire arresting party for the role they

---

91. Scott, *Domination*, 157.
92. Scott, *Domination*, 37.
93. Scott, *Domination*, 37–38.

played in executing Jesus. The humiliation and loss of dignity that Johannine Christians likely experienced due to the ignoble death of their messiah cannot be channeled into overt resistance without risk. They may not be able to express their frustration openly in society, but within the narrative world of the Fourth Gospel they can vent this anger safely by imagining Jesus' captors toppling forward, prostrating themselves before Jesus in the face of his overwhelming power.[94] The actions of retaliation and revenge that they are unable to perform in public are depicted in a sharply ironic moment in the Gospel narrative that humiliates the Roman cohort and the Jewish police.

There is also a hint of *schadenfraude*—joy or pleasure gained because of someone else's misfortune—in this scene. Scott says that *schadenfraude* "represents a wish for negative reciprocity, a settling of scores when the high shall be brought low and the last shall be first."[95] The humiliating collapse of the entire Roman cohort and the Jewish police at Jesus' feet represents such a moment, and one can imagine members of the Johannine audience smiling or laughing at this point in the narrative. This moment in the text may function comically for readers: it is humorous to imagine an entire cohort of Roman soldiers toppling feebly to the ground. Furthermore, as Michaels notes, there may also be "more than a touch of comedy" when Jesus repeats his question to his captors, "Whom are you looking for?" while they are apparently still lying prostrate on the ground.[96] It is intriguing, given the elaborate staging otherwise provided in this scene, that the evangelist never reports that the arresting party stands up again.[97] It is as if they are rendered prone throughout the rest of the scene, and it is not difficult to imagine members of the Johannine community chuckling at the reversal that befalls the massive, intimidating arresting party.

---

94. One also wonders if this prostration before Jesus signifies their unwitting acknowledgment of Jesus' divine identity!

95. Scott, *Domination*, 41–42.

96. Michaels, *Gospel of John*, 891.

97. In the arrest scene, Jesus *goes out* across the valley, Judas *brings* the Roman cohort and the Jewish police, Jesus *comes forward*, and they *step back* and *fall to the ground*. But the narrator never reports that they again stand on their feet.

The arrest scene in the Fourth Gospel exhibits resistance to Roman imperialism, particularly through its use of irony. With this literary device, the Fourth Gospel critiques aspects of Roman imperialism and undercuts public transcripts of the elite while promoting faith in Jesus. The irony becomes a weapon that strikes sharply against Jesus' captors in the narrative, while also appealing for readers to believe—or continue believing—in Jesus.

Chapter 4

The Roman Show Trial

INTRODUCTION

THE ROMAN SHOW TRIAL (18:28—19:16) showcases the theological and literary genius of the Fourth Evangelist.[1] It is the centerpiece of the passion narrative, its lengthiest scene, and a monumental showcase of many of its major themes and motifs. The evangelist has crafted a well-staged, dramatic, and intense scene of conflict among Jesus the king, the Roman governor, and the Jewish authorities as they engage questions of ultimate concern. Who has access to truth, power, and authority? Who is the true judge and sovereign of the world? To whom ought one give one's allegiance? Life and death hang in the balance while the participants wrestle with these questions.

This scene represents the most direct clash between Jesus and representatives of Roman imperial power in the Fourth Gospel. Not only is the Roman governor Pilate the most powerful Roman official in the province of Judea, but the members of the Jewish elite who appear are local allied elites who are complicit with Pilate in the maintenance of the imperial status quo. The narrative works to alienate the Johannine audience from both parties as it emphasizes Jesus' own sovereignty in a remarkable way.

All of the people with whom Jesus interacts in this scene are at the upper end of the socioeconomic spectrum; there is no mention of a

---

1. Recall my assertion that it is anachronistic to speak of Jesus' appearance before Pilate simply as a "trial." See pp. 67–68 above.

crowd composed of a broad section of the Jewish populace, as in the Synoptic Gospels.[2] Only representatives of the Jerusalem-based Jewish elite appear, interact, and collaborate with Pilate to execute Jesus. Throughout the proceeding, whenever the "Jews" ('Ιουδαῖοι) are mentioned (18:31, 36, 38; 19:7, 12, 14), the term never indicates a more general crowd. No frenzied multitude of commoners shouts for Jesus' death or chooses Barabbas over Jesus. The Jewish authorities alone, who are collaborators with and agents of imperial power, hand Jesus over to Pilate and negotiate with the governor throughout the scene.[3]

1. Jesus' Appearance before the Jewish Authorities (18:13-27)

Before Jesus is handed over to Pilate, he is interrogated by two members of the Jewish elite, Annas and Caiaphas.[4] While the Synoptics devote considerable attention to Jesus' appearance before the Jewish elite, John gives much more attention to the Roman show trial with Pilate. As Moore observes, "the Johannine narrator seems to want to march us briskly through Jesus' interrogations by Annas and Caiaphas in order to get us as expeditiously as possible to the interrogation by Pilate."[5] Neither Annas's nor Caiaphas's interactions with Jesus can properly be described as a "trial."[6] Of Annas, the Gospel reports simply that "the high priest questioned Jesus about his disciples and about his teaching" (18:19), and Jesus offers little in defense. Jesus' appearance before Caiaphas is not narrated at all; readers can only assume that Jesus is interrogated by him (18:24-28). Furthermore, the outcome of Jesus' appearances before these two Jewish authorities is established from the outset; this Jewish inquiry is a sham, as the Jewish authorities already intend to send Jesus to Pilate for execution. The presence of Roman soldiers alongside Jewish police

---

2. Cf. Mark 15:8-15; Matt 27:15-24; and Luke 23:13-23.

3. When Pilate says, "Your own nation and the chief priests have handed you over to me," he does not mean the entire nation has handed him over, but only the Jewish leadership (18:35).

4. Peter's denial scenes (18:15-18, 25-27) are interwoven with Jesus' appearances before Annas and Caiaphas, although a full discussion of these scenes is beyond the scope of this chapter. However, they certainly display Peter's challenging negotiation of imperial power as he seeks to maintain his loyalty to Jesus.

5. Moore, *Empire and Apocalypse*, 54.

6. Note that neither Annas nor Caiaphas is given a voice at this point in the narrative.

in the arrest scene (18:3, 12) suggests that both Roman and Jewish elites perceive that Jesus is a threat. They have already collaborated to capture him; soon the Jewish elite will send Jesus to Pilate to ensure his execution.

Howard-Brook insists that there is no real Jewish "trial" in the passion narrative because the entire Gospel narrative has been cast in the form of a trial of sorts.[7] The Jewish authorities send temple police to arrest him (7:32), Nicodemus argues that Jesus must first have a hearing (7:51), and Jesus gives testimony (8:12–20). Following this, Jesus is accused of being a "Samaritan" and demon-possessed (8:48), and then escapes a stoning attempt (8:59). Howard-Brook says that there is a second "hearing" in chapter 10 when the Jewish authorities ask Jesus to tell them "plainly" about his identity as the Messiah (10:22–30); Jesus' response warrants a second stoning attempt (10:31). Howard-Brook concludes that "the Fourth Gospel does not provide a passion-setting narration of the hearing before Caiaphas and the Sanhedrin or condemnation of Jesus because it has *already happened* in chs. 7, 8, and 10."[8] Skinner is like-minded, arguing that the Fourth Gospel does not need to linger over Jesus' appearance before Caiaphas because "Caiaphas has already spoken his mind in 11:45–53."[9] At 18:14, the narrator explicitly recalls Caiaphas's previous statements, reminding the audience that "Caiaphas was the one who had advised the Jews that it was better to have one person die for the people."

Nevertheless, the Fourth Gospel uses this brief scene to make significant claims. Jesus says just enough in his appearance before Annas to indict the Jewish authorities for their lack of belief. Jesus insists in 18:20 that he has "spoken openly to the world," and has "said nothing in secret"; the world and its people, however, are incapable of understanding him (1:10; 3:19; 7:7; 14:17; 15:18–19; 17:25). He has already stated his case and has witnessed to the truth, but the Jewish authorities, who are "of this world" (8:23), have rejected him. They have no answer to give when he says, "If I have spoken wrongly, testify to the wrong. But if I have spoken rightly, why do you strike me?" (18:23).[10] They can give no good response because they have none.

---

7. Howard-Brook, *Becoming Children of God*, 392–93.
8. Howard-Brook, *Becoming Children of God*, 392.
9. Skinner, *Trial Narratives*, 89.

10. Even in something as simple as a slap, the vast power deferential between Jesus and the elite Jewish authorities is on display. The degrading action seeks to humiliate Jesus and remind him of his lowly, subordinate status.

It would be a mistake to conclude that Jesus' appearances before Annas and Caiaphas constitute strictly religious interrogations rather than political ones because they only involve the Jewish authorities. Recall that the Jewish authorities are dependent upon and allied with elite Roman power, and are instrumental in maintaining the imperial system.[11] Both groups are instrumental in preserving order in Judea and share power—at times tensely—as allies. Jesus' interrogations by the Jewish authorities and Pilate are both assuredly political in nature. The Jewish authorities originally plotted to kill Jesus after he raised Lazarus from the dead (11:45), and their concern was not religious, but rather explicitly political in nature: "If we let him go on like this, everyone will believe in him, and the Romans will come and destroy both our holy place and our nation" (11:48). In Jesus they saw a threat to the imperial status quo that jeopardized the stability of the Judean province and their place within the Roman imperial system as local allied elites. The political nature of their concern is also reflected in Pilate's first question to Jesus: "Are you the king of the Jews?" (18:33). Such a charge establishes him not only as a threat to the status quo in Judea, but also as a threat to the Emperor.[12] Thus, Jesus is handed over to Pilate the governor, setting the stage for their complex interaction that is the centerpiece of John's passion narrative.

2. Structure of the Roman Show Trial

The Roman show trial has been carefully crafted by the evangelist into seven episodes, which create a chiastic structure based on the location of the action.[13] The episodes alternate between two settings, with Pilate moving back and forth between them: outside the governor's headquarters where the Jewish authorities await, and inside where Jesus is bound. Indeed, the Fourth Gospel is unique among the Gospels to have Pilate's back-and-forth movement into and out of the Roman headquarters. Jesus' appearance before Pilate in the Synoptic Gospels appears to take place strictly in public settings. Jesus' isolation within the headquarters

---

11. See, for example, Josephus, *Ant.* 20.247–51, which describes the Roman control of the high priesthood in Jerusalem, at first through client kings, and then through Roman governors. It also observes that the chief priests are entrusted as the rulers of Judea (20.251).

12. Brown, *Gospel According to John*, 2:861.

13. See further Moore, *Empire and Apocalypse*, 59; and Brown, *Death of the Messiah*, 1:758.

makes Pilate's interrogation of him much more intimate and personal in the Fourth Gospel.

The structure largely follows Pilate's explicit movement into and out of his headquarters. Pilate "goes out" (ἐξῆλθεν) to meet the Jewish authorities (18:29, 38; 19:4) and then "enters" (εἰσῆλθεν) back inside to interact with Jesus (18:33; 19:9). However, since Pilate's movement is not always explicitly noted (e.g., 19:1, 12), the structure of the unfolding drama is chiefly determined by the shifts between his interactions with the Jewish authorities and with Jesus. Thus, an outline for the Roman interrogation emerges as follows:[14]

	Section	Location	Participants	Movement
1	18:28–32	Outside	Pilate and "the Jews"	Pilate went out (18:29)
2	18:33–38a	Inside	Pilate and Jesus	Pilate entered the headquarters (18:33)
3	18:38b–40	Outside	Pilate and "the Jews"	Pilate went out (18:38b)
4	19:1–3	Inside	Pilate, Jesus, and Soldiers	Pilate took Jesus (19:1)
5	19:4–8	Outside	Pilate, Jesus, and "the Jews"	Pilate went out again (19:4)
6	19:9–11	Inside	Pilate and Jesus	Pilate entered the headquarters (19:9)
7	19:12–16a	Outside	Pilate, Jesus, and "the Jews"	Pilate brought Jesus out (19:13)

It is clear from the outline that, even though Jesus is the most significant figure of the Fourth Gospel as a whole, Pilate becomes the central figure of this scene as the narrative traces his movements back and forth between Jesus and the Jewish authorities. This should give pause to commentators who claim that the narrative focuses primarily on the culpability of the Jewish authorities.[15]

3. John's Presentation of Pilate

Pilate is the only Roman with whom Jesus interacts in the Fourth Gospel, apart from the Roman soldiers and their officer who arrest Jesus in the

---

14. This table is adapted slightly from Carter, *Pontius Pilate*, 138.
15. E.g., Keener, *Gospel of John*, 2:1103.

garden (18:3, 12). Thus, Moore observes that, for John, "the face of Rome . . . is the blurred face of the Prefect of Judea, Pontius Pilate."[16] The Fourth Gospel's presentation of the governor is unique and complex, and one's interpretation of it influences one's understanding of the entire Roman interrogation scene, which his character dominates.

In one such interpretation, Neil Azevedo's poem "Pontius Pilate," the poet imagines what might be going on inside the mind of the Roman governor himself, as he assesses the situation before him:

> As we emerged out onto the pavement,
> I could hear the mob, fervent for frailty,
> feel its way toward us. We were each alone.
> To divert its attention is always best, to calm;
> yet this time I would distort its motive
> and its claim on him. Such was my dignity.
> But I wrongly gauged my powers to persuade
> and saw my words swallowed with his mouth.
> Still, I tried having slowed it by dressing him
> to calm its taste—until it revealed its maw
> and its dull voice. I let go. If only I hadn't
> been so similar to something weakened,
> displayed before the image of my hid belief,
> chosen but useless. We were both forsaken.[17]

Azevedo imagines the Jewish crowd, swelling in numbers, which has assembled to watch the proceedings. The intensity of the event is palpable, as the religious fervor of a major, sacred festival threatens to erupt into hostility. In the face of such a political nightmare, Azevedo portrays Pilate as having no "powers to persuade." The governor and the condemned man stand in solidarity, both "alone" before the powerful, dangerous multitude. Pilate attempts to calm the crowd by dressing up the accused, but their demands are not assuaged by this mocking gesture. He ends up feeling "so similar to something weakened," that is, to the one about to be executed on Rome's cross. Azevedo's Pilate is powerless and cannot control the events as they unfold.

Such a perspective is characteristic of most interpretations of the Johannine Pilate throughout history. Rensberger observes that, "[b]y

---

16. Moore, *Empire and Apocalypse*, 52.
17. Azevedo, "Pontius Pilate," 45.

virtually universal consent, Pilate is seen in John as a more or less sympathetic figure, a man who wants to be fair, who would gladly acquit Jesus, but who through lack of resolve and susceptibility to political pressure all too easily becomes the tool of 'the Jews' and their malevolence."[18] Brown's view is typical of the majority of scholarly perspectives on Pilate until the late twentieth century.[19] Acknowledging the presence of the Roman cohort in the arresting party, Brown insists that "Pilate himself is presented as favorable to Jesus."[20] In his view, Pilate believes that Jesus is politically harmless and so is keen to release him. Yet the governor is presented as weak, vulnerable, and ultimately ineffective in his maneuvering with the Jewish authorities. Thus he is unable to negotiate for Jesus' freedom. Though Pilate three times declares that he finds no case against Jesus, he does not have the political strength or resolve to release him. Pilate finally accedes to the political pressure of the Jewish authorities and hands Jesus over to be crucified. Brown argues that Pilate is "typical . . . of the many honest, well-disposed men who would try to adopt a middle position in a struggle that is total."[21] Pilate's attempt at neutrality ends up serving the interests of the world that is hostile to Jesus.

It is hard to imagine, however, that the Johannine audience would have perceived the Roman governor as "weak"; Pilate was the most powerful representative of imperial power in the Judean province. He has a network of the elite governing class, as well as the backing of Rome's military might, which already looms large within the narrative. The Jewish authorities have acknowledged the threat of Israel's destruction (11:48), indicating that they are fearful of the military power to which Pilate has access. And of course, the might of Rome appears in the presence of the cohort in Jesus' arrest (18:1–12). Furthermore, the interactions between Pilate and the Jewish authorities seem more complex than one-sided intimidation. Pilate seems to ridicule the Jewish authorities by repeatedly referring to Jesus as their "king." Finally, should Pilate be called "weak" if he does, in fact, successfully eliminate a possible threat to Rome by having Jesus crucified?

---

18. Rensberger, *Johannine Faith*, 92.

19. Brown, *Gospel According to John*, 2:863–64, 872, 885–96. See also Barrett, *Gospel According to St. John*, 531–46; Dodd, *Historical Tradition*, 96–97, 104–7, 119–20; and Schnackenburg, *Gospel According to St. John*, 3:241–67.

20. Brown, *Gospel According to John*, 2:863.

21. Brown, *Gospel According to John*, 2:864.

Rensberger has made a groundbreaking contribution to contemporary discussions of the Johannine Pilate.[22] He is dissatisfied with such older views of Pilate as weak and ineffectual, a governor who is sympathetic toward Jesus yet powerless to release him, due to manipulation by the Jewish authorities. Rensberger notes reasons to question any such understanding of Pilate. For example, he observes Pilate's repeated taunts to the Jewish authorities by calling Jesus the "King of the Jews." It is also difficult to maintain that Pilate is favorable to Jesus when he violently scourges the prisoner in the middle of the show trial. Finally, Pilate appears triumphant when the Jews make their final pledge of Roman allegiance: "We have no king but Caesar!" (19:15).[23]

Much of the scholarly insistence that Pilate is favorable to Jesus yet fails to secure his release stems from his proclamations that he finds "no case" against Jesus (18:38; 19:4, 6). Rensberger argues, however, that it is "possible in John for a character to proclaim Jesus' innocence without himself believing in it or caring about it."[24] He proposes instead that Pilate is indifferent to Jesus' innocence and fate, and that his ultimate aim in the "trial" is "to humiliate 'the Jews' and to ridicule their national hopes by means of Jesus."[25] Pilate mocks and antagonizes them by presenting Jesus as their "king" on several occasions (18:39; 19:5, 14, 15). He is also bent on reminding the Jewish authorities that they are not an autonomous people: they cannot kill Jesus without Rome (18:31; 19:6-7) and their true "king" is the emperor (19:15). Furthermore, it is hard to imagine that Pilate might truly find Jesus "innocent" if he deems him an unsanctioned king. Such figures were deemed rebels and were dealt with harshly by the agents of imperial Rome.[26]

---

22. Rensberger, *Johannine Faith*, 87-100.

23. Rensberger, *Johannine Faith*, 92.

24. Rensberger, *Johannine Faith*, 92.

25. Rensberger, *Johannine Faith*, 92.

26. See, for example, a number of accounts from Josephus. He recounts the stories of a certain Simon, who "assumed the diadem" and was decapitated by Roman forces (*J.W.* 2.57-59; *Ant.* 17.273-77); Athronges, a shepherd who aspired to the throne and whose brothers were killed as a result (*J.W.* 2.60-65; *Ant.* 17.278-84); and Simon bar Giora, who surrendered in the attire of a king by rising out of the rubble of the Jerusalem temple and who was later ritually executed in Rome (*J.W.* 7.29-31, 153-55). Horsley describes the messianic revolt and independent Judean state led by Simeon Bar Kosiba from 132-35 CE. By committing significant military resources toward the effort, the Romans were finally able to violently eliminate the movement (Horsley and Hanson, *Bandits, Prophets, & Messiahs*, 127-29). These four examples, of course, were

However, the Jewish authorities do exhibit power in the Roman show trial, too. Because they are local allied elites who are part of the power structure of the empire, Pilate cannot make unilateral decisions without threatening their necessary alliance. Pilate does not bend completely to their will, yet they do get something that they want, too: Jesus' death. They do not go home licking their wounds.[27]

Thus, in the Fourth Gospel, the evangelist presents a Pilate who is primarily concerned not with justice, but with the maintenance of the Roman imperial order. He is certainly not "favorable to Jesus," since he tortures and then crucifies him.[28] Nor is it a fair trial by modern standards. Yet Pilate cannot make unilateral decisions. Both elite parties—Pilate and the Jewish authorities—negotiate successfully to get something that they want.

4. Irony and the Roman Interrogation of Jesus

Irony abounds in this major section of the Fourth Gospel narrative. Josef Blank is right to claim that Jesus' kingship is the dominant theological motif of the "trial" narrative,[29] and irony contributes tremendously to the development of this motif. Though he does not know he speaks the truth, Pilate himself declares that Jesus is king several times in the show trial episodes. The Jewish authorities, however, tragically renounce the kingship of God and Jesus in favor of Caesar. Both of these are examples of verbal irony. Meanwhile, the text cleverly and ironically presents Jesus as a king undergoing coronation, proceeding to his enthronement upon the cross. Jesus is the one who possesses true power and authority, not Caesar or Pilate. Jesus' kingdom is also presented in sharp contrast with Rome's empire because nonviolence is one of its characteristics (e.g., 18:36).

The text also uses irony to present Jesus as the supreme judge of the Roman "trial." While Pilate is the one who ostensibly leads the proceedings, the text suggests that Jesus is not the one being tried but rather the one judging Pilate and the Jewish authorities. As O'Day points out, "Employing some of the Gospel's most painful irony, John 18:28—19:16a

---

all violent anti-imperial movements. Nevertheless, it is not difficult to see why Jesus, a popular kingly figure, might make the agents of imperial Rome nervous.

27. They are, however, dissatisfied with the inscription Pilate places on the cross during the crucifixion (19:19–22).

28. In contrast to Brown, *Gospel According to John*, 2:863.

29. Blank, "Die Verhandlung vor Pilatus," 62.

shows that it is the world, not Jesus, who is on trial."[30] The Fourth Gospel pronounces judgment upon Pilate, Rome's empire, and the allied Jewish elites as they all reject Jesus.

While Jesus appears as a weak, abused, condemned prisoner, he remains in full control during the Roman interrogation, as he does throughout the passion narrative. Early on, the narrator notes that the events proceed toward crucifixion in fulfillment of Jesus' words (18:32). Jesus goes obediently to his death at the will of the Father (e.g., 10:18). It is God's will, not Rome's, that directs the events of the narrative and the course of history.

Furthermore, the Gospel presents Jesus in ironic fashion as the paschal lamb who takes away the sin of the world (1:29). He is tried and then crucified on the day of preparation for Passover, when the sacrificial lambs are being slaughtered, and he functions as the supreme sacrificial lamb for the Passover festival. The Roman interrogation ultimately does not serve imperial purposes but God's life-giving purposes. It leads to the fulfillment of God's plan; Jesus will be "lifted up" on the cross, and this is the means by which he draws all people to himself (12:32).

Finally, the narrative paints both Pilate and the Jewish authorities in an exceedingly negative light. Both prefer darkness and death to God's life-giving plans and are impervious to the truth that Jesus represents. They are agents of Rome and Satan who stand diametrically opposed to God's agent, Jesus. Irony surrounds the Gospel's presentation of Pilate, ridiculing him. Over and over again, the Gospel employs what Duke calls "irony of identity" to mock the Roman governor.[31] Pilate repeatedly fails to grasp the fullness of Jesus' identity as the show trial progresses and thus consistently responds to him in an inappropriate manner. "What is truth?" Pilate wonders, blindly ignorant of the fact that "truth" stands embodied right in front of him (18:38; cf. 14:6). When the governor does correctly verbalize Jesus' identity, it is always unwittingly. Pilate sarcastically calls Jesus the "king of the Jews," but fails to realize that his statement is ironically true.

---

30. O'Day, "Gospel of John: Introduction," 800.
31. Duke, *Irony in the Fourth Gospel*, 100.

Scene 1: Jesus Is Handed Over to Pilate (18:28-32)

1. Setting

The context of the Roman show trial is firmly established in this first scene, which signals both its attention to the Roman setting and its timing at the beginning of the Jewish Passover festival. This scene also exhibits convoluted political negotiations and collaboration between Pilate and the Jewish authorities that will continue throughout the proceedings. However, it also suggests that the outcome of show trial is predetermined. The Jewish authorities indicate their intention to kill Jesus from the outset, yet the narrative aside in v. 32 reveals that Jesus is actually in control and the proceedings move toward the fulfillment of his words.

The Roman show trial begins at v. 28, which establishes both the location and the timing of the events that will soon unfold in dramatic fashion. The narrator describes Jesus' transfer from Caiaphas to Pilate's headquarters, the *praetorium*. The Greek word πραιτώριον is a transliteration of the Latin word for a residence of a chief Roman official in an occupied territory. Of the eight occurrences of this word in the New Testament, four are in this scene in the Fourth Gospel, which is the only Gospel to mention the *praetorium* at the beginning of the Roman proceedings.[32] It is clear that John takes seriously the setting of this show trial in the very center of imperial power in the province.[33]

The very use of the term *praetorium* here recalls for readers the presence of Rome's occupying forces. Judea was a colonized land, and such an imposing building would have been a constant reminder of Roman occupation. Carter notes that the very use of this term creates a "display of power [that] is intimidating."[34] Howard-Brook says that "the praetorium symbolized the ability of the distant imperial government to radiate its power into every land it held in colonial subjugation."[35] This text also evokes for John's audience the umbrella of Roman imperialism under which they, too, live. The chief local representative of this distant

---

32. Matt 27:27; Mark 15:16; John 18:28 (twice), 33; 19:9; Acts 23:35; and Phil 13. It is rendered variously as "Pilate's headquarters," "the palace of the Roman governor," "the Roman governor's residence," and "hall of judgment" in English translations.

33. Pilate's main headquarters were at Caesarea, but he would relocate temporarily to Jerusalem for potentially volatile holidays such as Passover.

34. Carter, *Pontius Pilate*, 138.

35. Howard-Brook, *Becoming Children of God*, 394.

imperial government, Pilate, will dominate the narrative that unfolds and will soon send Jesus to his death on a Roman cross.

The evangelist describes the prisoner transfer taking place "early in the morning" (πρωΐ), which indicates the fourth and final division of the night, the period right before daybreak.[36] Howard-Brook maintains that this term is significant. He highlights the fact that πρωΐ is a Roman term and argues that its use "moves the narrative out of Judean and into Roman time," further grounding the setting of the narrative in the Roman imperial world.[37] Furthermore, "it signals the coming return of the light, the approaching end of the long night through which Jesus and his disciples have traveled."[38] Indeed, as we observed that the nighttime setting of the arrest scene was symbolically and theologically significant, Bultmann argues for a symbolic (though depoliticized) reading here. He contends that 18:28 signals that "the day of the victory of Jesus over the world is breaking."[39] The "light of day" will soon overcome the darkness (1:5).[40] Though the outcome of the Roman interrogation appears as a defeat, it will make possible the fulfillment of God's plans.

Even more significant than this note about the early hour is the date on which the interrogation unfolds (18:28): the day of preparation before the celebration of the Jewish Passover festival. Indeed, this is a distinctive chronological feature of John's Gospel. In the Synoptics, Jesus' final meal with his disciples is a Passover seder, and he is executed on the following day, the 15th of Nisan, after Passover has begun.[41] In the Gospel of John, however, Jesus is tried and executed on the day of preparation before Passover (18:28; 19:14, 31). The last meal that he shares with his disciples thus is not a Passover seder (13:2). Rather, Jesus is slaughtered on the day of preparation before Passover begins at sunset, a full day be-

36. Brown, *Gospel According to John*, 2:844.
37. Howard-Brook, *Becoming Children of God*, 394.
38. Howard-Brook, *Becoming Children of God*, 394.
39. Bultmann, *Gospel of John*, 651.
40. Haenchen maintains that "the temporal notice, early in the morning, has no symbolic significance: it was a part of the tradition beginning with Mark 15:1" (Haenchen, *John 2*, 178). Brown points out that "John does not mention light here and there is no clear indication he intended symbolism, but it would fit in with Johannine theology" (Brown, *Gospel According to John*, 2:866). John 4:6 only mentions that it "was about noon" as the Samaritan woman and Jesus meet. There is almost certainly symbolism present in that indication of time, suggesting that the evangelist does not need to mention light or darkness explicitly to intend symbolism.
41. Cf. Matt 26:18–19; Mark 14:12–16; Luke 22:7–13.

fore he is executed in the Synoptic Gospels. Symbolically and ironically, the Johannine Jesus becomes the sacrificial Passover lamb, a theologically loaded image. The Passover festival recalled the Israelites' liberation and exodus from Egypt, which would have been a provocative, politically charged image for Jewish persons living under the domination of imperial Rome.

2. The Jewish Authorities

It is profoundly significant that the Jewish authorities hand over Jesus on the eve of the Passover. The evangelist notes that they do not enter the *praetorium* themselves, "so as to avoid ritual defilement and to be able to eat the Passover" (18:28).[42] It is clear that these Jewish elite want to be able to participate in the festival that begins at sunset, but it is unclear why they believe that they would become ritually impure if they enter the *praetorium*.[43] However, the motives and rationale of the Jewish authorities are less important than the rhetorical effect of this comment from the evangelist, which does two things. First, it sets up the staging for the Roman proceedings that are about to unfold: Pilate will have to move between his interrogation of Jesus inside and his negotiations with the Jewish authorities outside. Second, it creates a scathing irony in the narrative that presents the Jewish authorities in an extremely negative light.

This irony can be understood in a number of different, overlapping ways. First, the narrative portrays the Jewish authorities, "soon-to-be murderers," as anxious to maintain their ritual purity.[44] They themselves are blindly unaware of this dramatic irony, and thus victims of it. Howard-Brook observes the "bitter sarcasm here, for those who are so worried

---

42. The narrative is actually ambiguous about who, specifically, hands Jesus over and the identity of those who want to participate in the Passover festival. The "they" of 18:28 has no clear antecedent. They are described simply as "the Jews" in 18:31. In 18:35, Pilate says that Jesus' "own nation and the chief priests" handed him over to the Roman governor. Immediately before Jesus arrives at the *praetorium*, he appears before Annas and Caiaphas. It seems clear that the Jewish police from the arrest scene escort Jesus around: they appear in 18:13 (which has a clear antecedent), 18, and 22. It seems probable that the Jewish police, along with the chief priests, are those who arrive at the *praetorium* and are the "they" in 18:28. Regardless, the principal Jewish characters in the Roman trial scene are agents of the Jewish elite.

43. For an overview of the things that might possibly render them impure, see Brown, *Death of the Messiah*, 1:744–46.

44. Duke, *Irony in the Fourth Gospel*, 128.

about this legal technicality are anxiously attempting to have a man of their own covenant killed."[45]

Second, as O'Day points out, "The trial narrative opens with 'the Jews' ' insistence on ritual purity and their meticulous attention to the demands of their faith, and it will end with their complete denial of the claims to that faith (19:15)."[46] They express concern that they would not be able to participate in the religious festival if they enter the *praetorium*, but by the end of the Roman proceedings, the Jewish authorities essentially renounce their faith in God by declaring, "We have no king but the emperor" (19:15). O'Day's claim ties this moment in the narrative to the end of the show trial.

Third, it is ironic that they wish to eat the Passover meal ($\pi\acute{\alpha}\sigma\chi\alpha$). The Passover meal symbolically recalls the liberation of the Jewish people from oppression under the domination of a foreign power: Egypt. The Jewish authorities wish to participate in this symbolic remembrance of victory over a foreign power, but by the end of the Roman proceedings they end up pledging exclusive loyalty to the emperor of a new, oppressive foreign power: Rome.

Finally, Brown also highlights the significance of Passover with respect to irony. He points out that the Jewish authorities "fear that ritual impurity will prevent their eating the Passover lamb, but unwittingly they are delivering up to death him who is the Lamb of God (1:29) and thus making possible the true Passover."[47]

These overlapping ironies convey sharp criticism of the Jewish authorities. The irony vilifies them as hypocrites, murderers, and imperial collaborators. But it also subtly suggests, as the quotation from Brown observes, that they are inadvertent participants in God's plan. Their participation makes it possible for Jesus to go obediently to his execution on Rome's cross.

3. Accusation and Charges (18:29–30)

Because the Jewish authorities do not wish to enter the *praetorium*, due to religious sensibilities, Pilate deigns to come out to meet them. Only the Fourth Gospel describes such movement on Pilate's part. As noted

---

45. Howard-Brook, *Becoming Children of God*, 394.
46. O'Day, "Gospel of John: Introduction," 815.
47. Brown, *Gospel According to John*, 2:866.

above, he will move repeatedly between the interior and exterior of his headquarters for the duration of the Roman show trial.

Pilate is mentioned by name for the first time in the Fourth Gospel in v. 29.[48] He is not referred to as "Pontius Pilate" or given the title "governor." He is identified simply as "Pilate."[49] Howard-Brook insists that this means that "readers are all too familiar with this infamous colonial despot."[50] One cannot help but wonder if the Fourth Evangelist's omission of Pilate's rank represents a subtle "de-throning" of him. Jesus is the only titled ruler present in this scene.[51]

An incongruity presents itself in Pilate's question to the Jewish authorities: "What accusation do you bring against this man?" (18:29). Why must Pilate ask this question if he has already collaborated with the Jewish authorities by sending his troops to arrest Jesus (18:1–12)? Does he not already know the allegations against Jesus and perceive him as a potential threat? It is unlikely that the Fourth Evangelist would create such an obvious logical inconsistency in an otherwise well thought-out passion narrative. Instead, Pilate is already aware of the threat that Jesus poses to Roman hegemony; this question likely represents Pilate's public posturing and political maneuvering with the Jewish authorities—he will, after all, taunt them and remind them of their subservience to Rome with his next statement in 18:31.[52] It does not imply lack of prior knowledge about Jesus.[53] As noted above in chapter 3, Pilate has been involved in the plot to arrest, try, and execute Jesus from an early point by sending his troops to the garden (18:3).

---

48. What the NRSV renders as "Pilate's headquarters" in v. 28 is simply πραιτώριον in Greek.

49. Matthew refers to Pilate as "the governor" (ἡγεμών) on several occasions (27:2, 11, 14, 15, 21; 28:14). Luke 20:20 describes Pilate as "the governor" as well (20:20). Mark does not use the term for Pilate specifically, but does use it in 13:9 to refer to governors in general. Only Luke 3:1; Acts 4:27; and 1 Tim 6:13 apply the full name "Pontius Pilate" to the governor.

50. Howard-Brook, *Becoming Children of God*, 395. This is quite probable, as early Christian creeds attested Jesus' crucifixion by Pontius Pilate (e.g., Ign. *Trall.* 9:1; Ign. *Smyrn.* 1:2).

51. The Roman emperor, of course, is mentioned, but is not present (19:12, 15).

52. Brown, on the other hand, argues that this statement from Pilate represents a formal request for an accusation (*Gospel According to John*, 2:866).

53. The Greek word κατηγορία ("accusation") and its related forms are legal terms. Cf. Matt 12:10; 27:12; Mark 3:2; 15:3–4; Luke 6:7; 23:2, 10, 14; Acts 22:30; 23:30, 35; 24:2, 8, 13, 19; 25:5, 11, 16, 18–19.

Within the larger context of the Gospel, Pilate's question mocks Jewish authorities. The Greek verb rendered "accusation" (κατηγορίαν) reminds the Johannine audience of Jesus' words in 5:45: "Do not think that I will accuse [κατηγορήσω] you before the Father; your accuser [κατηγορῶν] is Moses, on whom you have set your hope." This echo reminds readers of an important motif: Pilate and the Jewish authorities, not Jesus, stand accused. Jesus' statement in 5:45 suggests that Moses and the law are "the accusation" that condemns the Jewish authorities. Ironically, the Jewish authorities themselves will play right into this claim by advocating for something that they acknowledge in 18:31 is "not lawful" (οὐκ ἔξεστιν) for them to do: to have Jesus killed. The sharp contrast is plainly evident between the accusation that stands against the Jewish authorities and their failure to give a legitimate accusation against Jesus.

The evangelist may insinuate an even more dramatic claim with Pilate's request for an accusation from the Jewish authorities. Howard-Brook maintains that the evangelist's word choice for "accusation" (κατηγοριαν) indicates that the Jewish authorities are doing more than just accusing Jesus; rather, they are playing the role of the "accuser"—the "Satan"—by bringing Jesus before Pilate.[54] In the Hebrew scriptures, a Satan's role was that of accuser (Job 1:6; Zech 3:1); the Hebrew verbal root śṭn can mean "to act as adversary" or "to accuse." Satan is also explicitly called "the accuser" (κατηγορῶν) in the New Testament (Rev 12:10). Jesus has already spoken sharply to a group of Jews, telling them, "You are from your father the devil" (8:44).[55] Here the Fourth Evangelist takes Jesus' allegation one step further by having the Jewish authorities fill Satan's role in v. 29. They are, ironically, more like their "father" than they know.

In responding to Pilate, the Jewish authorities do not offer a legitimate accusation against Jesus. The Jewish authorities give an exasperated answer to the governor who is already aware of the threat that Jesus poses: "If this man were not a criminal, we would not have handed him over to you." Yet their answer contains a "rather vague untruth."[56] Readers of the Fourth Gospel know that he is not an "evil-doer" (κακὸν ποιῶν; NRSV: "criminal"). Jesus "does" (ποιέω) a number of things in the Fourth Gospel: he performs signs (e.g., 2:11, 23; 3:2; 4:54; 6:2; 9:16; 11:47; 12:18, 37), he makes disciples (4:1), he makes people well (e.g., 5:11, 15), he

---

54. Howard-Brook, *Becoming Children of God*, 396.
55. The Greek διάβολος was used in the LXX to translate the Hebrew śṭn.
56. Duke, *Irony in the Fourth Gospel*, 128.

executes judgment as the Son of Man (5:27), he does the works that the Father has given him (e.g., 5:36; 8:29; 10:25, 37-38; 14:31), and he washes the disciples' feet (13:7).[57] He does not, however, do "evil" (κακός).[58] The Jewish authorities are either mistaken or are lying outright; that they are lying is suggested by the fact that they cannot list any of Jesus' "wrongs" (κακός), either in 18:23 or here in 18:30.[59] The audience knows that they speak falsely and that Jesus is not an "evil-doer."

Duke defines an "irony of self-betrayal" as "whenever the words or deeds of a person clearly divulge a different character than he or she claims to be."[60] Such is the case here. The Jewish authorities' lie incriminates them as children of the devil. Jesus had accused them of as much in 8:44: "You are from your father the devil" who "is a liar and the father of lies." The irony also has the positive effect of reminding readers that Jesus is *not* an "evil-doer." Jesus has lived in accordance with the will of his Father and now goes obediently to the cross.

The Jewish authorities' statement that they are "handing [Jesus] over" to Pilate (18:30) is also an ironic and unwitting self-betrayal. This verb has been used numerous times in the Gospel to describe Judas's actions in handing over (παραδίδωμι) Jesus (6:64, 71; 12:4; 13:2, 11, 21; 18:2, 5). The devil had prompted Judas to hand over Jesus (13:2). Now the Jewish authorities do the same thing. In doing so, they too assume responsibility for Jesus' death. As we saw in chapter 3 above, however, irony surrounds the use of the Greek verb παραδίδωμι throughout the arrest, interrogation, and crucifixion scenes.[61] Jesus is only "handed over" because he intends it and has predicted it (6:64, 71; 12:4; 13:2, 11, 21). The Jewish authorities and Pilate are unwitting pawns who help fulfill God's purposes and Jesus' intention to die on the cross. Haenchen says that the appearance of the phrase "to hand over" (παραδίδωμι) "has the effect of a clock sounding the death knell" because of its regular appear-

---

57. In each of these cases, the Greek verbal root is ποιέω.

58. This is not to say that he is "innocent" in the eyes of imperial Rome. The text has already indicated that Jesus is perceived as a threat to Rome and the Jewish authorities (11:48).

59. In Luke 23:2, the Jewish authorities provide three charges of wrongdoing to Pilate: "They began to accuse him, saying, 'We found this man perverting our nation, forbidding us to pay taxes to the emperor, and saying that he himself is the Messiah, a king.'" Mark 15:1 and Matt 27:13 speak of "many" charges with which the Jewish authorities accuse Jesus.

60. Duke, *Irony in the Fourth Gospel*, 26.

61. See pp. 95-96 above.

ance throughout the rest of the show trial narrative (18:35, 36; 19:11, 16), but it will also provide a consistent, ironic reminder in the Roman show trial of Jesus' foreknowledge and predictions of his pending death.[62]

4. "Take Him Yourselves" (18:31)

Pilate responds to the Jewish authorities by taunting them: "Take him yourselves and judge him according to your own law" (18:31). His response cannot mean that he does not intend to try Jesus himself. The Roman governor has already sent an entire cohort of soldiers to arrest Jesus (18:3, 12); the narrative presumes Pilate's belief that Jesus is a threat. Surely Pilate would not leave such a delicate matter up to the Jewish authorities. Instead, Pilate is taunting them to remind them of their dependence on Rome. Their response in v. 31, that they are "not permitted to put anyone to death," reveals their recognition of their dependence upon Rome; they cannot legally execute Jesus without collaborating with Pilate. He has the final power in their tensive alliance. Furthermore, Pilate's use of the pronoun "you" (ὑμεῖς) is emphatic, suggesting a sarcastic edge. The Fourth Evangelist also mocks the Jewish authorities by placing these words on Pilate's lips. Duke notes that "since ch. 5 'the Jews' have been trying furiously to judge Jesus by their own law, with embarrassing results. The law of Moses simply will not condemn him. Thus Pilate's words mock their impotence to kill Jesus; and they themselves are more correct than they know in confessing they have no legal ground for the deed" in the second half of v. 31.[63]

The response of the Jewish authorities, "We are not permitted to put anyone to death" (18:31), has puzzled many interpreters who have debated whether or not the Jewish authorities could impose a death sentence under Roman rule.[64] The Roman governor, of course, possessed the power of *imperium* to execute criminals.[65] Brown contends that the Romans may have permitted the Jewish authorities to execute under certain circumstances, but in most cases capital punishment was reserved for the governor's final judgment. Josephus, for example, describes an

---

62. Haenchen, *John 2*, 178.
63. Duke, *Irony in the Fourth Gospel*, 128.
64. For an overview of the discussion, see Brown, *Death of the Messiah*, 1:363-72.
65. Josephus describes how the first prefect of Judea, Coponius, was sent to the province in 6 CE with "full powers, including the infliction of capital punishment" (*J.W.* 2.117-18).

episode in which Titus recalls the Roman permission granted to the Jewish authorities to execute those who infringed upon a particular temple ordinance (*J.W.* 6.124–26). In another instance, Josephus recounts how a high priest was removed from office after having some early Christians stoned without first gaining permission from the governor to convene the Sanhedrin for the capital case (*Ant.* 20.200–203). Brown suggests that the unauthorized execution of a messianic claimant—Jesus—during the volatile Passover festival would certainly have drawn Pilate's attention and punishment.[66] Thus, the Jewish authorities confess their dependence on, and their need to collaborate with, Pilate in this matter; both parties perceive Jesus as a threat, but only Pilate has the final decision to see the matter through.

However, Ramsey's view that the legal domain in question is the Mosaic—not Roman—law is plausible. He points out that the Greek verb ἔξεστιν ("it is permitted/lawful") is used in the Gospels "predominantly to refer to what is either permitted or forbidden to Jews *by the Law of Moses*."[67] The narrator has already expressed the Jewish authorities' concern to observe the Mosaic law by maintaining ritual purity for the Passover. Ramsey suggests that they also convey that desire here.

If we follow Ramsey's interpretation, deep irony may be discerned. He says that their statement is "an unintentional word of self-condemnation" which serves to confirm Jesus' own words to them earlier in the Gospel: "Did not Moses give you the law? Yet none of you keeps the law. Why are you looking for an opportunity to kill me?" (7:19).[68] Even though they will not kill Jesus themselves, they will lobby passionately for his execution and see to it that he is killed. Ironically, they will forsake both their law and their faith by the end of the proceedings.

It is possible that both Roman and Mosaic laws are signified by the text. The Jewish authorities cannot legally kill Jesus according to either law. Regardless, they reveal their intentions with their response: "We are not permitted to *put anyone to death*." Their use of the word ἀποκτείνω ("to kill") in v. 31, as opposed to θανατόω ("put to death"), suggests that

---

66. Brown, *Death of the Messiah*, 1:371–72.

67. Michaels, "John 18:31," 474–79. Michaels says that, "aside from John 18:31 itself, 20 of 21 uses of ἔξεστιν and ἐξόν in the Gospels fit this category" (475). However, elsewhere in the New Testament, the verb does refer to Roman legal matters (e.g., Acts 16:21; 22:25).

68. Michaels, "John 18:31," 478. See also John 8:37, 40.

their intention is to *murder* him, not to hold a legal execution.[69] The word θανατόω is typically used for legal killing in the LXX (cf. Exod 21; Lev 20, 24), while ἀποκτείνω is commonly used to refer to murder, as in the story of Cain's murder of Abel (Gen 4:8).[70] The Jewish authorities have not given a formal charge and they have already attempted to kill (ἀποκτείνω) Jesus throughout the Gospel (e.g., 5:14; 7:1, 25; 8:37, 40, 59; 10:31; 11:53). The outcome is settled in their minds; Jesus will be executed. Jesus' "trial" is thus not conducted in the service of justice, but rather for the benefit of the Jewish and Roman elites and therefore, by extension, the maintenance of the imperial status quo.

Unbeknownst to them, the Jewish authorities' statement that they cannot kill Jesus also serves a theological purpose: "This was to fulfill what Jesus had said when he indicated the kind of death he was to die" (18:32). From the perspective of the Fourth Gospel, the Jewish authorities cannot kill Jesus by stoning (8:59; 10:31) because he predicted that he would die by another method, by being "lifted up" (3:14; 8:28; 12:32). Jesus' prediction will come true when he is executed by Roman crucifixion in John 19.

This narrative aside in 18:32 echoes 18:9: "This was to fulfill the word that he had spoken, 'I did not lose a single one of those whom you gave me.'" The theme of fulfillment that surfaced in the arrest scene surfaces again as the Roman interrogation is about to begin. The Johannine audience can feel the incongruity between appearance and reality: the Jewish and Roman elites exert control of the proceedings, but the evangelist emphasizes that the events are happening according to Jesus' predictions and the will of the Father. Jesus is the "master over his own life and death," as he himself declared earlier: "For this reason the Father loves me, because I lay down my life in order to take it up again. No one takes it from me, but I lay it down of my own accord. I have power to lay it down, and I have power to take it up again" (10:17–18).[71] Jesus will die, but only because he chooses to do so in obedience to the Father's divine plan.

The stage is thus set in 18:28–32 for the Roman show trial that follows. The evangelist has anchored the context firmly within its Roman imperial setting and its overlap with the Passover festival. Irony

---

69. Howard-Brook, *Becoming Children of God*, 397.

70. The verb ἀποκτείνω is also used to describe the killing of enemy combatants. See Josh 7:5; 1 Sam 15:8; and 1 Macc 5:28.

71. Brown, *Gospel According to John*, 2:867.

has already emerged, marking the Jewish authorities as hypocrites, liars, murderers, and imperial collaborators. The evangelist has also employed irony to remind the Johannine audience that the entire proceedings will not move toward Pilate and the Jewish authorities' goals, but rather toward the fulfillment of Jesus' words.

Scene 2: Questioning the "King of the Jews" (18:33–38a)

Satisfied with the admission by the Jewish authorities that they are dependent upon him to secure Jesus' execution, Pilate returns to the interior of the *praetorium* to begin questioning Jesus. Pilate's first question deals with Jesus' sovereignty and kingship, a theme that will be prominent throughout the proceedings. Before long, however, Jesus, the true king and judge, turns the tables and begins questioning the governor. The Gospel uses irony in this scene to undercut Roman claims to sovereignty while presenting Jesus as the true king.

1. "Are you the King of the Jews?"

Pilate's first question to Jesus articulates the nature of his concern regarding the prisoner and why he sent his soldiers to arrest Jesus in the first place: "Are you the King of the Jews?" (18:33). This is the first explicit mention of Jesus' kingship in the passion narrative. Pilate is concerned that Jesus, who claims unsanctioned power, is a political claimant who might threaten Rome's hegemony and the stability of the Judean province. The expression "the King of the Jews" is not strictly a religious, messianic title, but rather has nationalistic political connotations.[72] Client rulers of Rome, such as Herod the Great and Herod Antipas, were called "kings" (e.g., Matt 2:1; Mark 6:14). The Greek term βασιλεύς was also used as a designation for the emperor in the Roman imperial world.[73] Pilate's use of this term for Jesus suggests his belief that Jesus may claim unsanctioned sovereignty over Judea. This would present a problem for

---

72. Brown, *Gospel According to John*, 2:868; and Lohse, *History*, 89–90. Herod, for example, was described as the "King of the Jews" (*Ant.* 14.9). See further p. 119 n. 26 above for a discussion of unauthorized "kingly" figures.

73. E.g., Josephus, *J.W.* 3.351; 4.596; 5.58–60, 563, as well as 1 Tim 2:2; 1 Pet 2:13, 17; and Rev 17:12. See also Carter, *John and Empire*, 192. The Fourth Gospel uses the term in relation to the emperor at 19:15: "We have no king but the emperor" (βασιλεύς and Καίσαρα).

Pilate because Jesus' purported rule is not authorized by Rome and thus contests imperial hegemony. More importantly, Jesus' kingship mimics and sets him in direct opposition to the Roman ruler himself. This title makes it abundantly clear that Pilate is concerned about a political charge and must determine whether Jesus is a threat to the emperor.

Kingship is not a prominent motif in the Fourth Gospel until Pilate's interrogation of Jesus begins. Indeed, the term "king" surfaces only four times prior to chapter 18. Nathanael calls Jesus the "King of Israel" when they first meet (1:49). Later, Jesus hastily escapes when a crowd of about five thousand tries to make him king by force (6:15). The theme of Jesus' kingship also emerges briefly but powerfully during his triumphal entry into Jerusalem, which itself mimics and mocks a Roman imperial procession.[74] A crowd takes up palm branches and quotes part of Ps 118, a psalm of royal triumph, shouting "Blessed is the one who comes in the name of the Lord—the King of Israel!" (12:13).[75] The Fourth Evangelist's depiction of the scene suggests that the people believe Jesus will re-inaugurate God's kingdom and governance over their nation. The fears that the Jewish authorities expressed in 11:48, that Jesus' popularity might incite Roman action, are not unfounded. In response to the quotation from Ps 118, Jesus himself sits upon a donkey, evoking the paradigmatic figure of Zech 9:9: "Look, your king is coming, sitting on a donkey's colt!" The following verse of Zechariah is not explicitly stated but is implied and clarifies Jesus' particular type of kingship in response to the crowd: "He will cut off the chariot from Ephraim and the war horse from Jerusalem; and the battle bow shall be cut off, and he shall command peace to the nations; his dominion shall be from sea to sea, and from the River to the ends of the earth" (Zech 9:10). The verse suggests that Jesus, as king, will rule "from sea to sea," stripping Rome of the breadth of its empire. The expansiveness of Jesus' empire mimics that of Rome's, but with a significant difference. Jesus is not depicted as a warrior king who will overthrow Rome's empire with military might; instead, he will banish the tools of war from the land.[76]

At least one further reference in the Fourth Gospel suggests Jesus' kingship. His identity as the "Son of Man" evokes Dan 7:13–14, which describes one who is given everlasting "authority" (ἐξουσία) and a

---

74. Borg and Crossan, *Last Week*, 2. See also Carter, "Church Bible Studies," 22–23.

75. O'Day, "Gospel of John: Introduction," 707. The words "the King of Israel" are added to the end of the quotation from Ps 118 and are probably taken from Zeph 3:15.

76. Borg and Crossan, *Last Week*, 4.

kingdom (βασιλεία) that shall never be destroyed.⁷⁷ The arrival of the "Son of Man" coincides with the end of all earthly empires (Dan 7:1–12) and the establishment of God's kingdom. Jesus refers to himself many times throughout the Gospel as this "Son of Man" (1:51; 3:13, 14; 4:50; 5:27; 6:27, 53, 62; 8:28; 9:35; 12:23; 13:31), a claim that threatens Roman hegemony. Although none of these references occur in the passion narrative, several do establish connections between Jesus' identity as the "Son of Man" and his passion. Jesus says that, as the Son of Man, he will be "lifted up" (ὑψόω) on the cross (3:14; 8:28; 12:32–34) and "glorified" in his death (12:23; 13:31). Jesus also claims "authority to execute judgment, because he is the Son of Man" (5:27). Jesus' identity as the "Son of Man" in the Fourth Gospel establishes him as the agent of God's sovereignty and signals that Rome's empire is under judgment.⁷⁸

Thus, while the kingship motif is not prominent in the first seventeen chapters of the Fourth Gospel, it is nevertheless significant. This theme resurfaces in force in 18:33 and will remain at the forefront of the narrative until Jesus is crucified.⁷⁹ It is striking that this kingship motif assumes prominence at the precise moment when Jesus finally comes face-to-face with Roman imperial power and its chief representative in the province. The Johannine audience is already aware of Jesus' kingship

---

77. The terms "authority" and "kingdom" both resonate with great significance in John's Roman trial (see 18:36; 19:10–11).

78. There is a tremendous amount of literature on the "Son of Man" expression in the Fourth Gospel, much of which deals with the background of the phrase and whether or not its background is Jewish apocalyptic literature. Some scholars suggest that there is little or no connection between the Johannine Son of Man and Daniel 7:13–14. Burkett, for example, contends that Jesus the Son of Man is preexistent in the Fourth Gospel, while the Danielic Son of Man is not (*Son of the Man*). He argues that the primary background for the Son of Man figure in John is Proverbs 30:1–4 and the figure of Ithiel, who is also the "Son of God" (*Son of Man*, 169–71). Rhea also argues for a non-apocalyptic background for the Johannine Son of Man expression, insisting instead that he is a Mosaic-Prophet-Messiah figure (*Johannine Son of Man*, 69–70). I, however, find Moloney's perspective most convincing. He argues that "the Johannine Son of Man is the continuation of a dynamic, growing interpretation of Daniel 7:13, which can be found in the Synoptic Gospels, 1 Enoch, 4 Esdras, the Fourth Gospel, and which even extends into the writings of the early Fathers" (*Johannine Son of Man*, 219). The apocalyptic Son of Man figure is widespread in both Jewish and early Christian literature surrounding the first century CE, as Moloney notes. Furthermore, John 5:27 links the Johannine Son of Man figure with judgment, a central theme in Daniel 7.

79. In fact, the occurrences of the word βασιλεύς are denser in John's Roman trial and execution than anywhere else in the entire New Testament. Of 115 occurrences in the New Testament, twelve are located in John 18–19.

from the few references to it earlier in the Gospel. It comes as no surprise, then, that Jesus' kingship clashes with Roman claims to sovereignty.

Pilate's question, "Are you the King of the Jews?" (18:33), expresses his skepticism that Jesus could be the liberator and sovereign of the Jewish nation. The Greek contains the emphatic pronoun "you" (σύ), as if Pilate is saying, "Are *you* the one who is going to seize dominion over Judea from Rome? How can you, a mere peasant, claim kingship?" The unspoken answer to Pilate's question, of course, is "yes, Jesus *is* the King of the Jews," although the governor will fail to understand both the veracity of Jesus' claim and the nature of his kingship.

2. Interrogating Pilate

Jesus' response, "Do you ask this on your own, or did others tell you about me?" (18:34), reverses the direction of the interrogation. This is not merely a request for information on Jesus' part. The Johannine audience knows that Jesus already "knew what was in everyone" (2:25). By answering Pilate's question with his own question, Jesus takes over as the judge of the scene; Pilate is now on trial and will have to make a decision about Jesus' identity. This stunning reversal is magnificent situational irony: one would not expect a Galilean peasant to interrogate a Roman governor! Furthermore, Jesus' question reminds the audience of the alliance between the Jewish and Roman authorities and suggests that Pilate has obtained prior knowledge about Jesus from them.[80]

Furthermore, Jesus' question raises the issue of the origin of their knowledge. Meeks notes the significance of the expression "*on your own*" (ἀπὸ σεαυτοῦ, literally "from yourself") in Jesus' question, "Do you ask this on your own, or did others tell you about me?" (18:34), in connection with similar constructions throughout the Gospel (5:19; 7:18; 11:51; 16:13).[81] There is an especially strong parallel between this statement and 11:49–51, in which Caiaphas advocates for Jesus' death: "'it is better for you to have one man die for the people than to have the whole nation destroyed.' He did not say this *on his own*, but being high priest that year he prophesied that Jesus was about to die for the nation." Meeks explains that Caiaphas's statement is unwittingly of divine origin. Likewise, Jesus' question suggests that Pilate's knowledge that Jesus is the "King of the

---

80. Carroll and Green, *Death of Jesus*, 94; and Carter, *John and Empire*, 192.

81. Meeks, *Prophet-King*, 63. The expression is nearly unique to the Fourth Gospel, appearing elsewhere in the New Testament only in Luke 12:57; 21:30; and 2 Cor 3:5.

Jews" is of divine origin even though he fails to see it. Meeks says it is "doubly ironic": so far as Pilate knows, his information is from the Jewish authorities, but ultimately it is from God.[82] As the conversation unfolds, Pilate will ironically testify to the truth of Jesus' kingship repeatedly during the Roman show trial.

Pilate sneers back at Jesus, "I am not a Jew, am I? Your own nation and chief priests have handed you over to me. What have you done?" The grammar of the first question indicates that Pilate expects a negative response: no, he is not a Jew.[83] This response emphasizes his role as the representative of a colonial power and implies his disdain for the Jewish people.[84] He is not a Jew; he is their Roman ruler.

However, in one respect, Pilate is remarkably similar to "the Jews" in the Fourth Gospel. Howard-Brook notes that throughout the Gospel, "geographic identity has been a matter not of birthplace or citizenship but of mythic allegiance.... To be a 'Judean' has meant... rejecting Jesus as the one sent from God and his commandment to love."[85] Howard-Brook elaborates, noting that "to the extent that Pilate is in league with the accusers who are seeking to kill Jesus, he, too, is a 'Judean.'"[86] O'Day also contends that "'the Jews' represent the world's resistance to the revelation of God in Jesus."[87] Therefore, Pilate's response suggests an ironic truth: while he is not technically a "Jew," in the symbolic world of the Fourth Gospel he is in fact one! His political alliance with the Jewish authorities is evaluated as one that is opposed to God. Pilate's true identity is up in the air even while he wonders about Jesus' identity. Like the Jewish authorities, he too will reject Jesus and the truth to which Jesus testifies.

Pilate's response is similar to the Pharisees' question in 9:40: "Surely we are not blind, are we?" They, too, expect a negative response, but are shown to be blind and unable to accept the truth. Both of these cases represent dramatic irony because the characters are unaware of the full implications of their questions.

---

82. Meeks, *Prophet-King*, 63.

83. The Greek particle μήτι indicates the expectation of a negative response.

84. Many commentators suggest that Pilate is expressing disdain for the Jewish people. See, for example, O'Day, "Gospel of John: Introduction," 816. This may be the case, given the emphatic Greek pronoun ἐγώ in v. 35.

85. Howard-Brook, *Becoming Children of God*, 398.

86. Howard-Brook, *Becoming Children of God*, 398.

87. O'Day, "Gospel of John: Introduction," 816–17.

Pilate continues: "Your own nation [ἔθνος] and the chief priests have handed you over to me. What have you done?" (18:35b). The mention of "nation" (ἔθνος) recalls 11:48–52, where Caiaphas recommended killing Jesus in order to save the nation (11:48, 50, 51, 52).[88] This textual link stresses the political motivations underlying the proceedings that will lead to Jesus' execution. Pilate's words also evince contempt for Jesus, a lowly provincial, by distancing Pilate from the distinct ethnic identity of the Jewish people. Pilate's question, "What have you done?," will not be followed by a denial of guilt from Jesus in v. 36, but rather a statement indicating that Jesus *does* rule a political entity outside of Rome's control.

3. "My Kingdom is Not from this World"

In v. 36, Jesus finally responds in dramatic fashion to Pilate's question concerning his kingship (18:33). Though he does not explicitly label himself a king, he does claim a "kingdom" (βασιλεία).[89] Jesus declares, "My kingdom is not from this world. If my kingdom were from this world, my followers would be fighting to keep me from being handed over to the Jews. But as it is, my kingdom is not from here" (18:36). The Greek term βασιλεία could be translated as "empire" here, highlighting a striking contrast between Jesus' empire and that of Rome.[90] Jesus claims an empire that is distinct from Rome's for two reasons. First, its origin is from God, not the world. Second, unlike Rome and its allies, Jesus' empire does not employ violence to maintain hegemony.

Jesus' statement that his "kingdom is not from this world" (ἡ βασιλεία ἡ ἐμὴ οὐκ ἔστιν ἐκ τοῦ κόσμου τούτου) refers not to the *location* of his kingdom but rather to its *origin* and *nature*.[91] Jesus' kingdom, like Jesus himself, is from above and has its source in the Father (8:23).[92] It would be a mistake to assume that Jesus speaks of his kingdom as entirely

---

88. These are the only five occurrences of the word ἔθνος in the Fourth Gospel.

89. While Jesus does not explicitly call himself "king," Pilate will do so on a number of occasions (cf. 18:33, 37, 39; 19:14–15, 19).

90. The word βασιλεία often describes "empires" in the LXX, as it does in Esther 10:1 and frequently in Daniel (e.g., 1:20; 4:30; 11:4). See also Carter, "Church Bible Studies," 17.

91. The Greek prepositional construction is best understood as indicating the source of Jesus' kingdom. See Wallace, *Greek Grammar*, 371. See also Meeks, *Prophet-King*, 63.

92. The parallelism between 18:36 and 8:23 is clearly evident in Greek. Jesus declares, "I am not of this world" (ἐγὼ οὐκ εἰμὶ ἐκ τοῦ κόσμου τούτου).

spiritual, absent from the physical world, and no threat to Rome's kingdom. Like Jesus' disciples who are "in the world" (17:11; ἐν τῷ κόσμῳ) but who do not "belong to the world" (17:16; ἐκ τοῦ κόσμου), Jesus' kingdom can exist in the world while maintaining a fundamentally different nature because its origin is from God. Rensberger supports this point, stating, "It is not a question of whether Jesus' kingship exists in this world but of how it exists; [it is] not a certification that the interests of Jesus' kingdom are 'otherworldly' and so do not impinge on this world's affairs, but a declaration that his kingship has its source outside this world and so is established by methods other than those of this world."[93]

How does the origin of Jesus' kingdom from above set it apart from Rome's kingdom? Jesus clarifies the difference between them: "If my kingdom were from this world, my followers would be fighting to keep me from being handed over to the Jews" (18:36). If Jesus' kingdom found its origin in the world, then it would reflect the violent nature of the Roman Empire.

The word typically translated as Jesus' "followers" (ὑπηρέται) in v. 36 is the same Greek word used to describe the Jewish temple police in 18:3–12, who employed the threat of violence as a strategy for maintaining the Roman imperial order; the soldiers and Jewish police arrived bearing weapons, prepared to take Jesus by force.[94] In stark contrast, Jesus' followers, with the exception of Peter (18:10), have not resorted to violence to keep him from being handed over—and Peter's outburst of violence is immediately and sharply criticized by Jesus.[95]

O'Day claims that this moment is infused with irony: "Jesus is ironically contrasting his 'officers' and the temple officers. His kingship, unlike that of the king Pilate serves (cf. 19:12, 14–16), is not secured by force (cf. 18:11)."[96] This is an instance of verbal irony, because Jesus says more than he explicitly states. Jesus promotes a nonviolent vision for his followers while condemning the violence employed by Rome and its allied elites. He does have a kingdom and followers, but they are fundamentally different from Rome's kingdom and the allied Jewish temple police, which

---

93. Rensberger, *Johannine Faith*, 97.

94. See also 18:18, 22; 19:6.

95. The Greek expresses this with a "contrary to fact" conditional statement, using an unreal, hypothetical condition to express a truth. *If* Jesus' kingdom were of this world, *then* Jesus' followers would be fighting, but it is *not* of this world so they *do not* fight to prevent Jesus from being handed over. See Wallace, *Greek Grammar*, 694–95.

96. O'Day, "Gospel of John: Introduction," 817.

use violence to maintain Roman hegemony. Jesus' statement reminds the Johannine audience that his followers did not resort to violence in the past, nor should they in the future in order to sustain his kingdom.

Furthermore, the word "world" (κόσμος) carries a special connotation within the Fourth Gospel. It refers not just to the physical world, but to the realm of unbelief and all who reject God's agent and purposes (cf. 1:10).[97] Jesus' statement in v. 36 suggests that Rome's empire is, in fact, "of this world." Rome is presented as opposing God's life-giving movement that Jesus advances.

Finally, in v. 36 we also glimpse a deep irony that runs through the entire Roman show trial. In describing his kingdom, Jesus "affirms that his appearance does not cohere with reality: he is a king."[98] Jesus stands before Pilate as a condemned prisoner, yet he claims sovereignty over an empire whose nature Pilate cannot grasp. The Fourth Gospel stresses the importance of drawing accurate conclusions about Jesus' identity (20:31) but Pilate will not be able to comprehend: he falls prey to the irony and cannot discern the deeper reality.

4. Truth

Pilate takes Jesus' statement as an affirmation of his kingship, responding, "So you are a king?" (18:37). Yet he fails to see the implications of Jesus' words regarding violence and the distinction between Jesus' empire and Rome's. The governor fixates solely on Jesus' kingship and the challenge it may pose to Roman hegemony. But again, his response suggests his skepticism and disbelief that Jesus is actually a king, judging from the emphatic "you" (σύ) in v. 37.

Jesus' response, "You say that I am a king," highlights the fact that the Roman governor himself is bearing witness to Jesus' identity as king.[99] Jesus continues, "For this I was born, and for this I came into the world, to testify to the truth. Everyone who belongs to the truth listens to my voice" (18:37). Jesus' response brings to mind earlier themes. The language of being born and entering into the world recalls Jesus' mission as the one sent by the Father (e.g., 1:9-13; 6:38). It also evokes Jesus' "otherworldliness" and reinforces that he is not "of the world."

---

97. Carter, "Church Bible Studies," 17.
98. Ehrman, "Jesus' Trial," 128.
99. Cf. John 18:39; 19:14-15, 19.

Jesus' final statement in v. 37, that "everyone who belongs to the truth listens to my voice," evokes Jesus' earlier comments in the Good Shepherd discourse, that "the sheep hear his voice" (10:3) and "the sheep follow him because they know his voice" (10:4). Jesus, in responding to a question about his kingship, invokes his identity as shepherd. Shepherd imagery in the Hebrew Bible was often used to describe Jewish leaders and kings (e.g., 2 Sam 5:2; 7:7; 1 Kgs 22:17; 1 Chr 11:2; Ps 78:71–72; Isa 44:28; Ezek 34:1–31; Mic 5:2–4). Such imagery was also used to describe the Roman emperors. Philo, for example, in describing how the emperor Gaius Caligula ought to behave, calls him "a shepherd and master of the flock" (*Embassy* 44). Dio Chrysostom explains that a good king is one who "has regard for his fellow-men" and who "extends his care to all" as a shepherd does for his flocks of sheep (*Kingship* 1.15–17). Thus, when Jesus identifies himself as the "good shepherd" who "lays down his life for the sheep" (John 10:11), his words carry political overtones. He is critical of the Jewish elite who are allied with Rome (10:8, 10, 12–13) because they "steal and kill and destroy" (10:10) and do not look after the interests of the "sheep."[100] The Good Shepherd discourse also evokes Ezek 34, which casts a critical light on the "shepherds of Israel," the Israelite leadership that works for its own benefit by taking advantage of the "sheep" (34:2). Read in this light, Jesus' identity as shepherd illuminates his role as king: his kingship is characterized by his willingness to lay down his life for his sheep (10:11, 17–18), in direct contrast to the self-serving motives of the ruling elite who control the Roman imperial system.

Pilate, of course, cannot grasp this point or the "truth" of Jesus' identity. He responds to Jesus' statement with a flippant "What is truth?" It would appear that he is not interested in an answer, because he does not wait to see if Jesus responds. Yet the Johannine audience knows the answer, making this a profoundly ironic moment. The question hangs in the air while Pilate goes out of the *praetorium* to address the Jews, yet the answer is practically ringing in the ears of the audience. Jesus has recently identified himself as "the truth" in the narrative (14:6), so the audience knows that Pilate cannot grasp the "truth" even as the one who embodies it stands right in front of him!

Because of the similar prepositional phrasing in Greek, there is a contrast evident in the text between those who belong "to the truth" (ἐκ

---

100. Taken within the narrative context, the "thief" and "bandit" of 10:1 describe the Pharisees whom Jesus has just criticized in 9:40–41. See Carter, *John and Empire*, 185; and Moloney, *Gospel of John*, 300–304.

τῆς ἀληθείας) in v. 37 and those who are "of the world" (ἐκ τοῦ κόσμου).[101] Jesus is "of the truth" and testifies to the truth. Pilate proves that he, like the empire he represents, is "of the world" by his failure to comprehend the truth that Jesus reveals. The governor can neither grasp nor accept the nature of Jesus' kingdom and his identity as truth.

Scene 3: Releasing Barabbas (18:38b–40)

While the Johannine audience reflects upon the answer to the question that Pilate has left hanging in the air, the narrative continues to follow the governor as he moves outside the *praetorium* to confront the Jewish authorities. His declaration to them that "I find no case against him" (18:38) cannot really mean that Pilate thinks Jesus is innocent. Carter remarks that Pilate's claim seems "quite strange after his previous consent to arrest Jesus, after Jesus talked about his empire (kingdom) and did not appear to dispute being a king!"[102] The context suggests that rather than being a sincere judgment on Jesus' case, Pilate's declaration is part of his ongoing negotiation with the Jewish authorities. As in their testy exchange at 18:29–31, Pilate mocks them again to remind them of their reliance upon him.[103]

In order to provoke the Jewish authorities, Pilate invokes a custom of releasing a prisoner during the Passover festival. Again, the governor cannot be sincere in his offer to release Jesus; Pilate has already deemed it necessary to send an entire cohort of troops to secure his arrest (18:1–12), and he already knows that the Jewish authorities are intent on having him killed (18:31). Nor is he acting out of fear or expediency to pacify a feverish crowd, as in the Gospel of Luke.[104] Rensberger contends that "We gain the impression that Pilate is merely going through a formality, well aware of what the outcome will be."[105] His derisive reference to Jesus as "the King of the Jews" is unlikely to move any of the Jewish authorities to ask for Jesus' release. Thus, this, too, can be interpreted as a political tactic intended to antagonize and display his power over the Jewish authorities. Pilate provokes the Jewish authorities by asking them if they want him to

101. Cf. 8:23; 15:19; 17:14, 16.
102. Carter, *John and Empire*, 304.
103. Carter, *John and Empire*, 304.
104. See Luke 23:18–25.
105. Rensberger, *Johannine Faith*, 93.

release for them "the King of the Jews" (18:39).¹⁰⁶ This is the first time that he refers to Jesus in this manner publicly, even though he surely does not really think that Jesus is their king and sovereign. Unwittingly, however, Pilate speaks a deep truth. Even as he speaks sarcastically to the Jewish authorities, he falls victim to dramatic irony once again. Jesus *is* king, and Pilate fails to perceive it.

The custom of releasing a prisoner is attested in all four canonical Gospels, although nowhere else in antiquity.¹⁰⁷ The Fourth Gospel has streamlined this Barabbas tradition and only provides a bare-bones picture of the event; it is the shortest Barabbas account of the four Gospels. O'Day says that the evangelist has narrowed the episode to one focus: "the choice between 'the King of the Jews' and Barabbas."¹⁰⁸ The Jewish authorities cry out (κραυγάζω) for Barabbas, and Pilate presumably allows him to go free.¹⁰⁹ Previously, the Fourth Gospel employed the Greek word κραυγάζω to describe the crowd's acclamation of Jesus as king at the triumphal entry (12:13). Even earlier, Jesus invoked his life-giving power, shouting (κραυγάζω), "Lazarus, come out!" (11:43). Here, the Jewish authorities renounce Jesus' kingship and demand his death, preferring Barabbas instead.¹¹⁰ They choose one "son of the father"—the Aramaic meaning of Barabbas—over Jesus, the incarnate Son of God the Father.¹¹¹ The choice that the narrative presents between Jesus and Barabbas is stark.

The evangelist includes an important narrative detail at the end of v. 40: "Now Barabbas was a bandit."¹¹² The Fourth Evangelist has withheld

---

106. Note that he does not offer to release to them "the one who is called 'the King of the Jews,'" but refers to Jesus as "the King of the Jews" as a statement of fact (cf. 19:21).

107. See Mark 15:6-15; Matt 27:15-26; and Luke 23:18-25.

108. O'Day, "Gospel of John: Introduction," 818.

109. At the very least, the narrative gives us no reason to doubt Barabbas's release. The focus is not on Barabbas's release but on the choice between him and Jesus. Note that the Synoptic tradition does attest to Barabbas's release (Matt 27:26; Mark 15:15; and Luke 23:25).

110. Later, the Fourth Evangelist employs the same Greek word to describe how the Jewish authorities demand Jesus' crucifixion (19:6) and resist Pilate's ploy to release Jesus (19:12).

111. Howard-Brook, *Becoming Children of God*, 403.

112. Meeks argues that the Fourth Evangelist has introduced this detail into the tradition, for only the Fourth Gospel notes that Barabbas was a λῃστής (*Prophet-King*, 68).

this fact from readers, even while Pilate and the Jewish authorities must have known it. The dramatic revelation at the end of this brief episode (18:38–40) prompts the Johannine audience to reconsider what has just taken place in light of this crucial information. Jeffrey Staley describes this narrative technique as "the victimization of the reader."[113] In such a technique, the narrator withholds significant information only to introduce it at a later time. This "forces the reader to recognize his or her misjudgments by supplying or implying the correct perspective."[114] In this case, the evangelist does not withhold the information that "Barabbas was a bandit" for long, but the sequential presentation of it *after* the Jewish authorities choose the release of Barabbas highlights their selection of Barabbas *the bandit* and forces the Johannine audience to reconsider the significance of that choice. Now that the audience knows that Barabbas is a λῃστής, the choice between Jesus and Barabbas is thrown into sharper relief. Such victimization is ironic because it depends on an audience that is lacking critical details known to characters in the story. In this case, the Johannine audience is the brief victim of irony, but the rhetorical force of this irony works to draw the audience closer to the truth.

The Greek term that the NRSV renders "bandit" has a significant bearing on interpretation of this passage. John is unique among the Gospels in describing Barabbas as a λῃστής (18:40), and the term can mean a number of things. On the one hand, it can signify a violent criminal such as a "robber," "highwayman," or "bandit."[115] K. C. Hanson and Douglas Oakman describe such "bandits" as those who are disaffected by colonial rule and who in turn lash out through theft and violence at local and imperial elites.[116] On the other hand, the term λῃστής can indicate one who participates in much larger-scale seditious activity, such as a "revolutionary," a "guerrilla" fighter, or an "insurrectionist."[117] After 70 CE, in the period when the Fourth Gospel was written, the word would recall the revolutionaries who took part in the Jewish Revolt (66–70 CE).[118] Josephus describes such "revolutionaries" on a number of occasions (*J.W.*

---

113. Staley, *Print's First Kiss*, 95–96.

114. Staley, *Print's First Kiss*, 95–96.

115. BDAG 594. E.g., Luke's Parable of the Good Samaritan includes "robbers" who attack the man going down from Jerusalem to Jericho (10:30–35).

116. Hanson and Oakman, *Palestine*, 80–85.

117. BDAG 594.

118. Brown, *Death of the Messiah*, 1:688.

2.254, 581–82; 4.135–39, 160–61; *Life* 77–79).[119] In the context of the Fourth Gospel, labeling Barabbas a λῃστής also reminds the audience of the "thieves" (κλέπται) and "bandits" (λῃστής) of 10:1–18 who threaten the Johannine flock and whose leadership contrasts sharply with that of Jesus, the "good shepherd" (10:11, 14).[120] Within the narrative context of chapter 10, these are the Pharisees, the Jewish leaders with whom Jesus clashes in chapters 9 and 10.[121] Thus, in choosing Barabbas, the Jewish authorities are choosing one of their own.

Whereas Jesus' followers know the voice of the Good Shepherd (10:4), they will flee from thieves and bandits because they "do not listen to them" (10:8). Jesus, the Good Shepherd, calls his sheep by name and leads them out to pasture, life, and salvation (10:3, 9–10). The Good Shepherd comes so that his sheep "may have life, and have it abundantly" (10:10), and even "lays down his life for the sheep" (10:11). In sharp contrast, Jesus suggests that the Jewish authorities, because they are thieves and bandits, sneak into the sheepfold with ill intent in order to "steal and kill and destroy" (10:10).

The shepherd imagery that 18:40 recalls also reinforces the motif of Jesus' kingship. Pilate has just offered to the Jewish authorities their king, the "King of the Jews" (18:39), and they have rejected him in favor of Barabbas. This brief scene is heavy with dramatic irony. The Jewish authorities and Pilate know not what they do. By drawing this linguistic connection between 10:1–18 and 18:38–40, the Fourth Evangelist cleverly highlights the Jewish authorities'—and Pilate's—rejection of Jesus, the Good Shepherd, the King of the Jews. They do not know Jesus' voice and do not belong to his flock. Instead they choose and thus align themselves with Barabbas, a violent λῃστής, who seeks devastation and death. Ironically, he is one of their own. Their failure to heed the voice of the Good Shepherd means that they will not find the life and salvation that Jesus offers.

This linguistic connection also points forward to Jesus' death on the cross. What makes the Good Shepherd *good* is that he "lays down his life for his sheep" (10:11, 15, 17). This subtly reinforces the motif that Jesus lays down his life of his own accord and at the will of the Father, and will

---

119. See Brown, *Death of the Messiah*, 1:687; Hanson and Oakman, *Palestine*, 84.

120. These are, in fact, the only three occurrences of the term λῃστής in the entire Fourth Gospel.

121. See Moloney, *Gospel of John*, 300–304.

take it up again (10:18). Further, the defining characteristic of his kingship is that he is enthroned upon, and reigns from, a cross.[122]

If anyone still doubts that there are political implications to this "trial," 18:38–40 should convince them otherwise. Because the Jewish elite choose to have Jesus executed rather than Barabbas, Jesus must be perceived as a political threat *greater* than Barabbas. Hanson and Oakman maintain that Jesus represented a different sort of threat to the ruling elite than Barabbas:

> If Barabbas was a threat to the social order because he led a violent band of bandits, at least these bandits usually concentrated on attacking country estates, Roman garrisons, and Roman supply lines. Jesus posed a different sort of threat to the urban elites. He gathered large crowds wherever he went, and he was recruiting members for a new group . . . Jesus was accused of actually being a pretender to the royal throne of Judea (a "messiah" [1.51]), meaning he was a threat to both the Roman rule of Palestine and the leadership role of the high priestly families.[123]

Jesus does not pose the threat of violence that Barabbas does, but Rome has proven that it can handle violent revolutionaries.[124] The threat Jesus poses is his potential to compromise the whole imperial system. Jesus, the "Son of Man," will possess an "everlasting dominion" and "all peoples, nations, and languages" will serve him (Dan 7:14).

The choice between Jesus and Barabbas is presented as the choice between two threats to imperial rule, but also between two competing visions of reality. Barabbas represents violence and death, while Jesus represents nonviolence and life. The Jewish authorities choose—and Pilate allows—the release of Barabbas. Whereas the Jewish authorities feared that Jesus' nonviolent movement would provoke Rome's wrath (11:48), they ironically elect to have an insurrectionist freed. This is exactly the type of person who would incite Rome to destroy their "holy place" and "temple" in 70 CE (11:48).

For the Johannine audience, this brief scene attacks the folly of Pilate and the Jewish authorities. The Fourth Gospel reveals the hypocrisy of the Jewish authorities who prefer—and of Pilate who allows—the release

---

122. Meeks, *Prophet-King*, 68.
123. Hanson and Oakman, *Palestine*, 87–88.
124. Carter, *John and Empire*, 304.

of a violent, political criminal over Jesus.[125] It also mocks them and exposes them as impervious to the truth that Jesus represents. Meanwhile it offers the audience a means of contesting Roman power and violence by choosing exclusive allegiance to Jesus, the Good Shepherd, the King of the Jews.

Scene 4: Torture and Jesus' Investiture as King (19:1–3)

Jesus is flogged and then dressed and mocked as a king in this central scene of the show trial's chiastic structure. Again, Pilate's movement and his interaction with Jesus set this apart as a separate scene within the larger show trial narrative. Though the narrative does not specifically state that Pilate returns to the interior of the *praetorium* at 19:1, it is implied because the Jewish authorities fade from view and the narrative focuses again on Pilate's interactions with Jesus. Furthermore, Pilate must be inside if he is to "go out again" to meet the Jewish authorities in 19:4. Although this scene is brief, it is suffused with deep irony that both ridicules the Romans and highlights Jesus' identity as king. The Romans inadvertently act and speak with more truth than they know by investing and hailing Jesus as king. Mimicry emerges in this scene, as well, as Jesus' investiture as king imitates imperial practices and power structures.

This central scene of the Roman show trial begins with Pilate having Jesus flogged (19:1).[126] Many English translations, mask the ambiguity of the Greek here, as in the NRSV translation of 19:1: "Then Pilate took Jesus and had him flogged." Such a translation assumes that the soldiers mentioned in the following verse carry out Pilate's wish. But the language of the Greek could suggest that it is the governor himself who is whipping

---

125. Bultmann, *Gospel of John*, 657–58.

126. The Fourth Gospel is the only Gospel to explicitly narrate the violent scourging of Jesus. Mark, Matthew, and Luke all mention it, but do not narrate the event itself. The Fourth Gospel uses μαστιγόω to relate the actual act of Jesus' scourging. Howard-Brook notes that this verb "refers to the particular Roman practice of flogging a criminal with a barbed whip, the *mastix*" (*Becoming Children of God*, 403). Matt 27:26 and Mark 15:15 both read (with only a small change in Greek word order) that "after flogging [φραγελλόω] Jesus, he handed him over to be crucified." The actual event is not narrated, but only mentioned as having been accomplished before Pilate hands Jesus over. Luke 23:16 only shows Pilate proposing that Jesus be "disciplined" (παιδεύω), but the text never explicitly confirms that he does so.

Jesus! Pilate is the subject of the verb rendered "to flog" (μαστιγόω).[127] If one interprets the verb with a simple active meaning, then Pilate is the principal agent and the one who lashes Jesus in the narrative world of the Fourth Gospel.[128] However, the verb could also carry a causative force, meaning that Pilate "is not the direct agent of the act, but the source of it."[129] In this case, the NRSV translation is appropriate. Regardless of how we interpret the verb, however, Pilate is still the primary agent of Jesus' scourging. Moore maintains that, even if the soldiers of vv. 2–3 are the direct perpetrators of the scourging, they are "every bit as much instruments in the hands of the prefect as are the scourges gripped in their own hands."[130] The chief representative of Roman power in the province brings Rome's violence to bear on this unauthorized king.

What is scourging doing in the middle of the Roman proceedings? In Mark and Matthew, Jesus is whipped at the end of the proceedings, after the verdict has been declared, and as a direct prelude to his crucifixion (Mark 15:15–20; Matt 27:26–31). Brown explains that such a scourging would weaken the condemned man and thus hasten a person's death by crucifixion.[131] That is not the case here, however. Half of the show trial remains before Jesus will be handed over to his executioners. Some scholars have suggested that Pilate has Jesus flogged in order to satisfy the Jewish authorities' desire to see Jesus punished, hoping that this will dissuade them from seeking the harsher death penalty.[132] Brown, for example, concludes that Pilate is trying to placate the Jewish authorities by showing them "a bloody and battered figure" that has received a lesser—but still harsh—punishment.[133] Bajsić takes Brown's argument a step further by insisting that Pilate was attempting to provoke the Jewish authorities into asking for Jesus' release by inflicting all of the violence

127. Τότε οὖν ἔλαβεν ὁ Πιλᾶτος τὸν Ἰησοῦν καὶ ἐμαστίγωσεν.

128. Historically speaking, we have cause to doubt that Pilate would have conducted the scourging himself, but here we are much more concerned with the Fourth Evangelist's presentation of the events rather than the historical proceedings of the trial.

129. Wallace, *Greek Grammar*, 411.

130. Moore, *Empire and Apocalypse*, 58. Brown, for example, argues that v. 2 "makes it clear that this was done by others at his order" (*Gospel According to John*, 2:874).

131. Brown, *Gospel According to John*, 2:888.

132. This is likely what Pilate intends in Luke 23:16.

133. Brown, *Gospel According to John*, 2:886. Cf. Barrett, *Gospel According to St. John*, 530; Bultmann, *Gospel of John*, 659; and Duke, *Irony in the Fourth Gospel*, 132.

upon him that Roman brutality could muster.[134] But the Jewish authorities have already shown themselves to be intent on having Jesus executed (18:31). Furthermore, this brutality is not done in view of the Jewish authorities. Nor does the Fourth Gospel emphasize Jesus' "bloody and battered" appearance in the following scene when he is presented to the Jewish authorities (19:4–8).[135] Thus, Jesus' scourging is neither a prelude to crucifixion nor an attempt to convince the Jewish authorities to approve his release. Instead, as Jennifer Glancy has argued, the violence that Pilate wreaks upon Jesus is best understood as torture.

Glancy contends that "in the Roman world, torture, conceived as a mechanism to extract truth from flesh, was used in interrogation, most commonly in interrogation of slaves and other low-status persons."[136] The *Digest of Justinian* describes Roman torture as "the infliction of anguish and agony on the body to elicit the truth" (48.10.15.41).[137] During Pilate's last interaction with Jesus, the governor wondered, "What is truth?" (18:38). Here, Glancy argues that Pilate tries to extract truth from Jesus by force. Though this torture is sparsely narrated, Moore maintains that Pilate's questions, which are intended to discover the truth of Jesus' identity are, in fact, present, but they are scattered throughout the "trial" rather than directly associated with the scourging (18:33, 37; 19:9, 10).[138] Thus, Pilate continues his quest to discover "truth" by means of torturing Jesus. Glancy asserts that "Pilate may not know the truth, but he thinks he knows how to get it."[139] However, as we have already seen, the irony that suffuses this moment is that Jesus *is* the truth, and Pilate cannot grasp this reality. Nevertheless, truth does emerge immediately following the scourging: Jesus is clothed as a king in vv. 2–3.

The manner in which the Fourth Evangelist describes Pilate's torture of Jesus exhibits dramatic irony. Note that Pilate "takes" (ἔλαβεν)

---

134. Bajsić, "Pilatus, Jesus und Barabbas," 7–28.

135. Instead, as we will see below, the following scene emphasizes Jesus' kingly appearance. When he is presented to the Jewish authorities, Jesus is described as wearing his crown of thorns and purple robe (19:5).

136. Glancy, "Torture," 108. Of course, the very acts of beating, abuse, and torture signify a status differential between the one inflicting and the one receiving the humiliation and abuse.

137. Quoted from Glancy, "Torture," 108. A number of historical sources attest Roman torture, including Acts 22:24, where the tribune orders Paul "to be examined by flogging [μάστιξιν], to find out the reason for this outcry against him."

138. Moore, *Empire and Apocalypse*, 61.

139. Glancy, "Torture," 121.

Jesus in v. 1 before torturing him. Howard-Brook points out the connection between this word and the Johannine prologue: "But to all who received [ἔλαβεν] him, who believed in his name, he gave power to become children of God" (1:12). Pilate does "receive" Jesus, ironically enough, but rather than "believing in his name," the Roman governor proceeds to *torture* him! The Fourth Gospel thus condemns Pilate's reception of Jesus and the Roman "justice" that Pilate carries out as a woefully inadequate response to the one whom God has sent into the world.

Moore argues that this scene of torture, located in the central scene of the show trial's chiastic structure, also implies a critique of Roman imperial ideology. Specifically, it critiques torture as a "central mechanism designed to keep every Roman subject—slave, peasant, every other non-citizen, and, in certain cases, even citizens themselves—firmly in their respective, and respectful, places in relation to Roman imperial authority."[140] Torture is a means of control, intended to protect imperial interests. Yet the Fourth Gospel indicts Rome's torture, and in turn, Roman justice, as decidedly unjust. The justice that Pilate is responsible for carrying out is not justice at all.

The torture that Pilate inflicts upon Jesus also functions within the narrative context to shame and humiliate Jesus, as the soldiers also intend to do in vv. 2–3. The primary focus of this scene is not the torture itself, but rather the solders' mocking of Jesus and their ironic acclamation of him as "king." After Jesus is tortured, the Fourth Gospel reports that an unspecified number of soldiers dress Jesus as a parodic king and then proceed to taunt him (19:2–3).[141] The kingship motif could hardly be more emphatically in view here. In the previous scene (18:38–40), Pilate sarcastically proclaimed Jesus the "King of the Jews." Now the soldiers take up this proclamation and go one step further by crowning him.

Ignace de la Potterie maintains that the Fourth Evangelist "leaves out several details given in the Synoptic accounts, but retains precisely those which serve to emphasize the royal dignity of Jesus: the crown of thorns, the purple garment and the words of the soldiers: 'Hail king of the Jews.'"[142] The soldiers do not strike Jesus' head with a reed or spit upon him (as in Mark 15:19 and Matt 27:30), nor do they blindfold him (as in Luke 22:64). Furthermore, the Gospel does not explicitly characterize

---

140. Moore, *Empire and Apocalypse*, 62.

141. Mark 15:16 and Matt 27:27 each describe an entire cohort's (σπεῖρα) presence for the investiture and mockery.

142. La Potterie, "Jesus: King and Judge," 106.

the soldiers as *mocking* Jesus, nor do they ultimately remove the royal clothing they dress him in (cf. Mark 15:20; Matt 27:29, 31; Luke 23:11). Ehrman suggests that, while the Synoptic accounts present this scene as nothing more than a cruel and brutal mockery, "the soldiers really do crown and hail the King of the Jews" in the Fourth Gospel.[143] Surely mockery is intended, but the scene ends up looking remarkably like a legitimate coronation.

The Gospel reports that the soldiers "wove a crown of thorns and put it on his head" and "dressed him in a purple robe" (19:2). Both items represent royal imagery. The crown (στέφανος) is at the very least symbolic of kingship, but may be intended specifically as a parody of the emperor's laurel wreath, which was also called a στέφανος.[144] Haenchen notes that the emphasis for this first item is on the crown itself, not its composition from thorns. He argues that the thorns are from a date palm, not the sharper spiney acanthus, and consequently insists that the crown is a "pseudo-insignia of a king, and thus not . . . an instrument of torture" intended to inflict pain on the victim.[145] The robe with which they clothe Jesus is dyed in the imperial color, purple, and suggests wealth, power, and kingship.[146] All of this is patently ironic imagery. The soldiers have set up Jesus as a parody of a king in order to mock him, but they fail to grasp the truth that they unintentionally proclaim. Furthermore, in contrast to the accounts in Mark and Matthew, Jesus will not be stripped of this royal attire when the scourging comes to a close.[147] The Johannine Jesus will go to the cross dressed fittingly as a king.

After Jesus is clothed as a king, the soldiers mockingly pay homage to him with "Hail, King of the Jews!" and repeatedly strike him on the face (19:3). Their greeting, "Hail" (χαῖρε), resembles the acclamation "Ave Caesar" rendered to the emperor; they address Jesus as they would their ruler![148] Meanwhile, their repeated slapping of Jesus (ἐδίδοσαν αὐτῷ ῥαπίσματα) reminds the Johannine audience of Jesus' confrontation with

---

143. Ehrman, "Jesus' Trial," 128.

144. Brown, *Gospel According to John*, 2:874-75.

145. Haenchen, *John 2*, 181.

146. Brown, *Gospel According to John*, 2:875. On purple as an imperial color, see Rev 17:4; 18:16. As a color of wealth, see Lam 4:5; Dan 5:7-29. As a color of power and kingship, see Judg 8:26; 1 Macc 8:14; 10:20; 2 Macc 4:38.

147. Mark 15:20 and Matt 27:31 describe the Romans stripping Jesus of the regal garb and returning him to his own clothes.

148. Brown, *Gospel According to John*, 2:875.

Annas, in which he was struck by one of the Jewish police (18:22; ἔδωκεν ῥάπισμα). Howard-Brook remarks on the connection that "the Johannine ideology is consistent throughout: Rome and Judea are equal partners in the violence against the king."[149] However, Pilate's disdain not just for Jesus, but for the entire Jewish people, is again evident as the Roman soldiers abuse Jesus: they repeatedly disgrace and humiliate the "King of the Jews." They treat Jesus as a powerless ruler, a fitting "king" for the "despised and subjugated [Jewish] people."[150]

There is tremendous incongruity in this central scene of the Roman proceedings. On one level, the Romans enact a brutal reminder of imperial domination and control over the Jewish people by torturing Jesus. They then proceed to mock and verbally abuse this pitiful, bloodied "King of the Jews." The Fourth Gospel, however, cleverly presents this traditional episode so that the ironic picture that emerges is not of a helpless, pathetic, battered figure, but rather a king undergoing coronation—one who mimics the Roman emperor himself. The Romans prepare Jesus for his "lifting up" and glorification upon the cross by dressing him with royal attire and hailing him as they would the emperor. As O'Day comments, "The Fourth Evangelist . . . has transformed the tradition of Jesus' mockery by the Roman soldiers into a narrative of Jesus' investiture as king."[151] The Gospel undermines what would be a public transcript of Roman domination and power in the narrative. In its place it creates an acclamation of Jesus as King, in which the Romans ironically and unwittingly announce Jesus' kingship as an alternative to that of Caesar.

This is powerful dramatic irony. The Romans are completely oblivious to the reality of Jesus' kingship even as they mock him as a king. The governor's apparent obsession with the title "King of the Jews" (18:33, 39; cf. 19:14, 15, 19) has carried over to the Roman soldiers who enact the power and brutality of the Roman imperial system. Jesus does not resist their violence, but goes willingly and peacefully to his death, and ironically, his glorification.

---

149. Howard-Brook, *Becoming Children of God*, 404.
150. Michaels, *Gospel of John*, 929.
151. O'Day, "Gospel of John: Introduction," 819.

Scene 5: The Presentation of Jesus as King (19:4–8)

After Jesus is flogged, dressed in kingly attire, and mocked, the governor returns to the exterior of the *praetorium* where the Jewish authorities wait. This time he brings Jesus out with him, but the Gospel does not emphasize Jesus' battered state. Instead, it stresses the fact that he is still clothed as a king: "So Jesus came out, wearing the crown of thorns and the purple robe" (19:5). The text makes no mention of Jesus' flogging or his wounds after the brief incident itself in 19:1. Nor is there any indication that Pilate brings Jesus out to the authorities to convince them that he has "had enough" and should be released.[152] Instead, Pilate presents Jesus as king, dressed in regal attire, to mock the Jewish authorities with their "king." Meanwhile, the Johannine audience is reminded that Jesus proceeds to his death still adorned as a king.[153]

1. Behold the Man!

As Pilate brings Jesus out, he makes an ironic understatement: "Here is the man!" (19:5; ἰδοὺ ὁ ἄνθρωπος). The audience knows that Jesus is much more than a mere "man." Jaime Clark-Soles notes that on several occasions, Jesus' opponents refer to him as a mere "man," but in such cases, they fail to grasp Jesus' true identity or significance. She observes that "this is true of Caiaphas (11:50), those who question the blind man (9:16, 24), the woman who questions Peter by the gate (18:17), and, famously, Pilate (19:5)."[154] Caiaphas wanted "one man" (Jesus) to die on behalf of the nation (11:50), and the blind man's interrogators mistakenly referred to Jesus as "a man who is a sinner" (9:16, 24). Jewish antagonists in Jerusalem took him to be "only a human being" (ἄνθρωπος) and attempted to stone him for blasphemy, for making himself God, when in fact he was of divine origin (10:33). In all these instances, it is not enough to call Jesus a mere "man." The incongruity between Jesus' true identity and who they think he is signals irony; this irony appeals to readers, inviting them to

---

152. Brown, for example, believes that the "scourging, instead of being part of the crucifixion punishment (as is the flogging in Mark/Matthew), becomes in John a lesser punishment that Pilate hopes will satisfy 'the Jews' by causing them to give up on this wretched Jesus" (Brown, *Death of the Messiah*, 1:827). Brown's reading is likely influenced by Luke's account, in which Pilate plans to have Jesus flogged and then released (Luke 23:16).

153. The Johannine emphasis on Jesus' kingship also continues to display imitation and mimicry of Roman imperial ideology by presenting Jesus as a king or emperor.

154. Clark-Soles, *Death and the Afterlife*, 116.

accept the fullness of Jesus' identity which the characters in the narrative fail to grasp.

However, Jesus' opponents are not the only characters in the narrative who speak of Jesus simply as a "man." Clark-Soles suggests that the use of ἄνθρωπος is also ironic in 2:10 and 5:7. In 2:10, at the wedding in Cana, the steward noted that "every *man* serves the good wine first," but readers, who know of Jesus' cosmic origin from the prologue (1:1–18), know that Jesus is much more than a man. Clark-Soles remarks that "if the steward had known who Jesus was, he might have asked Jesus for living wine, or wine that does not perish."[155] In 5:7, the lame man at the Pool of Bethzatha claims that there is "no one [ἄνθρωπος οὐκ] to put me into the pool." Clark-Soles detects irony here too, observing that his statement is "true enough, but Jesus, who is much more than an *anthrōpos*, is available to heal him."[156] In such instances, Culpepper would say that the author "winks at the reader," who knows Jesus' true identity and divine origin.[157]

Pilate's statement also brings to mind Jesus' "Son of Man" (υἱός τοῦ ἀνθρώπου) sayings throughout the Gospel (1:51; 3:13, 14; 6:27, 53, 62; 8:28; 9:35; 12:23, 34; 13:31). The title "Son of Man" simultaneously recalls Jesus' divine origin (3:13), his authority to carry out judgment (5:27), his life-giving role (6:27, 53), and his prediction of his death (8:28) and glorification (12:23; 13:31). The title is also evocative of Dan 7:13–14, which, as we have noted, declares that one like a "son of man" (LXX: υἱὸς ἀνθρώπου) will receive "dominion and glory and kingship, that all peoples, nations, and languages should serve him" and proclaims that "his dominion is an everlasting dominion that shall not pass away, and his kingship [βασιλεία] is one that shall never be destroyed." As Jesus is presented as a king to the people, Pilate's statement recalls Jesus' status as the "Son of Man" whom the Fourth Gospel presents as an eschatological judge and eternal king with an everlasting kingdom. Pilate, of course, does this inadvertently, impervious to the truth. But the audience of the Fourth Gospel knows that Jesus is the "man," namely the "Son of Man," who judges the Jewish authorities and Pilate, and whose reign portends the end of—yet also mimics—the Roman imperial system that they both represent.

155. Clark-Soles, *Death and the Afterlife*, 114–15.
156. Clark-Soles, *Death and the Afterlife*, 115.
157. Culpepper, *Anatomy*, 171.

Pilate's statement "Here is the man!" is thus an ironic understatement and an example of irony of identity. The Johannine audience knows that the Jesus whom Pilate presents to the Jewish authorities is much more than a "man." The truth of Jesus' identity eludes the governor's grasp even as Jesus stands beside him dressed in regal attire. The audience, however, is reminded of Jesus' true identity as king and as the "Son of Man" who will possess an everlasting dominion vis-à-vis Rome.

2. Acclaiming the King

Brown observes that this moment in the text represents the next step in Jesus' coronation ritual, in which Jesus is "brought out, royally bedecked and empurpled, to be presented to his people for acclamation," mimicking Roman imperial practices.[158] Jesus does receive acclamation here, but it is unusual for a king: "When the chief priests and the police saw him, they shouted, "Crucify him! Crucify him!" (19:6).[159] The verb κραυγάζω recalls the crowd's cries of acclamation during the triumphal entry, when they shouted, "Hosanna! Blessed is the one who comes in the name of the Lord—the King of Israel!"[160] The cries of the Jewish authorities, however, call for his crucifixion. The Fourth Evangelist also uses κραυγάζω when Jesus shouts for Lazarus to come out of his tomb, providing a striking contrast between "the crowd's shout that brings death to Jesus and Jesus' shout that brings life to Lazarus."[161] As Jesus stands in regal garb before them, they shout for his death rather than acclaim him as king.[162] The Jewish authorities reject him, preferring the imperial status quo over the progress of God's plan.

Yet Carter points out the situational irony of their desperate request for Pilate to crucify him: "in calling for Jesus' crucifixion, the leaders demand that Jesus be lifted up, the very means by which he said he will draw all people to himself."[163] In 12:32–33, Jesus announces: "I, when I am lifted up from the earth, will draw all people to myself"; the narra-

---

158. Brown, *Gospel According to John*, 2:890.

159. The Greek text literally reads "Crucify! Crucify!" There is no explicit direct object following the imperative.

160. The verb κραυγάζω appears rarely in the NT. Of its nine occurrences, six are in John. Matt 27:23 and Mark 15:13 use κράζω to describe this request for crucifixion. Luke 23:21 uses ἐπιφωνέω.

161. Brown, *Gospel According to John*, 1:427.

162. Brown, *Gospel According to John*, 2:890.

163. Carter, *John and Empire*, 306.

tor then observes that Jesus "said this to indicate the kind of death he was to die." The verb ὑψόω ("to lift up") has been used throughout the Gospel to allude to Jesus' death on a cross (3:14; 8:28; 12:32, 34), but it is not until 19:6 that *crucifixion* is explicitly mentioned in the text as the means of his death. In this example of situational irony, the Jewish leaders demand Jesus' death in order to remove the threat he poses to them, but it becomes the means by which Jesus is "lifted up" and thus glorified. They have also expressed concern that "everyone will believe in [Jesus]" if they do not kill him (11:48–50) and the Pharisees have lamented that "the whole world has gone after him" (12:19). Ironically, their request for Jesus' crucifixion will allow him to fulfill his intent to "draw all people to himself" (12:32). The Jewish authorities might as well be shouting, "Lift him up! Lift him up!"

3. "Take Him Yourselves"

In response to the Jewish request for crucifixion, Pilate responds, "Take him yourselves and crucify him; I find no case against him" (19:6). This is the third and final time that Pilate declares that he finds no grounds for legal action against Jesus (cf. 18:38; 19:4). Yet again, this cannot be a sincere offer from Pilate to the Jewish authorities; he knows they cannot kill him themselves (18:31), and if they were to do so, they would certainly not crucify him.[164] Instead, his comment reminds them that in the tensive alliance between Roman and provincial elites, the latter are dependent upon Rome for executing the prisoner. The Jewish authorities are reduced to begging in order to have Pilate kill Jesus, thereby expressing their submissiveness. Further, there is a sharp incongruity between the statement that Pilate finds "no case" against Jesus and Jesus' kingly attire. Can he really see no case against Jesus when Jesus is so royally garbed? The irony is palpable.

4. The Governor's Fear

The Jewish authorities attempt to force Pilate's hand by insisting that "we have a law, and according to that law he ought to die because he has claimed to be the Son of God" (19:7).[165] Upon hearing this, Pilate

---

164. Presumably they would stone him, as they attempted in 8:59 and 10:31.

165. The Jewish authorities are wrong on one point: Jesus never "claims" to be the Son of God (19:7; υἱὸν θεοῦ ἑαυτὸν ἐποίησεν). He *is the Son of God*. Attentive readers know the truth.

suddenly and inexplicably becomes "more afraid than ever" (μᾶλλον ἐφοβήθη) (v. 8). While some commentators would attach v. 8 to the following scene (19:9–12), it is more appropriate as the conclusion to this scene (19:4–8) for two reasons.[166] First, Pilate does not return inside the *praetorium* until v. 9. Pilate's movement frequently signals scene changes in the show trial drama (18:33, 38; 19:4).[167] Second, the Greek conjunction οὖν ("therefore") in v. 8 indicates that Pilate's fear is a direct response to the Jewish authorities' statement in v. 7.

An interesting problem is presented by the Greek term μᾶλλον, however. Many interpreters render it as a comparative; thus the NRSV translates v. 8 "[n]ow when Pilate heard this, he was *more afraid than ever*." Interpreted this way, readers are led to believe that the governor perhaps has been afraid for the entire duration of the interrogation, though the narrator only now reveals it. Certainly Pilate knows that Jesus presents a threat to Roman imperial rule, but has he doubted before now that he has the power and authority to handle the situation? O'Day maintains that the scholars who read fear back into the prior scenes of the "trial" are depending on "excessive psychologizing about the character and motives of the Johannine Pilate."[168] Instead, it is preferable to render the term μᾶλλον as elative or intensive: "Now when Pilate heard this, he was *very much afraid*."[169] Pilate has not been afraid for the length of the interrogation; he is only now stricken with fear.

As mentioned above, the οὖν in v. 8 signals what it is that evokes Pilate's fear, namely, the Jewish authorities' declaration that Jesus "claimed to be the Son of God" (19:7). Why might this statement cause Pilate alarm, though? There are three options.

One possibility is that the claim to be "the Son of God," suggests a religious charge of blasphemy in the eyes of the Jewish authorities. This recalls 8:59 and 10:31 where the Jewish authorities attempt to stone Jesus

---

166. E.g., O'Day, "Gospel of John: Introduction," 820; Michaels, *Gospel of John*, 933; Meeks, *Prophet-King*, 72. Howard-Brook and Thatcher resist this trend. See Howard-Brook, *Becoming Children of God*, 404–7; and Thatcher, *Greater Than Caesar*, 76–78.

167. Note the exception at 19:1. We have also pointed out above that Pilate's principal conversation partner is the best indicator of scene changes throughout the trial. Pilate will not verbally engage Jesus again until v. 9.

168. O'Day, "Gospel of John: Introduction," 820.

169. Barrett, *Gospel According to St. John*, 542; and O'Day, "Gospel of John: Introduction," 820. Barrett concedes that the translation "he was more afraid" may be justified if one interprets 18:38 as implying fear in Pilate's voice, but there is nothing in the text itself to suggest such an interpretation.

for what they deem blasphemous statements regarding his relationship with God. They may have in view Lev 24:16, which prescribes death for "one who blasphemes the name of the LORD."[170] Jesus' title, "Son of God," which has repeatedly been used to describe him throughout the Gospel (1:34, 49; 3:18; 11:27) and which he has used to describe himself on a number of occasions (5:25; 10:36; 11:4), forms the basis for this indictment. Even more often in the Gospel, Jesus is simply called "Son" and refers to God as his "Father" (e.g., 3:35). Jesus himself makes an explicit connection between the claim to be "God's Son" and blasphemy in 10:36 (cf. 10:33).

Within this perspective, the Jewish authorities are pressuring Pilate by threatening his post as governor of the province if he does not accommodate their local laws and practices by executing a blasphemer.[171] Thus, their "religious" charge is not strictly "religious" because it holds political consequence for the governor. Brown observes that "Roman provincial administrators characteristically respected regional religious practices."[172] Pilate has already accommodated himself to Jewish religious practices by going out to meet the Jewish authorities rather than forcing them to come inside the *praetorium* before the Passover (18:28–29).[173] The Jewish authorities are appealing to their own law to condemn Jesus, and if Pilate does not oblige them, then they will appeal to a higher authority—Caesar—who has the power to remove Pilate from his post. Pilate's fear is thus explained as a valid concern that he might lose his lucrative appointment as governor of Judea if he fails satisfy the Jewish authorities.

D. A. Carson offers a second possibility for why "Son of God" strikes fear in Pilate. He maintains that the expression "Son of God" would have sounded quite different to Greco-Roman ears. Rather than sounding like a religious charge of blasphemy to Pilate, Carson suggests that this charge would situate Jesus in "an ill-defined category of 'divine men.'"[174] In the Hellenistic world, such persons enjoyed divine powers. Pilate might be unnerved at the realization that he has just scourged such a man, fearful that Jesus might enact divine revenge upon him. However, there is little in the text itself to support this position.

170. For example, Brown, *Death of the Messiah*, 1:829; Meeks, *Prophet-King*, 47–57; and Michaels, *Gospel of John*, 932.

171. Brown, *Gospel According to John*, 2:891.

172. Brown, *Gospel According to John*, 2:891.

173. Carter, *John and Empire*, 306.

174. Carson, *Gospel According to John*, 600.

A third option emerges when this text is considered in light of the broader Roman imperial context. While the Jewish authorities in the Fourth Gospel consider the title "Son of God" blasphemous, it is also a title that might well rattle the governor's imperial sensibilities. "Son of god" (Latin: *divi filius*) was an honorific often used to describe Roman emperors, beginning with Augustus.[175] Augustus strategically promoted the deification of Julius Caesar, his adoptive father, in order to assert his own divine origin and authority with this title. Later emperors followed suit. Tilborg lists numerous inscriptions in Ephesus alone that designate various emperors as "sons of god": Augustus, Nero, Titus, Domitian, Trajan, and Hadrian are all accorded this title.[176] The broad use of imperial propaganda, such as coins circulated throughout the empire, meant that the title "son of god" would have been strongly associated with the person of the emperor.[177] The Jewish authorities' statement that Jesus claimed to be a "Son of God" would surely sound to Pilate and to John's audience much like the attribution of the title "king" to Jesus. It mimics the imperial title and sets Jesus up in imitation of and as rival to the emperor. While the Mosaic law prohibits blasphemy, Pilate and his local allies (including the Jewish authorities) are also concerned about maintaining another "law of the land," namely the Roman one that stipulates execution for treasonous provincials.[178]

While the blasphemy charge is likely in view for the Jewish authorities, owing to the textual connections with 8:59 and 10:31–36, this third option makes the most sense of Pilate's fear. He is concerned that Jesus intend to contest the emperor's throne. Pilate's duty is to protect imperial interests against such a threat, and his status as governor of Judea is endangered if he does not. With this in mind, other features of the text become clear. For example, Pilate's immediate question to Jesus as he returns inside the *praetorium* in the next scene, "Where are you from?" (19:9), makes little sense if Pilate interprets the claim of the Jewish authorities strictly as a blasphemy charge. Yet, as we shall see, it makes better sense if Pilate is concerned that Jesus is more than a mere messianic pretender and has lofty imperial aspirations. Further, it makes sense of the opposing claims that Pilate and Jesus make regarding authority in

---

175. Richey, *Roman Imperial Ideology*, 99.
176. Tilborg, *Reading John in Ephesus*, 39.
177. Richey, *Roman Imperial Ideology*, 99–100.
178. Hanson and Oakman, *Palestine*, 87.

19:10–11. Finally, it resonates with the accusation by the Jewish authorities in 19:12: "Everyone who claims to be a king sets himself against the emperor." In this view, "Son of God" becomes a synonym for "king" or "emperor."[179]

5. Summary

The primary irony that permeates this scene is the fact that Jesus *is* the king, even though neither Pilate nor the Jewish authorities perceive this reality. Jesus' regal attire as he is presented to the Jewish authorities emphasizes this point. Meanwhile, Pilate is the target of irony when he mischaracterizes Jesus as a mere "man." But he inadvertently says more than he knows: Jesus is the Son of Man, the one who will have an everlasting dominion over all the peoples of the earth. Likewise, he unwittingly presents Jesus as a "king" worthy of acclamation. Still, the Jewish authorities call for Jesus' death rather than acknowledge his kingship. However, the crucifixion they call for will be the means by which Jesus draws all people to himself. The execution they seek will be Jesus' moment of exaltation.

The Jewish authorities' assertion that Jesus claimed to be a "Son of God" strikes fear in Pilate. This is an occurrence of situational irony: the most powerful, highest-ranking Roman official in the province of Judea is terrified of a man who seems, ostensibly, to be a poor, lowly, powerless peasant. Yet Pilate cannot help but wonder if Jesus represents a genuine threat to the imperial throne. He will pursue this question in the next scene.

Scene 6: Origins of Power (19:9–11)

1. "Where Are You From?"

Pilate, now afraid, re-enters the praetorium to interrogate Jesus. His question, "Where are you from?" (πόθεν εἶ σύ), might seem on the surface to be a simple request for information regarding Jesus' geographic origin. Brown suggests that this straightforward question might be a way of seeking a "legal loophole" by which Pilate could dismiss the case; he might be able to send Jesus to be tried by Herod if Jesus falls within Herod's

---

179. Carter, *John and Empire*, 195.

jurisdiction.[180] However, taken in context, this question is certainly asked in response to what Pilate has just learned from the Jewish authorities: that Jesus claimed to be God's Son. Pilate wants to know if Jesus is indeed from heaven or from "which god or ruler . . . Jesus descended."[181] Could he possibly contest the emperor's throne? However, within the broader context of the Fourth Gospel, this question bears a particular theological significance. As O'Day emphasizes, "the question of Jesus' origins is one of the most important christological and theological issues in the Gospel."[182] It is a pervasive question that surfaces throughout the narrative (e.g., 6:41–42; 7:25–29, 41–42; 8:14; 9:29–30; 16:27–28). To know where Jesus is from is to acknowledge his origin in, and authority from, the Father. By asking this question, therefore, Pilate falls victim to the Gospel's irony and exhibits his ongoing and utter lack of knowledge about Jesus' identity. He has no idea where Jesus comes from. The question says much about Pilate's character and lack of understanding even while it reminds the audience of what it already knows: Jesus' origin is from God, his Father (e.g., 1:1–3, 18; 3:34; 7:29; 8:42; 16:28).

The presence of the Greek word πόθεν ("from where"), which has appeared frequently throughout the Fourth Gospel, signals irony here. Duke insists that repetition is often a clue to the presence of irony in texts: "When a word, phrase, or image is often repeated, its importance is stressed, and its ironic content may be heightened."[183] Throughout the Gospel, πόθεν is used when characters lack necessary knowledge regarding spiritual matters. In the Gospel's opening chapter, Nathanael asks Jesus "Where did you get to know me?" when Jesus identifies him as "an Israelite in whom there is no deceit" upon meeting him for the first time (1:47–48). At the wedding at Cana, the steward tastes the water that becomes wine and does not know "where it came from" (2:9). In his conversation with Nicodemus, Jesus enigmatically declares, "The wind blows where it chooses, and you hear the sound of it, but you do not know where it comes from or where it goes" (3:8). The Samaritan woman asks Jesus incredulously, "Where do you get that living water?" (4:11). Jesus

---

180. Brown, *Gospel According to John*, 2:878. In Luke, Pilate determines that Jesus, a Galilean, falls under Herod's jurisdiction and sends the prisoner to be interrogated by him (Luke 23:7).

181. Carter, *John and Empire*, 307.

182. O'Day, "Gospel of John: Introduction," 821.

183. Duke, *Irony in the Fourth Gospel*, 33. The word πόθεν appears thirteen times in the Fourth Gospel and only twelve times in the other three Gospels combined.

tests Philip by asking him "Where are we to buy bread for these people to eat?" when a large crowd gathers (6:5). People of Jerusalem assume that Jesus cannot be the Messiah because they mistakenly believe that they know where he comes from: "Yet we know where this man is from; but when the Messiah comes, no one will know where he is from" (7:27). The Pharisees question Jesus' testimony, but he contends that "[e]ven if I testify on my own behalf, my testimony is valid because I know where I have come from and where I am going, but you do not know where I come from or where I am going" (8:14). Finally, when the man born blind is interrogated by the Jewish authorities, he remarks on the irony of the situation. They reject Jesus simply because they do not know "where he comes from," and the healed man responds, "Here is an astonishing thing! You do not know where he comes from, and yet he opened my eyes" (9:29–30). Each of these occurrences of πόθεν involves a misunderstanding and lack of knowledge. The characters in the story fail to grasp what the Johannine audience already knows: Jesus has been sent from his Father above.

Thus, when Pilate asks Jesus "Where are you from?" he, too, falls victim to the Gospel's irony. He exposes his own ignorance even as he underlines for the audience one of the major themes of the Gospel: Jesus' origin from God. If Pilate were to know that Jesus is sent from God, then he would presumably know God, as well.

Jesus does not respond to Pilate's inquiry about his origin; instead he lets the question linger in the air. Brown suggests that "the refusal to answer may be a recognition that Pilate . . . will never understand [Jesus'] origins from above."[184] Carter proposes that Jesus' silence emulates Isaiah's suffering servant (Isa 53:7), a "classic pose of the powerless (who accomplish God's redeeming purposes) before the 'powerful.'"[185] Whatever the reason for Jesus' silence, its rhetorical effect on the Fourth Gospel's audience is significant. The audience is able to infer the answer to Pilate's question based on many occasions on which Jesus' origin from God has been alluded to or described (e.g., 1:1–3, 18; 3:34; 7:29; 8:42; 16:28). Duke points out that this process of discovering or realizing the ironic meaning of a text is gratifying for the audience: "[R]eaders are generally delighted to discover that they have been entrusted with the task of

---

184. Brown, *Death of the Messiah*, 1:841.
185. Carter, *John and Empire*, 307.

rising above a rejected surface of meaning in search of a better one."[186] Such is the appeal of this ironic moment in the text. The audience can smile knowingly and feel a sense of superiority to the Roman governor because they perceive the answer to his question. Jesus is from God. This elevated perspective that the audience shares with the author creates and reinforces belief in Jesus as sent from God.

2. Authority

Jesus' silence is momentary, of course; he will speak soon enough (cf. 19:11). As a reaction to Jesus' silence, Pilate seethes, "Do you refuse to speak to me? Do you not know that I have power [ἐξουσία] to release you, and power to crucify you?" (19:10). Pilate's response is that of an aggravated judge reminding a prisoner that if cooperation is not forthcoming, a grave outcome awaits. Unbeknownst to Pilate, his statement also recalls Jesus' words at 10:17–18: "For this reason the Father loves me, because I lay down my life in order to take it up again. No one takes it from me, but I lay it down of my own accord. I have power [ἐξουσία] to lay it down, and I have power to take it up again." This earlier declaration indicates that Pilate's claim to authority is hollow.[187]

Jesus' retort is bold: "You would have no power over me unless it had been given you from above; therefore the one who handed me over to you is guilty of a greater sin" (19:11). With this compelling statement, Jesus decisively undermines Roman imperial claims to ultimate power and authority. Carter insists that "Pilate thinks that his will is being done, that the interests of Roman power are being furthered."[188] The Fourth Evangelist, however, contests—and mimics—such claims and imperial theology. History and the events of the passion are directed by neither Rome, its emperor, nor its gods, but rather by Jesus' Father alone. Pilate has no power over Jesus except what God allows and wishes.

Jesus' claim that Pilate has no power over him unless granted from above bears irony, in that Pilate no doubt interprets this statement to mean that the Roman emperor Tiberius has granted him *imperium* (the Latin word for the Greek ἐξουσία, "authority") to govern Judea. Jesus' statement, however, implies much more: that any authority or power that Pilate possesses comes from God.

186. Duke, *Irony in the Fourth Gospel*, 36–37.
187. O'Day, "Gospel of John: Introduction," 821.
188. Carter, *John and Empire*, 308.

The Greek term ἄνωθεν, translated here "from above," resurfaces for the first time since Jesus' conversation with Nicodemus in chapter 3.[189] In his conversation with the Pharisee, Jesus baffles the teacher with the statement, "Very truly, I tell you, no one can see the kingdom of God without being born *from above*" (3:3). The word ἄνωθεν is a double entendre in chapter 3, as it can mean both "again" and "from above." Nicodemus evidently takes it to mean "again"—very literally—as he goes on to ask, perplexed, "How can anyone be born after having grown old? Can one enter a second time into the mother's womb and be born?" (3:4). Nicodemus humorously misunderstands Jesus, thinking that one must physically be born again. Jesus, however, goes on to describe how one must be born "of the Spirit," that is, "from above" (3:5–7). The Fourth Evangelist uses wordplay to poke fun at Nicodemus while making a profound theological point. This same term carries a double entendre of a different sort in Jesus' response to Pilate. Pilate assumes one meaning of the term—that his authority comes from Caesar—while Jesus refers to a deeper level of meaning. Pilate believes that he is acting in this "trial" as an agent of Rome, but Jesus insists that the governor is acting unwittingly as a pawn of God in a cosmic drama much larger than he can fathom. Howard-Brook states that "Pilate is but a tool in the larger drama of the descent and the ascent of the messiah."[190] Neither Nicodemus nor Pilate grasps the intended sense of ἄνωθεν, and both find themselves on the receiving end of irony's mocking sting. For his part, Pilate fails to see that he is advancing God's cosmic plan.

Carter observes that in many scriptural traditions, "earthly rulers carry out God's will even without recognizing it."[191] For example, Babylon exacted God's punishment upon Jerusalem (2 Kgs 24:1–7). Later, Cyrus of Persia defeated Babylon and allowed the exiles to return home in fulfillment of God's plan for deliverance (Isa 44:28). Isaiah even calls Cyrus God's "anointed" (Hebrew: מָשִׁיחַ), who "shall build my city and set my exiles free (45:1, 13). Carter points out that "this traditional theological perspective undermines the claims of empires and rulers like Pilate to have absolute power by setting them in the context of God's greater,

---

189. This term appears five times in the Gospel (3:3, 7, 31; 19:11, 23). The narrator uses the term at 3:31, but Jesus has not used the term since his conversation with Nicodemus.

190. Howard-Brook, *Becoming Children of God*, 408.

191. Carter, *John and Empire*, 308.

though often unseen, purposes."¹⁹² Pilate will put Jesus to death, but he fulfills God's plans by doing so. Readers who remember Jesus' words at 10:17–18 also know that, though Pilate will execute Jesus, Jesus has "power to take [his life] up again." Jesus' power and authority mimic and trump those of Rome.

Duke contends that Pilate is presented here as an *alazōn* when he claims power and authority over Jesus.¹⁹³ In Greek comedy, an *alazōn* is a character who considers himself to be greater than he actually is. Duke suggests that "alazony in comedy is the exact counterpart of hubris in tragedy: downfall follows. The agent of this downfall, the wily one who triumphs over the pretender, is the character who seemed so little and emerges so large."¹⁹⁴ In this case Jesus, whom Pilate thinks is utterly at his mercy, is one who channels God's authority. Pilate's downfall is not a literal one in the text, but the Fourth Gospel ironizes him in order to contest Roman claims to authority and power while asserting God's greater authority and power.

3. A Greater Sin

The second half of Jesus' response to Pilate is difficult to interpret: "[T]herefore the one who handed me over to you is guilty of a greater sin" (19:11). The text is ambiguous regarding just who it is that Jesus signifies. Does Jesus mean that Judas is guilty of a greater sin? Or does he speak of Caiaphas or the Jewish authorities instead? Brown admits that the logic of this verse is convoluted, and has given rise to widely varied scholarly suggestions regarding the identity of the guilty one.¹⁹⁵ Howard-Brook suggests that "Judas's fault is greater, for in addition to being part of the ancient covenant, he had walked with Jesus in the new covenant."¹⁹⁶ Brown, however, thinks that Jesus speaks of the Jewish authorities who were identified in 18:35: "Your nation and the chief priests have given you over to me."¹⁹⁷ Moloney believes that the text points only to Caiaphas's

---

192. Carter, *John and Empire*, 308.
193. Duke, *Irony in the Fourth Gospel*, 149. He does not, however, elaborate further.
194. Duke, *Irony in the Fourth Gospel*, 9.
195. Brown, *Gospel According to John*, 2:878.
196. Howard-Brook, *Becoming Children of God*, 408.
197. Brown, *Death of the Messiah*, 1:842. See also Lindars, *Gospel of John*, 569; Bultmann, *Gospel of John*, 662; and Schnackenburg, *Gospel According to St. John*, 3:261–62.

guilt, because the "one who handed [Jesus] over" is singular.[198] Michaels argues that the text ultimately implicates Satan, who sets Judas's betrayal in motion (13:27).[199] What are we to make of these varied possibilities? Who is "guilty" of this sin? Carroll holds that, in the Fourth Gospel, "sin" primarily refers to a failure to believe in Jesus.[200] This helps to clarify Jesus' claim. Judas, Caiaphas, and the Jewish authorities all have participated in handing over Jesus, and thereby signaled their failure to accept Jesus as the one sent by God. Thus, they all fall under judgment. The Fourth Evangelist has used the Greek word παραδίδωμι in relation to each of these parties (18:2, 5, 30, 35).[201] In 19:11, then, the Greek text uses the singular participle with collective force: each can be designated as "the one who handed [Jesus] over."[202] The ambiguity forces the audience to reflect upon this question and sweetens their realization that Pilate, too, will soon join them by handing over (παραδίδωμι) Jesus at the conclusion of the show trial (19:16). Thus, Jesus' response in 19:11b by no means exculpates the Roman governor. Instead, it ultimately implicates Pilate, too, of this "greater sin."[203]

Jesus' statement about the "greater sin" also makes it clear that he has the power and authority to judge people and to discern sin. Contrary to appearances, he is not judged by the Jewish authorities or Pilate. This should come as no surprise to the Johannine audience, which has already perceived that Jesus, as the Son of Man, has the authority to judge people (5:27).

---

198. Moloney, *Gospel of John*, 500. See also Beasley-Murray, *John*, 340–41.

199. Michaels, *Gospel of John*, 937.

200. Carroll and Green, *Death of Jesus*, 103. See also Carter, *John and Empire*, 308; and O'Day's discussion of John 9, where she claims that, in the Fourth Gospel, "sin is defined not by what one does, but almost exclusively by one's relationship to Jesus, and more specifically, by whether one believes that God is present in Jesus ("Gospel of John: Introduction," 664).

201. We must assume that Caiaphas is included in the group that hands over Jesus to Pilate (18:30, 35).

202. BDF 77.

203. O'Day makes a similar claim: "By the end of the trial, however, when Pilate himself hands Jesus over to be crucified (19:16a), Pilate will share their sin, because he, too, will have rejected the revelation of God in Jesus" ("Gospel of John: Introduction," 821).

4. Summary

This section has dealt directly with the crucial issue of power and authority. While this theme surfaces at other points throughout the narration of the arrest and interrogation, this brief exchange between Jesus and Pilate conveys the most straightforward claim about the authority and power of Jesus and God vis-à-vis Rome. And within the context of the Roman imperial world, that claim is astonishing. It is God, not Caesar or the Roman gods, that is the one true sovereign, the ultimate source of all true power and authority. Jesus' origin from the Father above allows him to share in this authority, and grants him the power to act as the legitimate judge. Meanwhile, Pilate is blind to the reality of Jesus' identity and erroneously assumes that as the highest-ranking imperial agent in the province, he is the one who is in ultimate control of the proceedings and who has the final say in matters. But this is not in fact the case. The Fourth Gospel declares that the sovereignty that Jesus and God share is decisive, mimicking and undercutting Roman imperial claims to ultimate power and authority.

Scene 7: Judgment (19:12–16a)

The boundaries between this section and the preceding one are ambiguous and difficult to establish conclusively.[204] Shifts in the show trial narrative often track Pilate's explicit movements into and out of the *praetorium* (18:29, 33, 38; 19:4, 9). However, this study maintains that the division of scenes is more clearly and appropriately delineated by noting the primary party with whom Pilate is interacting. In 19:1, for example, movement back into the *praetorium* is only implied, but Pilate's shift in focus from the Jewish authorities to Jesus indicates that a new scene has begun. Although Jesus is in view in 19:12, Pilate now begins to interact primarily with the Jewish authorities, signaling the beginning of a new scene. Further, one can also presume that Pilate has shifted back to the setting outside the *praetorium*. Finally, kingship language (vv. 12, 15), which is so

---

204. Carter, for example, groups v. 12 into both vv. 8–12 and vv. 12–16a (*John and Empire*, 307–10). Howard-Brook suggests grouping vv. 8–11 and vv. 12–16a (*Becoming Children of God*, 407–12). O'Day joins v. 12 with vv. 8–11 rather than vv. 13–16a ("Gospel of John: Introduction," 820–22). Giblin argues that Pilate actually heard the shouts of the Jewish authorities from inside the *praetorium*, since his departure from the Roman headquarters is not narrated until v. 13 ("John's Narration," 232).

significant here at the end of the proceedings, binds vv. 12–16a together as a discrete unit. For all these reasons, the seventh and final scene of the show trial drama now begins with Pilate's attempt to release Jesus in v. 12.

1. Attempt to Release Jesus

What should John's audience make of Pilate's attempt to release Jesus in v. 12? The imperfect tense of the verb ἐζήτει suggests either an inceptive or an iterative meaning: "Pilate began seeking to release Jesus," or "Pilate repeatedly tried to release Jesus." Is this a sincere attempt by Pilate to free Jesus, or is it a bluff?[205] The narrative context suggests that this is yet another political maneuver by Pilate to provoke the Jewish authorities, rather than an earnest attempt by the governor to free a wrongfully accused man. Pilate has already judged Jesus to be enough of a threat to send a cohort of troops to arrest him (18:3) and to have him tortured (19:1). Yet Pilate has suggested that the Jewish authorities deal with him themselves (18:31) and has thrice declared that he finds no case against Jesus (18:38; 19:4, 6). Although it appears that Pilate's actions are inconsistent, we have observed above that several of Pilate's interactions with the Jewish authorities are best understood as attempts to mock them and remind them of their dependence on Rome. For example, his proposal "Take him yourselves" (18:31) forces them to admit that they must rely on Rome to execute Jesus. Likewise, the Jewish authorities display their subservience to Rome by asking Pilate to release Barabbas (18:38–40). When Pilate brings Jesus out in 19:4–7, the scene is staged as a parody: Pilate finds "no case" against a regally dressed Jesus, and he mockingly suggests that the Jewish authorities crucify him themselves. Reading Pilate's attempt to release Jesus in 19:12 as a political stunt to antagonize the Jewish authorities makes the best sense of the wider narrative context. They respond, not yet with a declaration of faith in and dependance upon Rome (cf. 19:15), but certainly with a display of concern for Roman

---

205. Lincoln argues that 19:12 represents Pilate's first earnest attempt to release Jesus, suggesting that, after much consideration, Pilate has found a "religious charge" against Jesus inadequate. See Lincoln, *Truth on Trial*, 133. He contends that it is only when the Jewish authorities make a political statement in 19:12b ("If you release this man, you are no friend of the emperor") that Pilate finally decides to crucify Jesus. Lincoln erroneously believes, however, that a sharp distinction can be made between religious and political charges in this scene, as if claiming to be the "Son of God" (19:7) does not carry any political implications.

hegemony: "Everyone who claims to be a king sets himself against the emperor" (19:12).

The Jewish authorities respond to Pilate's attempt to release Jesus by crying out angrily (19:12). The translation "crying out" renders the Greek verb κραυγάζω, which we have already seen is significant within the Fourth Gospel. This verb was also used to characterize the shouts of the Jewish authorities for Pilate to "Crucify, crucify" in v. 6 and will be used again in v. 15 when they shout "Away with him! Away with him! Crucify him!" The same verb is also used when Jesus cries out for Lazarus to "Come out" of the tomb (11:43).[206] Jesus' cry is life-giving and fulfills God's purposes, while the cries of the Jewish authorities, who are accommodated to Roman imperial power, seek death.

2. "No Friend of the Emperor"

The Jewish authorities respond to Pilate's ploy to release Jesus with a significant challenge: "If you release this man, you are no friend of the emperor. Everyone who claims to be a king sets himself against the emperor" (19:12). The Jewish authorities insinuate possible consequences of any such action, namely, that Pilate might fall into disfavor with the emperor. Yet their response also reveals that they are, in fact, profoundly loyal advocates for Caesar's sovereignty, so much so that they question Pilate's loyalty and authority as the official representative of the emperor if he releases Jesus.

The expression "friend of the emperor" (φίλος τοῦ Καίσαρος) was an honorific title granted to some who were loyal to the emperor in the first-century Roman Empire. It is unclear, however, whether or not the evangelist uses it as an official title for Pilate here; it may simply describe anyone loyal to the emperor.[207] Whether or not the historical Pilate held

---

206. This verb is also used when the crowd cries out during Jesus' triumphal entry into Jerusalem (12:13) and when the Jewish authorities call for Barabbas's release (18:40).

207. While there is some discussion in the scholarly literature regarding when the title came into use and whether or not Pilate had this title, the cumulative evidence suggests that the title would have been widely known by the late first century, when the Fourth Gospel was written. For example, by the Hellenistic period, a similar appellation, "friend of the king," was already used to designate members of a select group of loyal supporters of a particular king (see 1 Macc 2:18; 3:18; 10:65; 3 Macc 6:23; Josephus, *Ant.* 12.298). The "friends of Augustus" were a recognized association during Augustus's rule (27 BCE to 14 CE). Coins stamped with *philokaisar* ("friend of Caesar") were minted during Herod Agrippa I's reign (37–44 CE). See Bammel,

this as an official title, the Jewish authorities' comment makes it abundantly clear that he has something at stake within the show trial narrative. The Jewish authorities threaten both his reputation with the emperor and his appointment as governor of Judea.[208]

Moreover, friendship with Caesar stands in striking contrast to the friendship that Jesus offers. Whereas the emperor's friendship is contingent on political expediency, Jesus' friendship is predicated on self-sacrificial love. Friendship language is prominent in chapter 15, where Jesus says, "No one has greater love than this, to lay down one's life for one's friends" (15:13). Jesus will fully manifest this ideal through his death on the cross.[209] Further, as a model for friendship, Jesus commands his disciples to love one another as he has loved them (15:12).

3. Sitting on the Bēma

After hearing these words from the Jewish authorities, Pilate brings Jesus out one last time to appear before those gathered. The Greek word οὖν, typically a marker of result, suggests that Pilate brings the prisoner out as a direct response to the words that the Jewish authorities have just spoken (19:13).[210] Michaels suggests that it is not Pilate but his guards who bring Jesus out, reasoning that Pilate already seems to be outside in the

---

"*Philos tou Kaisaros*," 205-10. Sherwin-White observes that "the connotation [of the phrase] . . . becomes markedly official in imperial documents, with the suggestion that so and so is the official representative of the Princeps" (*Roman Society and Roman Law*, 47). Bernard presents an opposing perspective, stating that the "official title is probably not found before Vespasian," but he gives no evidence to support his position. See Bernard, *Commentary on the Gospel*, 2:621.

208. Parallels have been drawn between this incident in the Fourth Gospel and an account by Philo, who reports an incident in which the Jewish authorities pressured Pilate to remove Roman shields from Herod's palace lest they report his misconduct to the emperor. He writes that Pilate "feared that if they actually sent an embassy [to the emperor] they would also expose the rest of his conduct as governor by stating in full the briberies, the insults, the robberies, the outrages and wanton injuries, the executions without trial constantly repeated, the ceaseless and supremely grievous cruelty," and thus imperil his governorship in Judea (*Legat.* 36.302-3).

209. O'Day points out that Jesus' statement regarding friendship is not novel in the first-century world; the philosophers Aristotle and Lucian both suggested that friendship might entail dying on behalf of one's friends. She says that "Jesus enacted the ancient ideal of friendship—he lay [sic] down his life for his friends" (22). See O'Day, "I Have Called You Friends," 20-27.

210. BDAG 736-37.

previous verse.[211] In the Greek text, however, Pilate is clearly the subject of the verb and thus continues to be the principal agent in this final scene of the Roman proceedings.[212]

According to the NRSV translation, Pilate "brought Jesus outside and sat on the judge's bench at a place called the Stone Pavement, or in Hebrew Gabbatha" (19:13). The word used to describe the judge's bench, *bēma* (βῆμα), indicates the raised platform from which legal decisions were considered and announced, but within a trial setting, a *bēma* typically refers to the judge's bench itself (e.g., Matt 27:19).[213] This elevated bench would have been in the forecourt of the governor's residence with steps leading up to it so that spectators could see the presiding judge. Accused persons would then stand before the judge during the trial. Such a picture emerges, for example, from Acts 18:12–17 and 25:6–12.[214] But a fascinating interpretive problem emerges at this point within the Johannine narrative: it is not at all clear who is sitting upon the *bēma*.

Though nearly all English translations convey that Pilate is sitting on the *bēma*, the Greek text is ambiguous on this point.[215] The Greek word in v. 13 rendered "sat" (καθίζω) can have an intransitive or transitive meaning. If intransitive, Pilate takes his own seat upon the *bēma*. If transitive, readers must supply the direct object that the text implies: Jesus. That is, Pilate *sat Jesus* upon the *bēma*. Who should the audience suppose is sitting upon the *bēma*? While a surface-level reading of the text assumes that Pilate sits upon the *bēma*, an ironic reading of the text would suggest that Jesus, as the true judge, is seated upon it.

Brown argues that an intransitive meaning is most appropriate, given the context. Pilate "is now about to render judgment" and announce

---

211. Michaels, *Gospel of John*, 940.

212. This is reminiscent of the scourging episode (19:1), in which the Greek text suggests that Pilate himself tortures Jesus. As we observed above, some scholars have argued that Pilate would not do such a thing himself, as it was beneath a person of his rank. Nevertheless, the Greek text depicts him as the principal agent, whatever the historical plausibility of the event as narrated.

213. Brown, *Gospel According to John*, 2:881. Cf. Josephus, *J.W.* 2.172 and *Ant.* 18.57, where Pilate sits upon his *bēma*; and *J.W.* 2.301, where the procurator Florus sits upon his *bēma*.

214. Matthew's entire Roman trial also seems to take place with Jesus standing before Pilate, while the governor is seated upon the *bēma* (Matt 27:11–26, esp. v. 19). See Brown, *Gospel According to John*, 2:881.

215. Many commentators conclude that Pilate is sitting upon the *bēma* (e.g., Howard-Brook, *Becoming Children of God*, 410; Michaels, *Gospel of John*, 940–41).

Jesus' fate; thus the Johannine evangelist renders the scene in a solemn manner by describing Pilate as taking his seat as he prepares to make his official decision.[216] Brown's argument is strengthened by the other occurrences of the Greek word καθίζω in the Fourth Gospel in 8:2 and 12:14. In both of these earlier cases the verbs are intransitive: Jesus sits down in the temple to teach (8:2) and he sits upon a young donkey as he approaches Jerusalem (12:14). Further, Blinzler argues that ἐκάθισεν ἐπὶ βήματος is nearly a technical expression for a judge taking his seat during a trial.[217] The strongest argument for an intransitive meaning is the historical implausibility of a transitive rendering: surely the Roman governor would not make a mockery of the "trial" or his authority to judge by seating the accused upon the *bēma*.[218]

However, there are compelling reasons to consider a transitive reading of καθίζω. The verb καθίζω is often used transitively (e.g., Acts 2:30; 1 Cor 6:4; Eph 1:20), which is to say that it commonly appears with a direct object, in contrast to the strictly intransitive κάθημαι, used, for example, to describe Pilate sitting upon the *bēma* in Matt 27:19.[219] Moreover, there is precedent for καθίζω appearing transitively without an explicit direct object: for example, there are no explicit direct objects in Acts 2:30 and Eph 1:20. It is also significant that two second-century texts use the verb transitively in a context very similar to John 19:13. The *Gospel of Peter* uses καθίζω transitively to describe Jesus' captors as seating him upon a "judgment seat" (καθέδραν κρίσεως) in order to mock him (*Gos. Pet.* 7). In fact, it was the publication of fragments of this apocryphal gospel by Adolf von Harnack that first prompted Johannine scholars to question whether the verb in John 19:13 might best be understood as transitive rather than intransitive.[220] Justin Martyr's *First Apology* from the mid-second century uses a nearly identical expression to the one in 19:13: ἐκάθισαν ἐπὶ βήματος (*Apol.* 35:6). In Justin's writing, the direct object is clearly Jesus, who is seated upon the judgment seat by his captors.[221]

216. Brown, *Death of the Messiah*, 1:845.
217. Blinzler, "Der Entscheid des Pilatus," 171-84.
218. Brown, *Gospel According to John*, 2:881; and Blinzler, *Trial of Jesus*, 237.
219. See BDAG 491-92.
220. Harnack, *Bruchstücke des Evangeliums*. Harnack argued that the author of the Fourth Gospel also meant καθίζω to be taken transitively.
221. Minns and Parvis, *Justin, Philosopher and Martyr*, 176-77. Meeks maintains that Justin Martyr and the author of *Gos. Pet.* probably did not use John 19:13 in composing their texts, because both of them place this incident within the soldiers'

Thus, we find in many early Christian accounts that it is Jesus, not Pilate, who sits upon the *bēma*.

La Potterie builds a compelling argument for a transitive reading of καθίζω in 19:13.[222] He insists that the two main verbs in 19:13, ἤγαγεν and ἐκάθισεν, are closely related and indicate one swift motion: Pilate *leads Jesus out* and *sits him down* upon the judgment seat. Thus, the direct object τὸν Ἰησοῦν serves both main verbs.[223] La Potterie further argues that because the term βῆμα is anarthrous, the verb describes the act of installing someone as judge, rather than the taking of one's own seat upon the βῆμα. According to La Potterie, a definite article would need to precede βῆμα if the text were to suggest that Pilate sits upon it.

O'Day argues for an ironic reading on the basis of the literary context: Pilate continues to mock the Jewish authorities here, so it makes logical sense for him to seat Jesus on the *bēma*. She observes that "it is fully in keeping with the character of the Johannine Pilate for him to taunt the Jews at this critical point by seating Jesus, still dressed in the purple robe and crown of thorns, on the judge's seat."[224] She notes the profound irony of such a reading, in which "Pilate, who intends to mock Jesus and the Jews by placing Jesus on the judge's seat, unknowingly places him in his rightful place as judge."[225] Pilate's action unwittingly points to Jesus' true identity, even while Pilate is blind to this reality.

The most compelling argument for reading καθίζω in 19:13 as transitive is provided by the Gospel's own theological perspective. Within the Gospel, Jesus is presented as the true judge (e.g., 5:22, 27; 9:39). As Andrew T. Lincoln writes,

> throughout the narrative Jesus the witness has also been seen to be Jesus the judge, and so the readers have been prepared for the climactic trial scene now to make this paradoxical point in the most graphic way. Within this trial scene itself, readers have also already been prepared by the discourse to view both Pilate and "the Jews" as those who stand exposed and judged before Jesus.

---

mocking of Jesus (*Prophet-King*, 74).

222. La Potterie, "Jésus, roi et juge," 217–47.

223. La Potterie, "Jésus, roi et juge," 223–25. La Potterie's argument is based on an examination of similar instances in the Greek text of the Fourth Gospel (e.g., 19:1, where "Jesus" serves as the direct object of both "took" and "flogged," and 19:6, where the pronoun "him" functions as the direct object of both "take" and "crucify").

224. O'Day, "Gospel of John: Introduction," 822.

225. O'Day, "Gospel of John: Introduction," 822.

Now, in the final scene, this irony becomes explicit and takes on narrative form.²²⁶

If one reads καθίζω as transitive, Jesus, seated upon the *bēma* by Pilate, is thus in an appropriate position to pass the final sentence upon both the Jewish authorities and Pilate.

Ultimately, however, the text is grammatically ambiguous. In all likelihood, a first-century audience would have found it ambiguous, as well. Fortunately, the audience does not have to choose between intransitive and transitive readings. An ironic reading of the text makes sense of both possibilities by viewing the text with two levels of meaning, the second of which stands in opposition to the first and implies some lack of awareness or understanding.²²⁷ Thus, on a superficial or strictly historical level, καθίζω can be understood intransitively. On the ironic and theological level, however, it is transitive. In sum, both Pilate and Jesus sit upon the throne. The audience of the Fourth Gospel knows that Jesus has the ultimate authority to act as judge, and thus can perceive correctly that it is he who sits on the *bēma*.²²⁸

4. The Stone Pavement

The Fourth Evangelist notes that the *bēma* that Pilate and Jesus ironically share is located "at a place called The Stone Pavement, or in Hebrew Gabbatha" (19:13). Both terms for this place, "The Stone Pavement" (λιθόστρωτον) and "Gabbatha" (Γαββαθα), must be significant; the author would not be sharing incidental historical details in a narrative that has been so carefully crafted to this point. Scholars acknowledge that the place referenced could be at one of two possible historical locations: either at King Herod's palace, which was on a hill in the western part of the

---

226. Lincoln, *Truth on Trial*, 135.

227. Brown argues that a double-reading is unlikely because in "previous Johannine instances of double meaning (vol. 29, p. cxxxv), the phenomenon has not been based on syntactical ambiguity, nor is it usual for the second meaning to be opposite of the first" (Brown, *Gospel According to John*, 2:881). La Potterie makes a similar claim, saying, "Grammatically, the two [meanings] are possible, but *not simultaneously*: it is necessary to choose" ("Jésus, roi et juge," 218; my translation). Ultimately, I do not find these arguments compelling; both meanings can coexist in the mind of the audience if we read the text ironically.

228. Barrett makes a similar argument, saying that Pilate sat on the *bēma*, but "for those with eyes to see," that is, for those who grasp the irony in my reading, it is Jesus who truly sits as judge (*Gospel According to St. John*, 452).

city, or at the Fortress Antonia, which Herod had constructed just to the northwest of the temple.[229] The name "Gabbatha" is most likely derived from an Aramaic root meaning "to be high, to protrude," which is consistent with the possible locations of the *praetorium*.[230] Both places stood on hills overlooking the city.[231] The inclusion of the name "Gabbatha" might subtly remind readers that Jesus is about to be "lifted up" (3:14; 8:28; 12:32); Ehrman says that the name "conforms with the Johannine conception of Jesus' Passion as his exaltation."[232] However, if this is the evangelist's intent, it is certainly an understated reminder.[233]

Ehrman also finds theological significance in the term λιθόστρωτος.[234] The word appears in 2 Chr 7:3 (LXX) when the people of Israel bow down upon the stone pavement (λιθόστρωτος) outside of the temple to worship God following Solomon's prayer that God should not reject God's "anointed one" (χριστός) (2 Chr 6:42). Although this connection is admittedly obscure, Ehrman contends that "if the Fourth Gospel does allude to this incident, a greater contrast can scarcely be imagined. No longer do the Jews beseech the Lord for the favor of his christ, the king; rather they reject the christ and condemn him to an accursed death by

---

229. Brown, *Death of the Messiah*, 1:845. It is also possible that the λιθόστρωτος does not refer to a fixed place. Steele proposes that it refers to a moveable "pavement" that would have traveled with a Roman official such as Pilate, and that would have been inlaid with mosaics depicting the lives of the Roman gods. Steele argues that Pilate, in Jerusalem for the festival, would have brought his *bēma* and this mosaic pavement with him, and that Jesus would have stood upon it: "The dramatic intensity of the scene . . . is sensibly heightened when it is realized that before the Prisoner were spread representations of episodes in the life and loves of the gods of pagan story . . . Christ confronted by Jupiter." No modern scholar seems to follow his proposal. See Steele, "Pavement," 562-63.

230. Brown, *Death of the Messiah*, 1:845; and Ehrman, "Jesus' Trial," 130.

231. Brown, *Death of the Messiah*, 1:845.

232. Ehrman, "Jesus' Trial," 130.

233. One cannot help but wonder whether the audience of the Fourth Gospel would pick up on the symbolism of an Aramaic term that the author does not define for them. The Fourth Evangelist has previously defined significant words for the audience (1:38, 41). The evangelist also gives place names in Hebrew or Aramaic on a couple of other occasions (5:2; 19:17). It seems likely that the evangelist is simply sharing the name "Gabbatha" here rather than implying any symbolic import.

234. Benoit notes that, in antiquity, the term λιθόστρωτος was used to refer to a number of different surfaces, including inlaid mosaic pavements, pavements of gold, silver, and precious stones (e.g., Esther 1:6), and simple yet colossal slabs. See Benoit, *Jesus and the Gospel*, 1:182-84.

crucifixion."[235] This subtle connection establishes the ancient Israelites who praised God as an antithesis to the Jewish authorities who call for Jesus' crucifixion and will soon confess Caesar as their one true king (John 19:15).

Howard-Brook submits a connection between the λιθόστρωτος and Roman imperial power, arguing that, regardless of whether it was at Herod's palace or at Fortress Antonia (which Herod built), "the Stone Pavement is associated with Herod, the Judean 'king,' who is never mentioned in the Fourth Gospel. By specifically linking the name with the 'Hebrew' (actually, Aramaic) Gabbatha, the narrator ties Pilate's place of judgment with the cooperation of the Judean authorities in their own friendship with Caesar."[236] Because Herod the Great was a client king of Judea, mentioning either of these structures associated with him recalls his status as an elite ally of Rome. It also evokes Roman sovereignty and dominion—as if readers needed any such reminder at this point! It is striking that Pilate is just about to present Jesus as "king" in 19:14. Jesus, whose own kingdom stands in stark contrast to Rome's, is brought out and presented to the allied Jewish elite at a place that recalls another king of the Jews—Herod—who once ruled the Jewish nation on behalf of Rome.

5. "Behold your king!"

While the significance of the place names is obscure, the next detail is not: "Now it was the day of Preparation for the Passover; and it was about noon" (19:14).[237] We have already observed that indications of time have theological significance in the Fourth Gospel, and that is the case here. Beasley-Murray maintains that three things are set in motion at this hour on the day of preparation: "Jews cease their work, leaven is gathered out of the houses and burned, and the slaughtering of the Passover lambs commences. The Passover festival, for all practical purposes, now begins."[238] The evangelist has already indicated that the Passover festival

---

235. Ehrman, "Jesus' Trial," 130.

236. Howard-Brook, *Becoming Children of God*, 410.

237. Literally, "the sixth hour," assumed to be the sixth hour after dawn. Note that Mark 15:25 indicates that Jesus is crucified at "the third hour," or approximately 9 AM; this detail is impossible to harmonize with John's account.

238. Beasley-Murray, *John*, 341. See *m. Pesaḥ.* 1:4–5. For further references within the Mishnah indicating the timing of events on the day of preparation, see Bonsirven, "Hora Talmudica," 511–15. Many scholars have attempted to explain the detail that

is imminent (11:55; 12:1; 13:1; 18:28), but this brings the timing of events back to the forefront of the audience's consciousness. A casual or uninformed reader of the Gospel might assume that these indications of time are incidental details within the narrative; however, informed readers will recognize the ironic note that the Fourth Evangelist strikes. Jesus, the "lamb of God" (1:29), will soon be slaughtered. While the Jewish nation celebrates their liberation from Egypt, Jesus will soon effect the eschatological liberation of the world.

Thus a pregnant silence hangs in the air as Pilate presents Jesus before the Jewish authorities. Once he does so, the scene moves quickly to its conclusion. Pilate declares to the Jewish authorities, "Here is your king!" Pilate points to Jesus, who is still wearing his royal garments and crown (v. 5). Brown contends that Jesus is presented as "a pathetic picture of royalty."[239] Yet the emphasis is not at all on Jesus as a beaten, bloodied, and defeated prisoner. The emphasis is on his kingship; it is thus an ironic picture of royalty. Pilate speaks sarcastically, mocking both Jesus and the Jewish authorities, but once again he makes an unwitting and ironic proclamation of truth. Jesus is king.[240] Pilate becomes irony's victim once more because he is unable to grasp the truth that he proclaims. Rome's sovereign representative unintentionally testifies to Jesus' true sovereignty.

The Jewish authorities reply furiously with three terse imperatives: "Away with him! Away with him! Crucify him!" (19:15).[241] The Greek imperative translated as "Away with him," ἆρον, from the root αἴρω, recalls other significant occurrences of the word in the Fourth Gospel.[242]

"it was about noon" (19:14) in connection with the specific time of the slaughter of the Passover lambs. Some suggest, as Schnackenburg does, that "the paschal lamb of the New Testament dies, according to the Johannine chronology, just when the paschal lambs of the Jews are being slaughtered in the temple, and none of his bones are broken" (*Gospel According to St. John*, 1:299). However, such arguments rest on assumptions that are unwarranted, as the text itself does not specify the exact timing of Jesus' death. For further information, see Keener, *Gospel of John*, 2:1129-31. I prefer Keener's argument that the connection intended by the text between Jesus' death and the slaughter of the lambs is "a link of the day rather than the hour" (*Gospel of John*, 2:1131).

239. Brown, *Gospel According to John*, 2:884.

240. Once again, mimicry is evident as Jesus' title (βασιλεύς) imitates that of the Roman emperor.

241. Note again the occurrence of the Greek word κραυγάζω to describe the shouts of the Jewish authorities (cf. 18:40; 19:6, 12).

242. That the Jewish authorities could have just cried "Crucify him, crucify him,"

As the Lamb of God, Jesus is the one who "*takes away* the sin of the world" (1:29). Within the context of chapter 19, which presents Jesus as the paschal lamb, the Jewish authorities call for Pilate to "take him away," which, ironically, will make it possible for Jesus to "take away the sin of the world." The same verb is used several times in chapter 5 to describe the healed man as "taking up" his mat to walk (5:8, 9, 10, 11, 12). Jesus' commands are restorative and life-giving, whereas the Jewish authorities seek death. In the Good Shepherd discourse, Jesus has stated emphatically that "No one *takes* [my life] from me, but I lay it down of my own accord" (10:18). From this perspective, the Jewish authorities are only playing into God's cosmic plan and Jesus' obedient intention to die on the cross. Finally, the verb is also used to describe the Roman Empire's ability to destroy the Jewish nation: "If we let him go on like this, everyone will believe in him, and the Romans will come and destroy [ἀροῦσιν] both our holy place and our nation" (11:48). It is a sad irony that the Jewish authorities do manage to have Jesus "taken away" and executed, yet the Romans still come in 70 CE and "take away" their holy place and nation. Thus, the cries of the Jewish authorities to "take him away" ring deeply and ironically in the ears of John's audience.

Pilate taunts the Jewish authorities one final time, asking, "Shall I crucify your king?" (19:15). The Jewish authorities have insinuated that Pilate might be disloyal to Caesar, so the governor responds that Jesus is *their* king, not his. As Michaels says, "If Jesus is in any sense 'King of the Jews' (18:33, 39; 19:3), then it is they, not he, who are disloyal to Caesar."[243] Pilate turns the accusation back on them and subtly reminds them of the fate that awaits imperial dissidents: crucifixion. His tactic evokes a response, and he gets a remarkable one.

The Jewish authorities reject any claim to Jesus as their king by declaring, "We have no king but the emperor" (19:15). Their statement could hardly be more dramatic, and they unknowingly say more than they intend. Lindars remarks that they "utter the ultimate blasphemy in the same breath as their final rejection of Jesus."[244] Not only do they reject Jesus; by declaring Caesar as their sole king they also reject God. They also abandon the testimony of the Jewish Scriptures, which declares God their only legitimate ruler: "O Lord our God, other lords besides you

---

as they did in 19:6, suggests there is significance to the use of this word here.

243. Michaels, *Gospel of John*, 944.
244. Lindars, *Gospel of John*, 572.

have ruled over us, but we acknowledge your name alone" (Isa 26:13).²⁴⁵ Meeks draws attention to a Passover hymn that celebrates God's kingship, one of the key themes of the Passover liturgy:

> From everlasting to everlasting thou art God;
> Beside thee we have no king, redeemer, or savior,
> No liberator, deliverer, provider
> None who takes pity in every time of distress and trouble.
> We have no king but thee.²⁴⁶

While it is uncertain whether this hymn would have been part of the seder by the time the Fourth Gospel was written, O'Day maintains that it still "captures the theological intent of the [Passover] celebration."²⁴⁷ At a time when the Jewish authorities should have been celebrating God's ultimate kingship, they insist instead that Caesar is their one, true sovereign.

Many scholars suggest that with this statement, the Jewish authorities renounce their faith in the God of Israel and their status as "Jews."²⁴⁸ Carter, for example, observes that "with these words, the Jerusalem leaders repudiate their centuries-old covenant with God as Israel's king."²⁴⁹ Perhaps it is more accurate to say that this climactic declaration confirms a repudiation that has consistently characterized their stance toward Jesus and God throughout the Fourth Gospel. The narrative has suggested repeatedly that their loyalties do not lie with God. From beginning to end, they have been accommodated to Roman rule and are a crucial part of the Roman imperial system in Judea. Their words reveal the depth of their involvement with Rome as elite members of Jewish society. Thus, rather than signifying a once-and-for-all abdication of their faith, their statement instead exposes the place they already occupy within the Roman imperial system. In the eyes of the Fourth Evangelist, they are not renouncing their faith in God in this moment; they have already done so. O'Day says that with their declaration, they "enslave themselves to Rome."²⁵⁰ In reality, and in spite of their mistaken and ironic claim that

---

245. Cf. Ps 47:2; 93:1–2.

246. Meeks, *Prophet-King*, 77.

247. O'Day, "Gospel of John: Introduction," 823.

248. E.g., Brown, *Gospel According to John*, 2:893; Michaels, *Gospel of John*, 944; O'Day, "Gospel of John: Introduction," 823.

249. Carter, *John and Empire*, 309.

250. O'Day, "Gospel of John: Introduction," 823.

they "have never been slaves to anyone" (8:33), the Jewish authorities have been subject to Rome for quite some time.

6. Pilate Hands Jesus Over to Be Crucified

With this, Pilate has apparently heard enough. He has elicited from the Jewish authorities their confession of faith and dependence (19:15), so he finally hands Jesus over to be crucified. This "handing over" (παρέδωκεν) completes the Roman governor's rejection of Jesus and places him in the company of Judas, Caiaphas, and the Jewish authorities, who have also signaled their failure to accept Jesus as God's agent by "handing him over." In the end, Pilate is not a weak victim, nor merely a pawn in the hands of the Jewish authorities. He is fully complicit and culpable in Jesus' death. He has even maintained and advanced Roman imperial interests by eliciting a declaration of faith in Caesar and dependence on Rome. And Pilate believes that he will now extinguish any threat that Jesus poses to the Roman imperial order by means of crucifixion.

7. A Choice of Two Kings

Familiar motifs emerge in this seventh and final scene of the Roman proceedings (19:12–16a). Themes of kingship, sovereignty, and loyalty are especially pronounced as the show trial draws to a close. Jesus is presented as the true king and judge even as Pilate and the Jewish authorities champion allegiance to Caesar. The irony is thick and censures Jesus' antagonists while appealing to the Johannine audience to maintain sole loyalty to God through Jesus. Pilate and the Jewish authorities reject Jesus as God's agent because they are unable to grasp Jesus' true identity as king. The Jewish authorities, who have collaborated with Rome throughout the passion narrative, consistently seek Jesus' death and cannot perceive God's life-giving purpose that he embodies. Meanwhile, Jesus, in full command of the situation, moves toward his final enthronement upon the cross. From there he will demonstrate self-sacrificial love through his death as the true Passover lamb.

For the audience of the Fourth Gospel, this final scene strikes the ultimate ironic note against the Jewish authorities. The elites allied with Rome expose their faith in Caesar by confessing him as their sole king, unwittingly confirming their abandonment of their faith in the God of Israel. The words of their declaration in v. 15 are a parody of Jewish claims to have "no king but God."²⁵¹ By affirming Caesar's lordship, they are rejecting God's exclusive claim to lordship. All those who perceive this irony find themselves faced with a choice. Whom will they confess as the true king: Jesus or Caesar? Will they choose God's life-giving purposes or the Roman imperial status quo?

IRONY, HIDDEN TRANSCRIPTS, AND NEGOTIATING ROMAN RULE

Jesus' appearance before Pilate in the Fourth Gospel serves as the centerpiece of the passion narrative and significant themes and motifs find their culmination in this scene. The Roman proceedings are flush with irony that creates and reinforces many of these themes. Most importantly, irony is used to promote the sovereignty of Jesus and God over that of Rome. It also displays Jesus' roles as judge and paschal lamb, his command of his own fate, and it lampoons the Roman governor and the Jewish elites. Furthermore, it functions as part of the Johannine hidden transcript of resistance, which contests imperial claims of the public transcripts while promoting an alternative vision of reality.

Sovereignty emerges as the most significant theme throughout these scenes. It is no coincidence that this Johannine theme finds its most striking expression at the moment when Jesus comes face-to-face with Pilate, the chief representative of imperial power in the province. The focal point of the entire interrogation rests in the center of its chiastic structure, in scene 4, when Jesus is invested as king. Herein lies the most prominent irony of this entire episode: the one who is mocked, tortured, and ultimately crucified as a royal pretender is actually the true king of the world.²⁵² Though Jesus will be crucified, it will not be a moment of defeat. Instead, it will be his moment of glorification as he is "lifted up," a king upon the cross. All of this conflicts sharply with—yet mimics—public transcripts of the Roman Empire that assert Roman dominion and present the emperor as the supreme ruler of the world. In contrast, the hidden transcript that emerges from the Fourth Gospel presents Jesus as the true king. Moreover, it is Jesus' Father who possesses power and authority; whatever power and authority Pilate has is granted to him by

---

251. Lincoln, *Truth on Trial*, 136.
252. Senior, *Passion of Jesus*, 69.

God. Rome's authority ultimately has no deep and abiding significance in the world.

The issue of sovereignty is presented as an "either/or" scenario for the Johannine audience. As Meeks claims, "what the trial suggests is that the disciple will always have to decide vis-à-vis the empire whether Jesus is his king or whether Caesar is."[253] The irony that the evangelist deftly employs throughout the narrative nudges the audience toward belief in, and loyalty to, Jesus as king. For example, Pilate himself is the unwitting chief witness to Jesus' kingship in the show trial (18:33, 37, 39; 19:14, 15), and this ironic presentation undermines his authority while elevating Jesus' authority. Likewise, the Jewish authorities provide a foil for the Johannine audience with their tragic declaration that Caesar—not God or Jesus—is their king (19:15).

Other aspects of the Johannine hidden transcript emerge from these proceedings. The presentation of Jesus as the "Son of Man" who judges the world and signals the end of all earthly empires contests and mimics Roman imperial claims of an eternal empire. Whereas the public transcripts of Rome declared "an empire without end" (Latin: *imperium sine fine*; Virgil, *Aeneid*, 1.279) and an "eternal city" (Latin: *aeternae urbis*; Tibullus, 2.5.23), Jesus' appearance as the Son of Man anticipates the end of Roman hegemony and the establishment of his own worldwide rule and "everlasting dominion" (Dan 7:14). However, Pilate and the Jewish authorities are blind to this reality. They think they are, in fact, securing Rome's dominion and maintaining the imperial status quo by crucifying Jesus.

Additionally, Rome and its emperor are not the agents of the divine will in the manner in which they suppose. Nor do Rome's gods direct the course of history. Whereas Rome's public transcripts suggested that the emperor ruled at the will of the gods and was the "viceregent of Jupiter" or even Jupiter himself on earth, the Fourth Gospel mimics and contests this claim by presenting Jesus as the agent of the Father who advances the Father's will.[254] Throughout the narrative, readers are reminded that the agents of the Roman elite do not engineer Jesus' fate. It is brought about, instead, by the Father's will and Jesus' obedience.

The explicit and implicit connections between the Roman show trial and the Passover celebration (18:28, 39; 19:14) suggest a hidden transcript

---

253. Meeks, *Prophet-King*, 64.
254. Fears, "Cult of Jupiter," 71; and Scott, *Imperial Cult under the Flavians*, 139.

of liberation that resists Roman public transcripts of dominance. If Jesus is the symbolic paschal lamb who takes away the sin of the world (1:29) and recalls the liberation of Israel from subjugation in Egypt, his sacrificial death portends liberation from both sin and Roman oppression. Furthermore, his identity as the "Son of Man" hints at the end of the Roman Empire. His identity as the lamb anticipates deliverance from the empire that obstructs God's life-giving purposes.

Jesus presents a nonviolent means of liberation, however, which contrasts sharply with the violence of imperial Rome. The Fourth Gospel calls out this violence and subverts public transcripts of Roman benevolence by connecting Rome to the violence characterized by "this world" (18:36). Whereas Rome employs violence to maintain control of its vast territory, Jesus demonstrates God's reign by means of his sacrificial death. The kingdom that Jesus advances is characterized not by violent struggle but by "relentless *witness* to the truth" as well as by disciples who ought to be distinguished by their "mutuality, self-sacrifice, and deep intimacy."[255] Jesus' kingdom, which is not "of this world" (18:36) but "of the truth" (18:37), presents an alternative to the world ruled by Satan and Rome that is cast in darkness and hostile to God's purposes.

A subtle critique of Roman justice can also be discerned. Carter's comments regarding the Matthean "trial" are also instructive for the Johannine account: "The narrative subtly exposes how 'justice' works in the Roman world, whose interests are being served, and in so doing, evaluates it negatively because of its opposition to God's agent."[256] In John, neither Pilate nor the Jewish authorities display concern that the non-elite Jesus be granted a fair trial.[257] Instead, they leverage the "trial" for their own political advantage. Jesus is destined to die from the moment of his arrest and detention.[258]

Other intersections between the Roman show trial and hidden transcripts are worth noting. According to Scott, symbolic inversions are typical of hidden transcripts. The peasant as king, judge, and agent of the gods upends the social order, with the Roman and Jewish elites on the receiving end of judgment. Inversions such as this "play an important

---

255. Howard-Brook, *Becoming Children of God*, 400.

256. Carter, *Matthew and Empire*, 150.

257. Recall the discussion on p. 69 above regarding the legal bias in Roman justice against provincials and non-elites. See further Garnsey, *Social Status and Legal Privilege*.

258. Herzog, *Jesus, Justice, and the Reign of God*, 240–41.

imaginative function" as they "create an imaginative breathing space in which the normal categories of order and hierarchy are less than completely inevitable."[259] They resist the public transcripts that reinforce social stratification and promote deference to elite representatives of power. Such symbolic inversions represent a form of disguised resistance; David Kunzle contends that "those satisfied with the existing or traditional social order [can] see the theme as a mockery of the idea of changing that order around."[260] Jesus the mock "king" is crucified in the end, after all. Yet the Fourth Gospel does not allow elite public transcripts to define the meaning of crucifixion; the Johannine audience knows that Jesus' crucifixion is not finally a shameful, humiliating death, but rather his glorification.

More than a hint of the Roman festival of Saturnalia surfaces during the show trial, as well, when Jesus, a non-elite, is dressed and mocked as king.[261] Saturnalia, celebrated annually in the month of December, was a remarkable occasion during which the usual social constraints and hierarchy were suspended.[262] Servants and masters dined and gambled together, food and drink were available in abundance, men wore women's clothing, and Roman citizens eschewed their togas and wore felt caps normally reserved for freedmen. At its most extreme expression there was a total inversion of power: masters served their slaves, who in turn were allowed to rebuke them, and a non-elite was appointed by lot as a mock king. Saturnalia offered revelers an alternative vision of life and a chance to express dissatisfaction, frustration, and complaints that they could not otherwise state publicly.[263] While many suggest that the Saturnalian atmosphere offered a type of "safety-valve" by giving oppressed peoples an opportunity to "get the hidden transcript off of their chest," Scott suggests that this festival was much more complicated—such a festival could "just as easily serve as a dress rehearsal or a provocation for actual defiance."[264] "After all," Versnel says, "the imagery is closely related,

---

259. Scott, *Domination*, 168.

260. Kunzle, "World Upside Down," 82.

261. Brown also notes the resemblance (*Gospel According to John*, 2:888).

262. See Versnel, *Transition and Reversal*, 146–63.

263. Scott, *Domination*, 173. Scott is specifically discussing the pre-Lenten carnival festival, which is comparable to the Roman Saturnalia, as both are occasions for "rituals of reversal, satire, parody, and a general suspension of social constraints."

264. Scott, *Domination*, 178.

if not identical, to that which is played out during revolutions."²⁶⁵ John's Roman show trial presents the audience an imaginative, alternative vision of Jesus as both king and judge who stands in sharp contrast to, yet imitates, Rome's emperor. This Saturnalian vision does not call for armed resistance, but it does present an ideological revolution.

Finally, double-meaning and ambiguity are vital to hidden transcripts, especially if they are to be expressed in public.²⁶⁶ The irony conveyed in the Johannine narration of the Roman interrogation is replete with both double-meaning and ambiguity. Much of the ironic communication is coded political speech—it is not self-evident for all readers. Indeed, as I have emphasized, ironic communication assumes two audiences: one that will get it and one (whether real or imaginary) that will not. Take, for example, Jesus' statement in 19:11: "You would have no authority over me except what is given you from above." These words are ambiguous, both to Pilate within the narrative and to potential readers as well. Jesus could be referring either to Caesar (acceptable from a Roman point of view), or to God (which would challenge imperial claims). Such a statement functions as part of a hidden transcript within the narrative. Jesus' statement is not openly defiant, but it would be meaningful as part of the Johannine community's hidden transcript, affirming that God, not Caesar, is the supreme source of power and authority.

The ambiguity regarding who is sitting on the *bēma* in 19:13 functions similarly. It is possible to discern in this image an innocuous statement of Pilate's preparation for delivering judgment. Yet for the Johannine reader who "gets it" by grasping the irony, the statement calls into question Pilate's legitimacy as judge. At the same time it promotes Jesus' status as the one who controls the scene and judges both Pilate and the Jewish authorities. In this fantasy scene Jesus imitates imperial power even as he overcomes it.

The irony helps create a powerful appeal to the Johannine community. The stated purpose of the Fourth Gospel is to promote belief in Jesus (20:31), and the irony in the Roman interrogation lends itself powerfully to this end. The Gospel presents two claimants to kingship—Jesus and Caesar—and irony challenges Caesar's representative while elevating Jesus in the eyes of the audience. Jesus is presented repeatedly as "king," and the appeal of this irony draws the audience toward the evangelist's

---

265. Versnel, *Transition and Reversal*, 162–63.

266. Recall Scott's third mode of political discourse: the politics of anonymity and disguise. See Scott, *Domination*, 18–19, 136–82.

perspective. Those who grasp it feel a sense of superiority to those within the narrative (e.g., Pilate and the Jewish authorities) who do not get it. The audience rides high above the proceedings and sees all of the follies that the Jewish and Roman elites commit. This promotes the hidden transcript of Jesus' sovereignty and encourages the audience's belief in Jesus as king.

Thus, in a remarkable variety of ways, the Roman show trial in the Fourth Gospel resists, critiques, and mimics elements of Roman imperialism. It subverts the public transcripts of the empire through its own hidden transcript that presents Jesus' sovereignty, affirms his own control over his fate, identifies God's will as the driving force of events, and presages the end of Roman rule. As Jesus moves forward toward the crucifixion, he obediently fulfills God's purposes and plans for the world. The king proceeds to his moment of glorification.

CHAPTER 5

Jesus' Crucifixion and Burial

INTRODUCTION

AT THE PINNACLE OF the Arch of Titus in Rome, an image depicts the apotheosis of the recently deceased Titus, as he is carried on the back of an eagle to heaven. Like many Roman emperors, he was deified upon death.[1] Imperial theology suggested that death did not end an emperor's influence upon the world; in death, an emperor could continue his worldly reign from a new divine vantage point.[2] Titus's death was thus portrayed as his ascent to the heavens, not his tragic demise. The significance of an individual's death can take on a number of different meanings, as the imperial stance regarding an emperor's death suggests. Death does not always represent loss or defeat.

This is decidedly the case in the Fourth Gospel. The Gospel contests the public meaning of Jesus' death by Roman crucifixion by means of

---

1. Price notes that, from the death of Augustus (14 CE) to the funeral of Constantine (337 CE), thirty-six of the sixty emperors of the period were granted apotheosis and deified (Price, "From Noble Funerals to Divine Cult," 57). In the first century alone, Augustus, Claudius, Vespasian, Titus, and Nerva were deified at death (Carter, *John and Empire*, 317). Other ancient traditions attest apotheosis and deification of great persons upon death, including Alexander the Great, Romulus (the mythical founder of Rome), and Moses (Cotter, "Greco-Roman Apotheosis Traditions," 130–49).

2. Kahl, "Acts of the Apostles," 149. Plutarch gives an account of the apotheosis of Romulus, in which he becomes a "propitious deity" who provides blessings from heaven (*Lives: Romulus* 28.1–3).

its presentation of Jesus' crucifixion and burial. The standard message and significance of the cross is subverted, disrupting public transcripts of Roman sovereignty, domination, control, and the threat of violence. While the crucifixion of Jesus is an experience of shame, humiliation, and defeat, the Fourth Evangelist reframes it as a moment of enthronement, glorification and supreme triumph.

At the same time, the Fourth Gospel mimics certain aspects of Roman imperial power even as it recasts the meaning of the crucifixion. Even in the presentation of Jesus' return to the Father, Jesus imitates the apotheosis of Roman emperors as he is "lifted up" to heaven.[3] John presents God's power as an alternative to Rome's power, and Jesus' sovereignty in contrast to the emperor's. The Gospel envisions an empire of God that extends across the entire world. Thus, the Gospel does not merely contest imperial power but adopts the language of empire in order to overpower Rome.

The Meaning of the Cross in Imperial Rome

Given the centrality of Jesus' crucifixion in Christian thought and its prevalence in artistic media throughout the ages, it is remarkable that the actual moment and means of Jesus' crucifixion are narrated so sparsely in the Fourth Gospel. The evangelist simply reports that "they crucified him, and with him two others, one on either side, with Jesus between them" (19:18).[4] Nothing is said of the precise means of crucifixion, nor are descriptive details provided of the cross itself or the degree of pain inflicted upon Jesus. Despite the brevity of the crucifixion account, however, John's audience would have brought many ingrained perceptions of crucifixion to bear on their understanding of this scene. In fact, the brevity of John's presentation of the act of crucifixion suggests that the audience knew a good deal about the reality of crucifixion in imperial Rome. We must turn to noncanonical sources for information about how crucifixion was understood and presented in first-century public transcripts.

---

3. However, the Fourth Gospel also contests the possibility of imperial apotheosis by claiming that Jesus is the only one who has "ascended into heaven" (3:13). See further Carter, *John and Empire*, 318.

4. Cf. Mark 15:27; Matt 27:38; and Luke 23:33.

Roman crucifixion was a cruel, violent form of execution, typically reserved for members of the lower classes, slaves, and provincials.[5] It was conceived as a slow, painful way to put someone to death, one that humiliated the victim and simultaneously functioned as a public warning to others. Other means of execution, such as impalement, would have been swifter. However, affixing a victim to a crossbeam hoisted on a pole made a public display of execution and drew out the dying process so that it was lengthy and excruciating.[6] Crucifixion itself was carried out in a variety of ways; executioners had some latitude in how they conducted it.[7] Seneca observes such variety on one particular occasion: "I see crosses there, not just of one kind but made in many different ways: some have their victims with head down to the ground; some impale their private parts; others stretch out their arms on the gibbet" (*Marc.* 20.3).[8] Likewise, Josephus recounts a disorderly scene as multitudes of Jewish rebels were crucified by Titus during the Jewish War: "the soldiers out of rage and hatred amused themselves by nailing their prisoners in different postures; and so great was their number, that space could not be found for the crosses nor crosses for the bodies" (*J.W.* 5.451). Death from crucifixion could occur relatively quickly or take several days. The cause of death could be one of any number of factors, including asphyxiation, dehydration, blood loss, infection, and exposure.[9] Josephus describes crucifixion as "the most pitiable of deaths" (*J.W.* 7.203) and Cicero calls it a "cruel and disgusting penalty" (*Verr.* 2.5.64.165).

Crucifixion was such an "utterly offensive affair" that Hengel observes a reticence on the part of ancient writers to describe it in detail, observing that "the relative scarcity of references to crucifixion in antiquity and their fortuitousness are less a historical problem than an

---

5. Brown, *Death of the Messiah*, 2:946. However, Martin Hengel contends that Roman citizens could also be executed by crucifixion for serious crimes such as treason. See Hengel, *Crucifixion*, 39–40.

6. Brown, *Death of the Messiah*, 2:945. In the seventh century, Isidore of Seville remarked that "hanging is a lesser penalty than the cross. For the gallows kills the victim immediately, whereas the cross tortures for a long time those who are fixed to it" (*Etymologia* 5.27.34; quoted in Hengel, *Crucifixion*, 29).

7. Hengel states this more strongly, suggesting that "the caprice and sadism of the executioners were given full rein" (*Crucifixion*, 25).

8. Quoted from Hengel, *Crucifixion*, 25.

9. Retief, "History and Pathology," 938–41; Zugibe, "Two Questions about Crucifixion," 34–43; and Brown, *Death of the Messiah*, 2:1090–92.

aesthetic one."[10] It was not in good taste to write about such a gruesome topic. Brown notes this too, commenting wryly that "at any period of history those who practice torture are not overly communicative about the details."[11] Cicero explains that "the executioner, the veiling of the head, and the very word 'cross' should be far removed not only from the person of a Roman citizen but from his thoughts, his eyes and his ears. For it is not only the actual occurrence of these things or the endurance of them, but liability to them, nay, the mere mention of them, that is unworthy of a Roman citizen" (*Rab. Post.* 5.16).

1. Crucifixion as Symbolic Annihilation

Beyond the sheer brutality and violence of crucifixion, it shamed and humiliated the victims even as it killed them. If death was the only desired outcome, decapitation would be much more efficient, requiring less time, space, and equipment. Thus, Thatcher explains a deeper meaning of the cross: "The violence of the cross went beyond physical punishment to symbolic annihilation, with the destruction of the victim's flesh narrating Rome's capacity to suppress every threat to the state's entire sovereignty."[12] Its symbolic import was every bit as significant as the physical death of the individual on the cross. It is what Scott describes as a "ritual of denigration"—an extreme one, to be sure—that emerges in systems where the dominant strip the dominated of dignity and autonomy.[13] The physical abuse inflicted upon subject peoples demonstrates the control that the dominant exercise over the oppressed, even over their very bodies, to the point of death. Alan Kirk observes that "torturous deaths—such as crucifixion was—can be highly symbolized forms of violence, with the disfiguring, distending, dismembering, smashing, and perforation of the human body routinized and choreographed to display and enact publicly the socially degraded status of the victim."[14] Crucifixion was much more than a means of execution.

For Jewish persons the shame and humiliation of crucifixion would be especially severe. Crucifixion would have evoked the declaration of Deut 21:22–23 that "anyone hung on a tree is under God's curse." Paul

10. Hengel, *Crucifixion*, 22, 38.
11. Brown, *Death of the Messiah*, 2:946.
12. Thatcher, *Greater Than Caesar*, 93.
13. Scott, *Domination*, 23.
14. Kirk, "Memory of Violence," 192–93.

reflects this attitude, reasoning that Christ redeems people "from the curse of the law by becoming a curse for us—for it is written, 'Cursed is everyone who hangs on a tree'" (Gal 3:13). To a person with typical Jewish sensibilities, a condemned man hanging on a cross would not appear to be God's Messiah, but one disgraced and utterly forsaken by God.

2. Crucifixion as Warning

Furthermore, crucifixion as a public means of execution served as an emphatic warning to onlookers. A quote ascribed to Quintillian explains that "when we [Romans] crucify criminals the most frequented roads are chosen, where the greatest number of people can look and be seized by this fear. For every punishment has less to do with the offense than with the example" (*Decl.* 274). Crucifixion was intended as a deterrent, warning those who might be tempted to follow in the footsteps of those crucified. The Fourth Gospel underlines this public nature of crucifixion, noting that many Jews read the inscription on Jesus' cross, "because the place where Jesus was crucified was near the city" (19:20). The onlookers would have read the inscription "the King of the Jews" and likely identified Jesus as a failed political agitator or treasonous royal pretender. The bruised, bloodied, naked body on the cross would broadcast the message: this is what happens to those who resist Roman sovereignty.

3. Crucifixion as Symbol of Roman Dominance

Roman crosses were also powerful symbols of Roman dominance. They served as reminders to all who viewed them that Rome alone had supreme authority over the land and would make use of all the violence and brutality it could muster to maintain control. Crosses impressed upon onlookers their subject status. Thatcher explains:

> [E]very crucifixion reenacted Rome's conquest of the victim's nation. In this drama, the officiating soldiers played the role of the conquering Roman legions, while the person on the cross represented his entire people group, beaten, broken, and subjugated. In Palestine particularly, every crucifixion reenacted Pompey's conquest of the region in 63 BCE, reminding both Rome and the Jews of exactly how things came to be the way they are.[15]

---

15. Thatcher, *Greater Than Caesar*, 93.

Crucifixion was a profound symbol for all provincials of their subject status.

Thus, as Jesus hangs on the cross in the Fourth Gospel, the public transcripts of Rome convey that he was a threat to the imperial order, one that Pilate has eliminated by means of execution. The cross presents Jesus as one who is shamed and humiliated, deserving of abuse, and certainly not worthy of imitation. In the Roman imperial world, Jesus' crucifixion is a moment of ultimate defeat that signals Rome's dominance both in Judea and across the empire. It showcases the power of the empire and the constant threat of violent punishment for would-be dissidents and rebels. It is a grotesque depiction of "the inevitable end of any story that begins with resistance to imperial rule."[16] Opposition to Rome ends in bloody, shameful death.

For Christians living toward the end of the first century, the cross thus would have represented a daunting problem: it would have been a formidable barrier to proclamation and belief in Jesus because it signified that Rome had defeated Jesus. Furthermore, it implied that Jesus himself was abandoned and cursed by God. Paul indicates this problem when he describes the "message about the cross" as "foolishness to those who are perishing" (1 Cor 1:18). He concedes that the proclamation of "Christ crucified" is a "stumbling block to Jews and foolishness to Gentiles" (1 Cor 1:23). The author of Hebrews also considers the humiliation of crucifixion, speaking of the "shame" of the cross (12:2). In short, the notion of a "crucified messiah" would have appeared oxymoronic.

4. The Ironic, Subversive Meaning of the Cross in the Fourth Gospel

In the public transcripts of Rome, the message of the cross is one of power, imperial triumph, and violent terror. The Fourth Gospel, in contrast, presents a brilliantly imaginative depiction of the message of Jesus' crucifixion. John radically transforms the meaning of the cross; the shameful, violent death becomes Jesus' glorious, crowning moment of triumph. This striking reinterpretation of the cross is a significant component of the Johannine hidden transcript of resistance that subverts Roman public transcripts. The Fourth Gospel deploys irony and other literary means to create incongruity between Roman and Johannine meanings of the cross,

---

16. Thatcher, *Greater Than Caesar*, 94.

to displace the dominant Roman meaning of the cross, and to promote belief in Jesus as King.

Already by the second century, creative efforts were made to challenge and negate the public meaning of Jesus' crucifixion. For example, Basilides, a gnostic teacher, maintained that Jesus was not actually crucified; he argued that the Romans unintentionally crucified Simon of Cyrene instead. Irenaeus records Basilides's view: "[Jesus] did not himself suffer death, but Simon, a certain man of Cyrene, being compelled, bore the cross in his stead; so that this latter being transfigured by him, that he might be thought to be Jesus, was crucified, through ignorance and error, while Jesus himself received the form of Simon, and, standing by, laughed at them" (*Adv. haer.* 1.24.4).[17] In order to overcome the challenge of Jesus' crucifixion, Basilides nullifies its meaning by proposing that Jesus was not crucified at all.

However, as we will see, the Fourth Gospel takes a strikingly different tack than Basilides. Rather than simply nullifying the public meaning of Jesus' crucifixion, it stands it on its head. Jesus does get crucified, but what is a defeat in Roman terms is reconstituted as his glorification (7:39; 12:23), triumph, and return to the Father (13:1, 3; 14:12; 16:10, 28; 17:11).

Thatcher describes such a view as a "countermemory," which he defines as "a radically different version of the past grounded in an alternative narrative framework."[18] A countermemory is not necessarily a completely ahistorical representation of the past. For example, in the Fourth Gospel, Jesus really is crucified and dies at the hands of the Romans. Yet a countermemory is a way of reframing the past that resists the dominant ideological understanding of this shameful death. The Fourth Gospel's narration of the crucifixion forms part of a hidden transcript that presents Jesus as the true King.

The Fourth Gospel can be said to "ironize" the meaning of Jesus' crucifixion. Recall Duke's definition: irony as "a literary device is a double-leveled literary phenomenon in which two tiers of meaning stand in some opposition to each other and in which some degree of unawareness is expressed or implied."[19] The two meanings of the cross—the Roman one and the Johannine one—stand in stark opposition to one another. The Johannine audience is able to grasp the deeper meaning of the cross

---

17. For other examples, see Brown, *Death of the Messiah*, 2:1093.
18. Thatcher, *Greater Than Caesar*, 90.
19. Duke, *Irony in the Fourth Gospel*, 17.

that the Gospel presents, while oblivious characters in the narrative attribute to it the usual significance conveyed by Roman public transcripts. By Roman standards, it represents Jesus' defeat; but from the Johannine perspective, it represents nearly the opposite. Jesus is enthroned as king, fulfills God's purposes, and draws all people to himself as he is lifted up from the earth to return to God and to the glory that was his before creation. This perspective has the power to deconstruct the Roman meaning of the cross, and the Fourth Gospel appeals to its audience to embrace the ironic Johannine vision. Let us turn our attention now to John's presentation of the cross, to see how this is accomplished.

Scene 1: Crucifying Jesus (19:16b-18)

After Pilate hands Jesus over to be crucified (19:16a), the deed is swiftly carried out in the narrative. Jesus carries his own cross to the site of the execution and the Roman soldiers affix him to it in the midst of two others. Even in this brief scene, significant Johannine themes emerge that contest the Roman imperial meaning of the cross and present Jesus as king, rather than as defeated.

1. Executioners

Who takes and crucifies Jesus (19:16, 18)? Scholars debate the identity of the "they" to whom these acts are attributed.[20] The immediate antecedent of the implied subject in Greek is the chief priests of v. 15.[21] However, within the narrative context, it is hard to imagine that the Fourth Evangelist conveys that the Jewish authorities take Jesus and crucify him. They have already stated explicitly that they cannot kill Jesus themselves (18:31). Furthermore, several verses later in 19:23, the Gospel clearly remarks that Roman soldiers crucify Jesus. However, the chief priests do bear responsibility for the slaughtering of lambs for the Passover festival.[22] The ambiguity of the pronoun leaves one wondering if perhaps both the

---

20. Those who that think that the ambiguous pronoun refers to the chief priests include Heil, *Blood and Water*, 84; Senior, *Passion of Jesus*, 101-2; and Michaels, *Gospel of John*, 947. Those who think it denotes the Roman soldiers include Beasley-Murray, *John*, 344; Brown, *Death of the Messiah*, 1:856-57; and O'Day, "Gospel of John: Introduction," 829.

21. Neither of the main verbs in 19:16b and 19:18 has an explicit subject pronoun in the Greek text.

22. Howard-Brook, *Becoming Children of God*, 415.

Roman soldiers and the Jewish authorities are in view. The soldiers will crucify Jesus, but the audience is not to forget that the Jewish authorities also share responsibility for slaughtering Jesus, the true Passover lamb.[23] Moloney has a similar view, arguing that "a combination of what the reader knows and what the text says indicates that both 'the Jews' and the Romans collaborate in the execution of Jesus."[24]

The Greek text reports that they "take" (παρέλαβον) Jesus. This word recalls 1:11, which declares, "his own people did not accept [παρέλαβον] him."[25] Ironically, here they do take him, but to execute him rather than to accept and believe in him and thereby become children of God (cf. 1:12). Indeed, far from being God's children, they stand in direct opposition to God.

2. The Way to the Cross

Once he is handed over by Pilate, Jesus' path to the cross is quite direct. In the Gospel of Luke, a "great number of the people" follow him, and women beat their breasts, wailing for him (Luke 23:27), but John includes no such reports. There is no reason to mourn for Jesus as he proceeds to the cross.

Nor is there any indication, as in the Synoptics, that Simon of Cyrene was compelled to carry Jesus' cross along the way.[26] Condemned criminals typically carried their crosses in the Roman Empire, so it should occasion no surprise that Jesus carries his own cross in the Fourth Gospel.[27] Yet this detail appears to matter to the Fourth Evangelist, who underlines the point emphatically by including a reflexive pronoun, ἑαυτῷ: Jesus goes to the site of the crucifixion "carrying the cross *by himself*" (19:17). The Simon tradition is well-attested in early Christianity, so it may be that the evangelist knows of it and intentionally contradicts it to stress

---

23. Of course, Pilate has been and will continue to be involved in the proceedings, so culpability rests upon his shoulders, as well (e.g., 19:1, 16, 19).

24. Moloney, *Gospel of John*, 506.

25. These are two of the three occurrences of this word in the Fourth Gospel (cf. 14:3).

26. Cf. Mark 15:21; Matt 27:32; and Luke 23:26. In all likelihood, it is merely the crossbeam that Simon carries in the Synoptics and that Jesus carries in the Fourth Gospel.

27. See Bultmann, *Gospel of John*, 668. Bultmann lists a number of primary sources which attest this (see 668n3).

Jesus' dignity, strength, and sovereignty as he makes his way to the cross.[28] Brown contends that there is most likely a "deliberate excision of the memory of Simon" in order to "continue the theme that Jesus went to his death as sole master of his own destiny."[29] This note recalls Jesus' contention in 10:18a: "No one takes it from me, but I lay it down of my own accord." And since this is the case, it also recalls Jesus' confidence that he will take up his life again on the other side of death: "I have power to lay it down, and I have power to take it up again" (10:18b).

As Jesus carries his cross, he goes out of the city to the "Place of the Skull" (Κρανίου Τόπον).[30] This is presumably a place where crucifixions were conducted with some regularity. Some scholars surmise that it may have been a rounded hill, since such a place might have had the appearance of the top of a skull.[31] A hill is a logical site for crucifixion, since it would maximize public visibility. Indeed, the evangelist will soon emphasize the public nature of the venue (19:20).

3. A Regal Crucifixion

Once they arrive at the site, Jesus is crucified between two others. The Fourth Gospel provides virtually no details about these two other men, in notable contrast to the Synoptic Gospels. Mark and Matthew both indicate that they are "bandits" (λῃσταί; Mark 15:27 and Matt 27:38), while Luke describes them as "criminals" (κακούργους; Luke 23:33) and features their exchange with Jesus (Luke 23:39-43). In John, they do not speak to Jesus or revile him (Mark 15:32; Matt 27:44; Luke 23:39), and are identified simply as "two others" (ἄλλους δύο; John 19:18), downplaying their identity as criminals. The emphasis is instead on the placement of the three crucified persons. In v. 18 the evangelist describes the two others as "one on either side" (ἐντεῦθεν καὶ ἐντεῦθεν) of Jesus and then reiterates that Jesus is "between them," or more precisely, that "Jesus [is] in the middle" (μέσον δὲ τὸν Ἰησοῦν). The evangelist is doubly emphatic that Jesus is the central figure. In this fashion, the two others mimic the appearance of a royal entourage. Senior observes that the two crucified

---

28. Of course, Jesus' carrying of his own cross also draws attention to the shame and cruelty intended by Rome in this prelude to the crucifixion itself.

29. Brown, *Gospel According to John*, 2:917.

30. Archaeological evidence has been unable to confirm this location outside of Jerusalem and no extrabiblical sources speak of such a place.

31. See Brown, *Death of the Messiah*, 2:937; and Michaels, *Gospel of John*, 948.

men with Jesus symbolically become "part of the crucified King's 'retinue' as he takes his place on the throne of the cross."[32] Though the Johannine Jesus is crucified among common criminals, his crucifixion is narrated in a manner that focuses attention on his kingship instead.

Even in these opening verses of the briefly narrated crucifixion account, the Fourth Evangelist presents the events in a manner that creates tension with the public transcripts of Rome. Viewed within the broader narrative context, Jesus is presented here with regality and strength. He carries his own cross and in crucifixion is accompanied by a symbolic, kingly entourage. The Roman meaning of the cross is subverted, for even as Jesus is nailed shamefully to the cross among criminals, the cross facilitates Jesus' exaltation.

Scene 2: The Inscription on the Cross (19:19–22)

After Jesus is crucified, the following episode focuses on the inscription that Pilate affixes to Jesus' cross. The Fourth Evangelist takes this event—common to all four Gospels—and transforms the charge against Jesus into a powerfully ironic indicator of the true meaning of Jesus' crucifixion. O'Day notes that "on the theological level ... this inscription positions the kingship motifs from the trial before Pilate (18:28–19:16a) as the interpretive lens through which to view Jesus' crucifixion."[33] By cleverly presenting the charge against Jesus and discussion of it between Pilate and the Jewish authorities, it becomes a major means of reframing the dominant meaning of the cross with the Johannine meaning.

1. A Worldwide Proclamation

Pilate once again moves to the foreground of the narrative in this scene. Though all four Gospels speak of an inscription upon the cross, only the Fourth Gospel credits its placement to the Roman governor himself.[34] Unfortunately, many English translations obscure Pilate's involvement, conveying that Pilate orders someone else to write and place the inscription.[35] The Greek text, however, suggests that he is the principal agent of

---

32. Senior, *Passion of Jesus*, 103.
33. O'Day, "Gospel of John: Introduction," 830.
34. Cf. Mark 15:26; Matt 27:37; and Luke 23:38.
35. E.g., the NRSV, which renders it as "Pilate also had an inscription written and put on the cross."

activity: "and Pilate also wrote an inscription and placed it upon the cross" (ἔγραψεν δὲ καὶ τίτλον ὁ Πιλᾶτος καὶ ἔθηκεν ἐπὶ τοῦ σταυροῦ; 19:19). Most likely, the verb carries a causative force, indicating that Pilate ordered others to have the inscription written and placed on the cross. Nevertheless, because he is the subject of both verbs, the Fourth Gospel highlights his agency in the actions, much as it did in the earlier flogging scene (19:1). With this inscription, Pilate once again provides ironic testimony to Jesus' kingship (cf. 18:37, 39; 19:14–15).

Only John among the evangelists describes the notice placed on Jesus' cross as a τίτλον, a direct transliteration of the Latin *titulus*. Mark calls it an "inscription of the charge" (ἐπιγραφὴ τῆς αἰτίας; Mark 15:26), Matthew calls it a "charge" (αἰτίαν; Matt 27:37), and Luke simply notes that it is an "inscription" (ἐπιγραφή; Luke 23:38). John's τίτλον (Latin: *titulus*) is a technical Roman word for a sign indicating the charge against a condemned criminal. Suetonius, for example, reports a slave being led out to the site of execution "preceded by a placard [Latin: *titulo*] giving the reason for his punishment" (*Cal.* 32). In a similar fashion, the placard placed on Jesus' cross indicates the reason he has been executed by Rome: Pilate labels him an unsanctioned "king of the Jews" who is thus a threat to imperial hegemony.[36] The Johannine audience, however, knows that it is also an ironic declaration of Jesus' true identity as the representative of God's sovereignty.

The Fourth Gospel underlines the fact that crucifixion was a public spectacle, explicitly stating that "many of the Jews read this inscription, because the place where Jesus was crucified was near the city; and it was written in Hebrew, in Latin, and in Greek" (19:20). John alone indicates that the inscription on the cross is read by many, and this is deeply ironic. Within the Roman imperial world, the public nature of Jesus' crucifixion is intended as a warning to others who might oppose the empire; it broadcasts the message that "threats to Roman rule would not be tolerated."[37] However, within the narrative of the Fourth Gospel, this public display actually works against Rome and threatens Roman sovereignty: it is evidence that Jesus' crucifixion is his glorification and that through it, he is drawing all people to himself. As Jesus himself predicted, "and I, when I am lifted up [Greek: ὑψωθῶ] from the earth, will

---

36. Jesus stands in contrast to a figure such as Herod, who was sanctioned by Rome to rule as "king of the Jews" (e.g., *Ant.* 14.9; 15.409). See further p. 119 n. 26 and pp. 132–133 on unsanctioned "kingly" figures.

37. Koester, *Symbolism in the Fourth Gospel*, 227.

draw all people to myself" (12:32; cf. 3:14 and 11:52). The verb ὑψόω conveys a double meaning throughout the Gospel (3:14; 8:28; 12:32, 34) that makes it deeply ironic; it indicates both the physical act of "lifting up" Jesus up on the cross and his exaltation as Son of Man and King. Jesus' crucifixion is the means by which he makes eternal life (ζωὴν αἰώνιον) available to all who believe (3:15).[38] The Fourth Gospel makes this point strikingly clear by emphasizing that the inscription is written in Hebrew, Latin, and Greek, signifying that it is a "universally comprehensible announcement" and a "world-wide proclamation of enthronement."[39] Only in John does the inscription appear in three languages. At this moment of the crucifixion, the Samaritan acclamation that Jesus is "Savior of the world" (4:42) rings particularly true; in his glorification upon the cross, the Gospel envisions that Jesus' kingship and rule extends to all people.[40]

There is a curious connection here with the beginning of the Gospel. Of the four Gospels, only John's placard declares the fact that Jesus is "of Nazareth." Nathanael, who wondered if anything good could come from Nazareth (1:46), was the first to pronounce Jesus "king" in the Gospel (1:49). By including the note about Jesus' origin from Nazareth, the Fourth Gospel recalls this early proclamation of Jesus' royal identity, drawing another subtle connection.

2. Pilate and the Jewish Authorities

Of course, Pilate's inscription also mocks the Jewish authorities, especially because the cross is staked in a public place. They have declared that Caesar is their sole king (19:15), yet Pilate ridicules them by identifying the humiliated, defeated one upon the cross as "King of the Jews," thereby

---

38. "Eternal life" is better rendered as "life of the age," or "age-ly life," that is, life that is characteristic of the eschatological age to come, in which God is truly known (17:3) and God's purposes are fully and finally established.

39. O'Day, "Gospel of John: Introduction," 830; and Brown, *Gospel According to John*, 2:919. O'Day contends that these are the three principal languages of the Judean province: Aramaic, the everyday language of the people; Latin, the language of the Roman Empire; and Greek, the language of business and commerce (830). Similarly, Howard-Brook notes that, while they do not cover every language in the Roman world, these languages are the "three languages of the Johannine world," and thus "tongues for the entire 'world' to understand" (*Becoming Children of God*, 417).

40. Mimicry is evident once again, as Jesus' title "Savior of the World" imitates titles used for Roman Emperors. See above p. 9 n. 26. For an extended discussion of the way in which Jesus' title intersects with Roman imperial claims, see Koester, "Savior of the World," 665–80.

reminding them of Rome's dominance and control of their province. Not surprisingly, it offends their sensibilities; Michaels says that Pilate is "rubbing salt in old wounds, the wounds that were opened when he repeatedly called Jesus 'the King of the Jews'" in the show trial (18:33, 39; 19:3, 5, 14, 15).[41] They insist that Pilate rewrite the inscription to read, "This man said, I am King of the Jews" (19:21), an alternative charge that distances them from Jesus.[42] They have no desire to be associated with one who is being executed as a representative of their subjugated people. Yet Pilate will not be deterred; he demonstrates (for those who would doubt his gubernatorial power) that he is no pushover in the Fourth Gospel. He has already gotten what he wanted from the Jewish authorities—most dramatically, their declaration of dependence on and submission to Caesar (19:15)—and has no reason to negotiate further with them. They, too, have gotten what they wanted: Jesus' execution.[43] They ask for more, but Pilate will not yield. His rigid position displays his strength and command in the midst of this situation. The Johannine audience, however, knows that Pilate is not the one in ultimate control of events as they occur.

When Pilate denies their request, responding, "What I have written, I have written [Greek: γέγραφα]," his words carry far more significance than he can know. The vast majority of the occurrences of the Greek verb γράφω in the Fourth Gospel refer to things written in the Jewish Scriptures (1:45; 2:17; 5:46; 6:31, 45; 8:17; 10:34; 12:14, 16; 15:25).[44] The few exceptions refer to the writing of the Fourth Gospel itself (20:30, 31; 21:24, 25). Because the evangelist uses the word γράφω repeatedly to describe Pilate's *writing* the inscription (19:19 [2], 20, 21, 22 [2]), it is imbued with authority and has a scriptural quality to it. Yet Pilate, whose purpose seems merely to antagonize the Jewish authorities, cannot see the deeper truth of his inscription. Duke calls this irony "unconscious testimony."[45] David Wolfsdorf says that dramatic irony is present when

41. Michaels, *Gospel of John*, 950.

42. Jesus never does say this precise phrase or explicitly call himself a "king" in the Fourth Gospel. At the narrative level, the Jewish authorities plead with Pilate to write something that is false in place of the profoundly true claim that Jesus is "King of the Jews."

43. Contrast this with O'Day's statement that the Jewish authorities have "won nothing," which does not cohere with the outcome of Jesus' appearance before Pilate ("Gospel of John: Introduction," 830).

44. Jesus writes on the ground in 8:8, although that pericope (7:53—8:11) is not original to the Fourth Gospel.

45. Duke, *Irony in the Fourth Gospel*, 89.

"the incongruity is between what a dramatic character says, believes, or does and how unbeknownst to that character, the dramatic reality is."[46] Pilate is once again irony's victim as he testifies unwittingly to the truth: Jesus is king (cf. 18:39; 19:14, 15). As before, Pilate, the chief representative of Roman imperial power in the Fourth Gospel, takes the lead in announcing Jesus' kingship to the world, mimicking and subverting the empire he represents! Furthermore, though Pilate flexes his political muscles in denying the request to change the inscription, the reality is that he could not change what he has written even if he wanted to: it is immutable and true, with authority like that of Scripture.

3. Summary

This inscription scene evinces the profound situational irony of the entire crucifixion: the crucified one is the world's true king. The Fourth Evangelist has transformed the inscription on the cross from a rationale for Jesus' crucifixion into a worldwide proclamation of Jesus' true identity. As Bultmann declares, "as the Crucified, Jesus is really the king; the kingly rule, awaited in hope, is not as such destroyed, but established in a new sense; the cross is the exaltation and glorification of Jesus."[47] This contradicts the public, imperial meaning of the cross and replaces it with the Fourth Gospel's hidden transcript. Jesus' crucifixion is his "lifting up" and his exaltation; the inscription placed upon the cross—"King of the Jews"—becomes his glorious title.

Scene 3: Dividing the Spoils of Crucifixion (19:23–25a)

Following Pilate's insistence that the inscription stand as written, the Fourth Evangelist describes the division of Jesus' clothes as spoils among the Roman soldiers, bringing to narrative life Ps 22. While some commentators have attributed considerable symbolic import to the untorn tunic, the major focus in this scene is on the fulfillment of Scripture: Jesus is presented as the paradigmatic righteous suffering one of Ps 22 who will be vindicated by God. O'Day observes that, for the Fourth Evangelist, "even in something as mundane as the disposition of Jesus' clothing God's plan for salvation is at work."[48] In this demeaning act, the evange-

---

46. Wolfsdorf, *Trials of Reason*, 246.
47. Bultmann, *Gospel of John*, 669.
48. O'Day, "Gospel of John: Introduction," 831.

list sees evidence that God's will is being enacted, unbeknownst to the Roman executioners. Furthermore, according to Ps 22, the divine plan culminates in God's dominion over all the world.

1. Mockery and Suffering

Psalm 22 (LXX Ps 21) speaks of a suffering righteous person who is beset by enemies who mock him and threaten death. The psalmist alternates between despair at his plight and reminders of God's faithfulness. The psalm acknowledges the reality of mockery and suffering, yet anticipates God's ultimate deliverance: "For he did not despise or abhor the affliction of the afflicted; he did not hide his face from me, but heard when I cried to him" (Ps 22:24). For early Christians, Ps 22 was extremely important in their understanding of Jesus' crucifixion. For example, the Gospel of Mark includes the opening of the psalm as Jesus speaks from the cross, "My God, my God, why have you forsaken me?" (Ps 22:1), a quotation that Matthew picks up from Mark. All three Synoptic Gospels employ Ps 22:26–27 as a paradigm for making sense of Jesus' crucifixion: "I am ... scorned by others, and despised by the people. All who see me mock at me; ... they shake their heads." Mark and Matthew depict passersby deriding Jesus and "shaking their heads," while the chief priests and scribes mock him (Mark 15:29–31; Matt 27:39–42). Though the common people stand by and watch in silence in Luke, the leaders "scoff" at him, the soldiers mock him, and even one of the criminals joins in the hostility by "deriding him" from an adjacent cross (Luke 23:35–39).

The Fourth Gospel includes no explicit mention of mockery like this during Jesus' crucifixion. Citing Ps 22:18, it singles out the division of clothing for inclusion in the narrative: "They divide my clothes among themselves, and for my clothing they cast lots." While the Synoptics focus on the mockery, the Fourth Gospel downplays its significance. Furthermore, the Fourth Evangelist does not direct attention to Jesus' suffering during the crucifixion. Jesus does not cry out in pain or abandonment from the cross, as in Mark and Matthew (Mark 15:34, 37; Matt 27:46, 50). Only one of Jesus' statements from the cross conveys his distress: "I am thirsty" (19:28). Yet mockery and suffering are evident (even if not prominent) within the passion narrative. While Jesus is still within the *praetorium*, the Roman soldiers taunt him, sarcastically acclaiming him king (19:2–3). Pilate also repeatedly ridicules Jesus as king, most recently by means of the inscription on the cross (19:19-22).[49] Like the suffering one of Ps 22, Jesus is presented as one beset by his opponents. The Johannine audience knows that, like the figure in Ps 22, Jesus will be saved by God. The Fourth Gospel acknowledges the reality of mockery and suffering, yet vindication is soon to come. In the theological perspective of the Fourth Gospel, this is Jesus' crowning moment; mockery and suffering will not have the final say in the matter.

2. The Division of Clothing

The division of clothing noted in Ps 22:18 ("they divide my clothes among themselves, and for my clothing they cast lots") is an example of Hebrew parallelism and indicates a single event. Whether intentionally or not, the Fourth Gospel divides this parallelism into a two-step process by which the soldiers split up Jesus' clothing: first they parcel out four pieces of his clothing and then they gamble for his tunic (19:23).[50] The first division is easy to accomplish for the soldiers: there are four of them and four parts of clothing.[51] The details of this event are sparse, directing the emphasis toward the fulfillment motif. Howard-Brook wonders whether there is any significance to the fact that there are four soldiers present who divide up the clothing. He speculates that they might be symbolic of "the Roman Empire's control of the 'four corners' of the world," but acknowledges that one cannot be certain of this.[52] Brown comments that "squads of four soldiers seem to have been common," so this detail may simply have been

---

49. In each of these instances, mockery serves to present Johannine truth in ironic fashion: Jesus is king.

50. While a number of scholars, such as Brown (*Death of the Messiah*, 954) and O'Day ("Gospel of John: Introduction," 831), state that the Fourth Evangelist has ignored or misunderstood the parallelism of the verse in the LXX, Michaels maintains that it is intentional and draws additional meaning from the text (*Gospel of John*, 952). Moo agrees that the Fourth Evangelist's treatment of the parallelism is intentional, arguing that "John is aware of the application of Ps 22:18 in the crucifixion narrative and that he has access to a tradition which mentions a seamless tunic that was gambled for. Not unnaturally, he sees in this incident a fulfillment of the other half of the psalm verse and accordingly records it" (Moo, *Old Testament*, 256-57).

51. Carson speculates that the four pieces might be the purple robe (19:2) as well as a belt, sandals, and head covering typical of a Palestinian Jew. See Carson, *Gospel According to John*, 612. He wonders further if the first division of clothing, like the division of the tunic, also might have been done by lot. Cf. Hengstenberg, *Commentary on the Gospel of St. John*, 2:412, who proposes that, "as the value of the four parts was unequal, the first distribution was probably by lot [as well]."

52. Howard-Brook, *Becoming Children of God*, 419.

included to lend realism to the account.[53] The primary emphasis is on fulfillment. By describing the division of Jesus' clothes and evoking Ps 22, the evangelist casts Jesus as the paradigmatic righteous sufferer of Ps 22 who will be vindicated by God.

3. The Seamless Tunic

The seamless tunic (χιτὼν ἄραφος) has garnered much attention in the history of the text's interpretation, especially since the word χιτών is not found in the psalm; only John among the evangelists mentions this article of clothing in relation to the crucifixion, reporting that the soldiers "also took his tunic; now the tunic was seamless, woven in one piece from the top" (19:23). This type of tunic probably would have been Jesus' undergarment.[54] Even though Michaels calls it the "grand prize" for one of the soldiers who will get "more than his share," there is not any indication in the text that this garment is particularly valuable.[55] Brown contends that "a seamless garment was not necessarily a luxury item, for it could be woven by a craftsman who had no exceptional skill."[56] The text only indicates that the soldiers do not want to destroy the item by splitting it (19:24). The detail that the tunic is "woven in one piece *from the top* [ἄνωθεν]" is intriguing in light of use of this word elsewhere in John's Gospel. Every time the word ἄνωθεν appears it bears theological significance, alluding to Jesus' origin from above (3:3, 7, 31; 19:11). Does it do so here? It is easy to imagine that the Johannine audience would recall these previous uses of this word and their significance.

In general, however, scholars more often point to two primary symbolic possibilities: the undamaged tunic as a symbol of Jesus' high priesthood or of the unity of the Christian community. Some seize upon a reference in Josephus to the robe (χιτών) of the high priest which he describes as of one, long, woven cloth (*Ant.* 3:161).[57] Both Exod 28:4 and Lev 26:4 also mention a χιτών worn by the high priest, although neither

---

53. Brown, *Death of the Messiah*, 2:954. Cf. Acts 12:4, where Peter is delivered to prison by four military units, each composed of four soldiers (Greek: τέσσαρσιν τετραδίοις).

54. BDAG 1085.

55. Michaels, *Gospel of John*, 952.

56. Brown, *Death of the Messiah*, 2:956.

57. E.g., Brown, *Gospel According to John*, 2:912-13, 920-21; and Heil, *Blood and Water*, 89-92. Josephus says that the tunic is not "stitched" (ῥαπτός; note the etymological connection between ῥαπτός and ἄραφος, which BDAG 128 also points out).

describes it as seamless. In each of these scriptural references, an outer robe, rather than undergarments, seems to be in view. Nevertheless, the possibility that this verse points to Jesus' high priesthood is intriguing in light of certain Roman imperial realities. For a number of years in the first century, the high priestly garments were controlled by the Romans.[58] If this connection is implicit, it suggests that Jesus is the true high priest, and that Rome does not control the high priesthood after all. Jesus does notably say that he will "consecrate" himself for his followers (17:19). However, interpretation of the tunic as symbolic of Jesus' high priesthood does not account for why it was not divided. Furthermore, the major emphasis in the crucifixion account is most certainly on Jesus' kingship, rather than on any priestly role that he plays.

The proposal that the tunic symbolizes the unity of Jesus' followers is more plausible. As early as the third century, Cyprian, the bishop of Carthage, suggested that the tunic symbolized unity.[59] Brown observes that, on the whole, the Fourth Gospel is concerned much more with communal unity than with Jesus' identity as high priest.[60] In particular, Jesus says that there will be "one flock" of his followers (10:16), and Caiaphas inadvertently prophesies that Jesus will die "to gather into one the dispersed children of God" (11:52). Furthermore, the theme of unity is emphasized during Jesus' lengthy final prayer before the passion narrative. There, Jesus prays for the unity of his followers, asking "that they may all be one" (17:21) and that "they may become completely one" (17:23). However, how would such symbolism make sense of a reading of this particular scene in which Jesus' tunic is ultimately taken from him by the soldiers?[61] If such symbolism is in view, it is obscured by the fact that Roman soldiers end up in possession of the tunic.

4. Fulfilling Scripture

Taking narrative context into account, the best explanation for the seamlessness of the tunic is that it requires the soldiers to cast lots to decide who will take ownership of it, thereby invoking Ps 22:18. O'Day, for example, asserts that "this episode seems to have no distinctive theological

---

58. Brown, *Gospel According to John*, 2:921.
59. Moloney, *Gospel of John*, 507.
60. Brown, *Death of the Messiah*, 2:957.
61. For Michaels, this is the major stumbling block for both speculative options regarding the symbolism of the tunic (*Gospel of John*, 953).

significance for the Fourth Evangelist other than what it had for all the evangelists: its fulfillment of Scripture (v. 24)."[62] Jesus takes on the guise of the afflicted figure of Ps 22 who will be rescued by God. Of the four Gospels, John is the most emphatic that the division of clothing fulfills this Scripture, for John alone explicitly connects this division of clothing with Ps 22; the Synoptics hint at this, but John states clearly that "this was to fulfill what the scripture says" (ἵνα ἡ γραφὴ πληρωθῇ; 19:24).[63] Furthermore, this fulfillment motif is especially prominent in the Johannine crucifixion scene; this is the first of three moments that are explicitly linked to the fulfillment of Scripture (cf. 19:28, 36).

This fulfillment motif plays a critical role in the evangelist's shaping of audience perception of imperial power. As we have seen, crucifixion served as a reminder to provincials of their subjugated status and Rome's might. Crucifixion declared loudly, "Rome's will is done." The Fourth Gospel contests this by insisting that Jesus' crucifixion occurs in fulfillment of Jewish Scripture and in order to fulfill God's purposes. Thatcher observes that "prophecy thus becomes an antidote for imperial power."[64] Furthermore, by evoking Ps 22, the Johannine audience is reminded that Jesus will be vindicated by God. Thus, the Gospel asserts that God's will, not Rome's, is accomplished by Jesus' obedient death on the cross.

Irony is surely at work here as well. Roman soldiers unwittingly fulfill Ps 22, just as Pilate unwittingly witnessed to the sovereignty of Jesus with the inscription affixed to the cross (19:19–22). Rome's agents scarcely have free will in this scene; they divide up the clothing and gamble for the tunic *so that* (ἵνα; 19:24) Scripture might be fulfilled. Like Pilate, they are unsuspecting participants caught up in the cosmic drama that God—not Rome—directs.

The evangelist's use of Ps 22 may also evoke further meaning for readers aware of the whole psalm. The psalmist appeals to God for salvation and receives it, declaring, "[Y]ou have rescued me" (22:21) and "[God] heard when I cried" (22:24). Like this righteous one, Jesus will be rescued, just as he has predicted: "I lay down my life in order to take it up again" (John 10:17; cf. 2:19–21). Jesus will die, but he will be resurrected on the other side of death. Furthermore, the end of Ps 22 envisions "all the

---

62. O'Day, "Gospel of John: Introduction," 831.

63. The statement ἵνα ἡ γραφὴ πληρωθῇ is formulaic, and appears several times in the Gospel, often word-for-word (13:18; 17:12; 19:36) or with similar wording (12:38; 15:25; 19:28).

64. Thatcher, *Greater Than Caesar*, 99.

families of the nations [who] worship before [God]" (22:27). The psalmist asserts God's exclusive sovereignty, declaring, "For dominion [LXX: βασιλεία] belongs to the LORD, and he rules over the nations" (22:28). In addition, the psalmist imagines that God's dominion is so broad that even those who have died and those yet to be born will worship God (22:29–31). Even Rome, which claims an eternal empire, cannot declare a reign as extensive as this. By evoking this psalm, the Fourth Evangelist mimics and contests assertions of Roman imperial ideology; God is the one exclusive sovereign who rules the entire world, not Caesar.

5. Summary

As the soldiers divide Jesus' clothing as spoils, the Fourth Evangelist depicts them enacting Ps 22:18. While Ps 22 is thoroughly enmeshed in early Christian tradition surrounding the crucifixion and surfaces in all the Gospels, the Fourth Gospel does something remarkably different with this tradition. The evangelist includes none of the allusions to mockery and suffering that are present in the Synoptics and uses the psalm primarily to emphasize that Scripture is fulfilled in Jesus' crucifixion. Even an event as routine as the division of his clothing bears witness to the fact that his death represents his exaltation and the unfolding of God's plan.

Scene 4: New Relationships at the Foot of the Cross (19:25b–27)

Jesus' interaction with some of his followers as he hangs on the cross in John is unique among the Gospels. All four Gospels depict women at the cross; in the Synoptics, however, they observe the proceedings from "a distance" (Mark 15:40; Matt 27:55; Luke 23:49). In John, they are close enough to the cross that Jesus can speak with them. The Fourth Gospel also presents the model disciple, the one whom Jesus loved, standing with the women. The presence of these figures attests to their steadfastness to the very end and to their exemplary faith in Jesus. While Jesus is suspended on the cross, he ensures that his mother is provided for, while also symbolically inaugurating a new family of God, embodied in the new relationship between his mother and the beloved disciple.

1. Women at the Cross

While the soldiers divide Jesus' clothing, a group of four women stand nearby, looking on as Jesus dies.[65] The women are appropriate foils for the four soldiers who have violently crucified Jesus and divided his clothing among themselves. The women represent faithful followers who are not afraid to stand near the cross (παρὰ τῷ σταυρῷ; 19:25), the powerful symbol of Roman dominance. They display no fear of being associated with Jesus, nor are they terrorized by the cross.

O'Day detects a contrast between these women and Jesus' male followers as well. She recalls that "Jesus predicted that all the followers would abandon him at his death, scattering to their own homes (16:32), but the women stand firm. In the face of death and the fear of reprisals, the women do not run away."[66] They serve as models for those Johannine Christians living at the end of the first century CE who find it difficult to maintain faith in Jesus in the midst of their imperial context.

2. A New Family of God

While Jesus hangs on the cross, he speaks calmly to his mother and "the disciple whom he loves," announcing "Woman, here is your son," and "Here is your mother" (19:26–27). Jesus' declarative words bring to mind adoption formulas in the ancient world.[67] Consider, for example, Ps 2:7: "You are my son; today I have begotten you." Similar formulas were also used to establish other familial relationships such as marriage. In the apocryphal Book of Tobit, Raguel speaks to Tobias regarding Sarah: "from now on you are her brother and she is your sister" (Tob 7:11). While the construction in John is apparently unique, employing

---

65. There is syntactical ambiguity regarding how many women are present in v. 25. The grammar could convey that the sister of Jesus' mother is synonymous with "Mary the wife of Clopas," in which case a total of three women appear at the cross. The NRSV, for example, presents only three women: "Meanwhile, standing near the cross of Jesus were his mother, and his mother's sister, Mary the wife of Clopas, and Mary Magdalene" (19:25). However, an explicit contrast between these women and the four soldiers in the previous scene is established by a μὲν ... δέ construction at the end of v. 24 and the beginning of v. 25. This contrast suggests that four women are likely in view. These four women—Jesus' mother, his mother's sister, Mary the wife of Clopas, and Mary Magdalene—mirror the four soldiers, yet stand in sharp distinction to them.

66. O'Day, "Gospel of John," WBC, 527.

67. Barrett observes this, too (Gospel According to St. John, 459). For a brief discussion of adoption formulas in the ancient world, see Vaux, Ancient Israel, 112–13.

ἴδε ("here" or "behold"), it still suggests the institution of a new, legal bond. From a practical standpoint, Jesus' instructions to his mother and the beloved disciple ensure her ongoing care and support after his death. No other male relatives appear to be available to tend to this. Jesus' brothers are mentioned early in the narrative (2:12; 7:3, 5, 10), but then fade from view, making their last appearance at 7:10.[68] Likewise, Joseph, Jesus' earthly father, is twice mentioned by others in passing (1:45; 6:42), yet makes no appearance in the narrative. Thus, by designating a legal male relative, Jesus ensures the wellbeing of his mother after his death, and the beloved disciple takes her "into his own home" (εἰς τὰ ἴδια).[69]

Jesus' attention to the quite practical matter of providing for his mother also has theological significance. Scholars debate the symbolic, theological import of the new relationship between Jesus' mother and the beloved disciple, and have advanced numerous proposals.[70] Many read far too much into the text, however. In the early church period, Mary was viewed as a "new Eve" who becomes the mother of all of Jesus' followers, symbolized by the paradigmatic beloved disciple. She has also been identified as "Lady Zion," a symbolic representation of the church that gives Christians new life through baptism.[71] Some contend that Jesus' mother symbolizes the ancient faith and heritage of Judaism, which now passes to Christianity, symbolized by the beloved disciple.[72] Bultmann proposed that the mother represents Jewish Christians who find a home with the beloved disciple, representing gentile Christians.[73] However,

---

68. Stauffer contends that Mary is in need of a male relative because she is no longer associated with Jesus' other brothers. By appearing at the cross, "[s]he confesses that she belongs to the community of the accursed one. That means cutting herself off from James and his brothers who still hold aloof of Jesus" (cf. 7:5). This may read a bit too much into the textual evidence, but the basic point remains: Jesus provides for her ongoing care in his absence. See Stauffer, *Jesus and His Story*, 113.

69. Note the contrast between the beloved disciple who takes Jesus' mother into his own home (εἰς τὰ ἴδια), and Jesus' other disciples who he predicts will scatter, "each one to his home" (εἰς τὰ ἴδια).

70. Brown enumerates a number of diverse views. See *Death of the Messiah*, 2:1019–26.

71. E.g., see Feuillet, "Les adieux du Christ," 477–80.

72. E.g., see Strachan, *Fourth Gospel*, 319.

73. Bultmann, *Gospel of John*, 673. He says, "The beloved disciple represents Gentile Christianity, which is charged to honour the former as its mother from whom it has come, even as Jewish Christianity is charged to recognize itself as 'at home' within Gentile Christianity, i.e. included in the membership of the one great fellowship of the Church."

none of these suggestions is well-supported by the text. The emphasis is not on the characters themselves; corresponding formulas emphasize the creation of new relationships: "Woman, here is your son" (γύναι, ἴδε ὁ υἱός σου; 19:26) and "here is your mother" (ἴδε ἡ μήτηρ σου; 19:27). More convincing, then, is to understand these verses as symbolizing "the beginning of the creation of the new family of God."[74] Early in the Gospel, the narrator declares that all who receive Jesus and believe in his name receive power "to become children of God, who were born, not of the blood or of the will of the flesh or of the will of man, but of God" (1:12–13). During the hour of Jesus' glorification and death, this new family is now a reality. Culpepper says that Jesus' mother and the beloved disciple "form the nucleus of the new family of faith."[75] New relationships are formed at the cross—not only between the beloved disciple and Jesus' mother, but also between believers, Jesus, and God. When Jesus appears to Mary Magdalene after his resurrection, he commissions her to "go to my brothers and say to them, 'I am ascending to my Father and your Father, to my God and your God'" (20:17). As a result of Jesus' passion and resurrection, Jesus' followers are now "children of God" and his own siblings.

Thatcher observes how calm and collected the Johannine Jesus appears while he hangs on the cross. He finds that the significance of this moment in the text extends to "the fact that Christ possesses the power and presence of mind to care for his mother and the Beloved Disciple, even in his darkest hour."[76] He displays none of the agony that the Markan Jesus appears to exhibit when he cries "My God, my God, why have you forsaken me?" (Mark 15:34; cf. Matt 27:46). In what was surely a moment of excruciating pain, suffering, and defeat, the Johannine Jesus attends to the needs of others. In what was surely a moment of unbearable agony, Jesus demonstrates his vitality and depth of love by inaugurating a new family of God.

Of course, this suggestion coheres with the Gospel's emphasis on the cross as Jesus' crowning moment of triumph; he does not writhe in pain, but rather manifests regal authority and full command of the events that transpire. Howard-Brook declares that "the Johannine Jesus uses the power of the cross to form new relationships, to heal wounds, to generate

---

74. O'Day, "Gospel of John: Introduction," 832.
75. Culpepper, *Anatomy*, 122.
76. Thatcher, *Greater Than Caesar*, 159.

new communities just when all seems dust and ashes."[77] Jesus' exercise of the power and authority that he has received from his Father subverts the power Rome sought to wield through the cross. Rather than dealing death to dissidents and exalting Rome's glory, the cross is co-opted by Jesus to establish something new and beautiful in the midst of the violence that Rome intends. Jesus' actions, along with the faithful presence of the four women and the beloved disciple, stand in stark contrast to the violence that Rome inflicts upon the crucified one.

Scene 5: Jesus' Death (19:28–30)

Having accomplished his final task by establishing new relationships between his mother and the beloved disciple and inaugurating the family of God (vv. 25b–27), Jesus has now finished his mission.[78] His moment of death is at hand, and the episode is rich with theological significance. Jesus' death is a carefully orchestrated moment that represents his monumental triumph. This scene displays Jesus' command of the events of the passion narrative all the way to the moment of his death. Furthermore, Jesus' moment of death is cast in terms of the completion of the work that the Father has given him to do. There is no agony or distress in Jesus' moment of death, either; Jesus dies calmly and of his own volition. In addition, the Fourth Evangelist once again draws upon a psalm depicting a righteous suffering one, Ps 69, shaping audience perceptions of Jesus' identity and the meaning and outcome of the crucifixion. Jesus takes on the appearance of the figure of the psalm, who is surrounded by antagonists and nearly overwhelmed by troubles, yet remains confident in God's imminent salvation. Such an end presents a radically different perspective on the significance of his death than the public transcripts of Rome suggest.

1. Fulfillment

The emphasis on the completion of God's plans and the fulfillment of Scripture could hardly be more pronounced in this scene. The evangelist employs the related Greek verbs τελέω and τελειόω three times in the brief span of three verses. In v. 28, the narrator indicates Jesus' awareness

---

77. Howard-Brook, *Becoming Children of God*, 423.

78. The phrase in v. 28, μετὰ τοῦτο, suggests that this episode follows immediately on the heels of the last scene.

that "all was now finished [τετέλεσται]." Thus, he proclaims his thirst "in order to fulfill [τελειωθῇ] the scripture." In v. 30, Jesus declares, "It is finished [τετέλεσται]." The evangelist has used τελειόω and related words on several occasions in the Fourth Gospel to describe Jesus' mission as one of completing the work of his Father. For example, at 4:34, Jesus declares, "My food is to do the will of him who sent me and to complete [τελειώσω] his work" (cf. 5:36; 17:4). It is now the end and he has completed "all things" (πάντα) that the Father has given to him to accomplish (cf. 3:35; 5:20; 13:3; 15:15; 17:7). He can now die because he knows that everything is accomplished.[79] Only his death and resurrection remain.

As Jesus endures his dying moments, the Fourth Evangelist reports that his final actions signal fulfillment of Scripture and his identification with the suffering righteous one of Ps 69.[80] As one might expect of a crucified and dying man, Jesus announces, "I am thirsty," a one-word statement in Greek: διψῶ (19:28). This is not, however, a cry of desperation. The evangelist reports that Jesus announces his thirst in order to evoke Scripture, making it "a profound expression of Jesus' awareness that his death is following a divine program."[81] He recalls a verse from Ps 69 (LXX Ps 68) in which the psalmist laments, "[F]or my thirst [δίψαν] they gave me vinegar [ὄξος] to drink" (Ps 69:21). The mere mention of thirst summons this psalm to mind—one the Fourth Evangelist has invoked on two previous occasions in the Gospel (cf. 2:17; 15:25). In addition, Jesus receives a sponge of wine (ὄξους) from his enemies, just as the psalmist does (Ps 69:21). The psalm describes one who is nearly overwhelmed and defeated by troubles, yet who maintains steadfast belief in God's deliverance and salvation. The Fourth Evangelist portrays Jesus as this paradigmatic figure. Because of this, even as Jesus suffers at the hands of Roman soldiers, the Johannine audience anticipates Jesus' vindication by God. Rome will not have the final word. Nor is its power ultimate, for Jesus' suffering will not end in death but with life. At Jesus' moment of death on the cross, all the events proceed in accordance with the divine plan.

---

79. This section is evocative of Isa 55:1–11, and v. 11 in particular: "[S]o shall my word be that goes out from my mouth; it shall not return to me empty, but it shall accomplish that which I purpose, and succeed in the thing for which I sent it."

80. Normally, πληρόω is used in the Fourth Gospel to indicate the fulfillment of Scripture (cf. 12:38; 13:18; 15:25; 17:12; 18:9; 19:24, 36). Here, it is evident that πληρόω and τελειόω are used virtually synonymously. See Moule, "Fulfillment-Words in the New Testament," 318.

81. Thatcher, *Greater Than Caesar*, 115.

This moment also emphasizes Jesus' fierce determination to complete the tasks God has entrusted to him. Recall that when Peter attacked a member of the arresting party, Jesus admonished him, "Am I not to drink the cup that the Father has given me?" (18:11). There, his "cup" was to embrace arrest and then death at the hands of the Romans. Here, Jesus' acknowledgment of his thirst also displays his resolution to drink "the cup" in order to accomplish his death for God's purposes.

2. Common Wine

A web of connections bind the opening and closing moments of Jesus' ministry in John 2 and John 19. Among other things, Jesus' mother appears in both scenes, and both feature wine. However, the wine in the two scenes is of far different quality. In Jesus' dying moments, the Roman soldiers offer Jesus ὄξος, a common, vinegary wine that was typical among the lower classes and Roman soldiers.[82] But at the very beginning of his public ministry, Jesus produced an abundance of superior wine (καλὸν οἶνον) at a wedding in Cana, thereby revealing his glory (2:10–11). In Jewish tradition, a profusion of wine was an eschatological symbol, a sign of God's reign and the fertility and abundance of the age to come (e.g., Amos 9:13; Joel 3:18). The common wine that Jesus receives on the cross in response to his thirst is a poor substitute for the wine that Jesus has made available to others, a miraculous gift of divine blessing. Soon thereafter, Jesus also offered the Samaritan woman at the well "living water" so that she might "never be thirsty" again (4:10–15). O'Day detects irony in the contrast now apparent in the crucifixion scene: "The world falsely attempts to assuage the thirst of the One who is himself the source of 'living water.'"[83] Moreover, Jesus' words to the Samaritan woman at 4:10 are appropriate also for the Roman soldiers: "If you knew the gift of God, and who it is that is saying to you, 'Give me a drink,' you would have asked him, and he would have given you living water" (4:10). The Roman soldiers fail to see Jesus as the source of life.

---

82. BDAG 715. On the cheap wine common to Roman soldiers, see Carson, *Gospel According to John*, 620. Note that the immediate antecedents of the "they" who offer Jesus the vinegary wine are Jesus' mother and the beloved disciple. Nevertheless, readers should probably understand that it is the Roman soldiers who have the wine available and also direct access to Jesus as he hangs on the cross (Brown, *Death of the Messiah*, 2:1074).

83. O'Day, "Gospel of John: Introduction," 832.

3. Hyssop and the Passover

The branch of hyssop that the soldiers use to offer Jesus the sponge recalls the Passover lamb tradition of Exod 12. The Fourth Gospel has already alluded to the Passover and the slaughtered lamb, evoking Jesus' identification with the lamb (1:29; 18:28, 39; 19:14); it will do so again shortly (19:33, 36). In Exodus, Moses instructs the Israelites to take hyssop and spread the blood of a slaughtered lamb (πάσχα) around their doorposts as a marker of Jewish identity (Exod 12:21–22). Consequently, God spares their children while passing through Egypt and killing every firstborn. This plague effects liberation; it persuades Pharaoh to release the Israelites from captivity (Exod 11:1–12:33). In John, the blood of the Lamb of God smeared upon the cross prompts reflection on the crucifixion as the means by which God effects the deliverance of God's people from oppression.[84] The reference to hyssop locates Jesus' death within the context of God's actions to overcome imperial domination.[85]

4. Jesus' Moment of Death

Jesus finally dies in a subtly narrated moment. It is a dignified, regal death of one who is calm and in control. He does not scream in agony, as in Mark, but simply states, "It is finished" (τετέλεσται; 19:30).[86] While a superficial reading of the text might take this as the dying gasp of a desperate victim, it is certainly not. As Thatcher observes, "'It is finished' means nothing like 'I'm done for.'"[87] Instead, it is Jesus' declaration that he has accomplished all that the Father has given him to do. Moloney concurs, noting that this cry is "an exclamation of achievement, almost of triumph."[88]

Having uttered his final words, Jesus bows his head and "hands over" (παρέδωκεν) the spirit, dying.[89] The verb παραδίδωμι has played a

---

84. See Howard-Brook, *Becoming Children of God*, 424.

85. The violent slaughter of firstborn children in the exodus story to effect liberation is troubling and seems to be at odds with the Fourth Gospel's resistance to the use of violence. In the exodus narrative, the violence employed by God is imitative of imperial power.

86. Cf. the death cries of Mark 15:37 and Matt 27:50, which are presented ostensibly as "incoherent death scream[s]" (Thatcher, *Greater Than Caesar*, 115).

87. Thatcher, *Greater Than Caesar*, 115.

88. Moloney, *Gospel of John*, 504.

89. There is some discussion regarding what it means for Jesus to "hand over the

prominent role throughout the passion narrative as Jesus is delivered into the hands of Rome's agents (see 18:2, 5, 30, 35, 36; 19:11). The series of events precipitated by Judas's betrayal, his "handing over" of Jesus (18:2), is now complete.[90] Ironically, though, neither Judas, nor the Jewish authorities, nor the Romans are the true masters of Jesus' fate. Instead, it is Jesus himself who ultimately "hands over" his own life. Thus, Jesus' claim in 10:18 is validated: "no one takes my life from me, but I lay it down of my own accord." He is in control, even at the moment of his death.[91]

5. Summary

The moment of Jesus' death in the Fourth Gospel is carefully crafted to emphasize key theological points. It also contests Roman public transcripts by presenting an alternative vision of the meaning of Jesus' death on the cross. Even in the midst of what Rome has designed as a shameful, humiliating execution, "Jesus remains a figure of dignity."[92] His crucifixion—which represents his defeat by Rome—represents his exaltation by God.

Jesus' words in this scene are especially significant. Both "I thirst" and "It is finished" convey that as he dies, Jesus completes God's work for him and fulfills Scripture, taking on the guise of the righteous sufferer of Ps 69 who is soon to be vindicated. Roman public transcripts would suggest that one who hangs on a cross is a condemned criminal, one who is condemned, broken, forsaken, and ultimately annihilated by the empire. The cross broadcasts its message of Roman domination. Yet the Johannine hidden transcript presents Jesus' moment of death on the cross in a strikingly different manner, as the completion of his mission and God's foreordained plan. God's will is done, not Rome's. Furthermore, Jesus is

---

spirit" (19:30). Moloney, for example, suggests that here, Jesus makes the Holy Spirit available to his followers (*Gospel of John*, 504–5). However, the Fourth Evangelist explicitly narrates Jesus' gift of the Holy Spirit to his followers in 20:22: "When he had said this, he breathed on them and said to them, 'Receive the Holy Spirit.'" At 19:30, the evangelist simply uses the Greek word πνεῦμα to mean Jesus' life force; πνεῦμα refers to "that which animates or gives life to the body" (BDAG 832). Cf. Matt 27:50, which describes Jesus' moment of death in a similar manner.

90. Howard-Brook, *Becoming Children of God*, 424.

91. Compare the wording of Jesus' moment of death in the Synoptics. Mark 15:37 and Luke 23:46 report simply that Jesus "expired" (ἐξέπνευσεν). In Matt 27:50, Jesus cried in a loud voice and then "let the spirit go" (ἀφῆκεν τὸ πνεῦμα).

92. O'Day, "Gospel of John: Introduction," 832.

the primary agent in this scene, fully in command of the events as they unfold.

Jesus' final words also express a Johannine hidden transcript. As Thatcher notes, "Christ's words from the cross are filled with what Christian audiences would recognize as *double entendre*. On one level, everything the dying Jesus says would fit neatly into any cross story; on another, the informed reader hears the pronouncements of a dying king."[93] A crucified and dying man might say "I am thirsty" and then announce his dying breath by muttering, "It is finished." But in the context of the Johannine narrative, these statements convey far more meaning than this. They are profoundly ironic words for those who grasp their significance, subverting Roman understandings of the cross. In Jesus' death, his suffering is muted and he is neither overcome by Rome nor forsaken by God.

Scene 6: Blood and Water (19:31–37)

The evocation of Jewish Scripture continues as the Jewish authorities make plans to dispose of the bodies before sunset and as the Roman soldiers ensure that the three crucified men are dead. This scene is unique among the Gospels and is theologically charged. The presentation of the aftermath of Jesus' death challenges the Roman meaning of crucifixion by demonstrating that the events surrounding Jesus' death are by no means haphazard; they are reframed within the context of Jewish Scriptures. Furthermore, this scene emphasizes that Jesus' death is life-giving and leads to belief.

1. Broken Bones

After Jesus' death in v. 30, the narrative directs attention to the Jewish authorities who now seek to hasten the deaths of the crucified men. It is the day of preparation (παρασκευή) both for the coming Sabbath and for Passover, so they do not want the bodies left exposed on the crosses after sunset (19:31). Because the two days overlap in John's narrative time, it is a particularly significant Sabbath (ἦν γὰρ μεγάλη ἡ ἡμέρα ἐκείνου τοῦ σαββάτου). The narrator has already noted that it was the day of preparation for Passover (παρασκευὴ τοῦ πάσχα; 19:14; cf. 18:28), so this second reminder is a "socially powerful time signal."[94] It illumines the motiva-

---

93. Thatcher, *Greater Than Caesar*, 110.
94. Howard-Brook, *Becoming Children of God*, 427.

tion of the Jewish authorities and also brings the Passover symbolism back to the forefront of this scene.

This motivation most likely derives from Deut 21:22–23, which instructs that corpses of those who are executed by hanging on a tree should be buried before sunset. As in 18:28, the Jewish authorities are concerned with conformity to the Mosaic law. And as at 18:28, irony pervades the moment and condemns them. As recently as 19:15, the Jewish authorities secured Jesus' death sentence by denying their faith in God and declaring exclusive allegiance to Caesar; now they show scrupulous concern for maintaining the Law. Sebastian A. Carnazzo calls attention to the "obvious irony in this concern to keep a statute of the Mosaic Law by those who had wrongfully accused and handed over Jesus for crucifixion and, contrary to the Mosaic Law, proclaimed a foreigner as their king (John 19:15; Deut 17:15)."[95] In the same vein, O'Day detects the "ironic symmetry" between 18:28 and 19:31, which frame Jesus' death, emphasizing "the Jewish leaders' preoccupation with religious ritual and propriety and their dependence on Roman rule to practice their own customs."[96] This irony casts a critical light on the Jewish authorities whose concerns are not authentic expressions of faith and who forfeit autonomy in favor of accommodation and collaboration with the Roman imperial elite.

Since those crucified could linger between life and death for several days, the Jewish authorities ask Pilate to hasten the process by having the legs of Jesus and his co-sufferers broken. Breaking the legs of the crucified, known as *crurifragium*, was a common Roman practice. Combined with crucifixion, it was a way to accelerate death from blood loss or asphyxiation.[97] While the primary intent of *crurifragium* was to serve as a cruel deterrent to others, "the severe punishment ironically turns into a merciful deed" for crucifixion victims because it brings suffering to a quicker end.[98] Mercy, of course, is not the intention of the Jewish authorities.

---

95. Carnazzo, *Seeing Blood and Water*, 64.

96. O'Day, "Gospel of John: Introduction," 833.

97. Crossan claims that by breaking the legs, executioners ensure that a crucified victim is unable to continue to breathe, hastening death from asphyxiation. See Crossan, *Cross That Spoke*, 163.

98. Koskenniemi et al., "Wine Mixed with Myrrh," 388–89. Crossan cites two examples where the legs of crucified men are *not* broken so that their suffering is prolonged (*Cross That Spoke*, 164). In such cases, mercy is withheld to make the punishment more severe.

The Evangelist narrates with brevity the breaking of the legs of the men crucified on either side of Jesus (v. 32). Yet when the soldiers approach Jesus, he is already dead. This establishes a notable contrast between Jesus and the two men whose legs are broken. Though crucified, Jesus ultimately dies of his own volition by "giving up his spirit" in v. 30. These other two crucifixion victims die as a result of further imperial violence.

2. Blood and Water

Readers are not given to understand why one of the soldiers pierces Jesus' side in 19:34; he probably seeks to ensure that Jesus is dead. At this point parenthetical testimony interrupts the narrative, minimizing the importance of the soldier's motivation while underlining the importance of the blood and water that spring forth from the wound: "He who saw this has testified so that you also may believe. His testimony is true, and he knows that he tells the truth" (19:35). The issue of blood and water—whatever it symbolizes—is reported in the narrative in order to promote belief.

This striking detail, present only in John, has long intrigued interpreters. A popular interpretation of the blood and water holds that they symbolize the sacraments of eucharist and baptism. Patristic and medieval exegetes found such an interpretation quite compelling.[99] Narrative context provides some support for this view. Eucharistic overtones are particularly pronounced earlier in the Gospel in the Bread of Life discourse, where Jesus says, "Those who eat my flesh and drink my blood have eternal life" (6:54), and describes his blood as "true drink" (6:55). Jesus' blood is life-giving.[100] For the Fourth Evangelist, participation in eucharistic celebration also draws the Christian community into unity with Christ: "Those who eat my flesh and drink my blood abide in me, and I in them" (6:56). However, eucharistic overtones are not the dominant

---

99. O'Day, "Gospel of John: Introduction," 834. For one example of patristic interpretation, see Augustine, *Civ.* 22.17. A number of modern commentators also hold a sacramental reading of this text. See, for example, Moloney, *Gospel of John*, 505–6, 509.

100. Carnazzo observes that, in the cultural milieu of the Fourth Gospel, blood would have been understood as the "seat of life" (*Seeing Blood and Water*, 65). In the context of the Gospel itself, Carnazzo notes that, "based upon the association with life," blood is "used as an image for natural birth (1:13)." He contends that Jesus' blood in particular is "described as a source of life which ... appeared to imply a purificatory and life-giving function to his death (6:53–56)" (*Seeing Blood and Water*, 66).

imagery in 19:34.[101] In contrast to 6:53-58, there is nothing in this scene that suggests the eating of Jesus' flesh. There is only blood, and blood is to be expected from the piercing. The water comes as a surprise.

Water is a potent symbol throughout the Fourth Gospel; water imagery flows abundantly through the narrative.[102] Baptisms are conducted with water (1:26, 31, 33), abundant wine is produced from water (2:9), and feet are washed with it (13:5). Jesus walks on the sea (6:16-21) and a man seeks healing in a pool (5:2-9). Two water-focused passages in particular resonate with 19:34. First, Jesus' interaction with the Samaritan woman at the well makes water imagery a central focus. After initially seeking a drink of water from the woman (4:7), Jesus then offers her living water (4:10), declaring, "those who drink of the water that I will give them will never be thirsty. The water that I will give will become in them a spring of water gushing up to eternal life" (4:14). Here, water is associated closely with belief in Jesus and the fullness of life that comes with it.

Second, Jesus' proclamation on the last day of the Festival of Booths is also germane to an understanding of the issue of blood and water in 19:34. On the final day of the festival, Jesus announces, "Let anyone who is thirsty come to me, and let the one who believes in me drink" (7:37-38). The rationale for Jesus' claim is based in Scripture (although it is unclear what text the evangelist has in mind): "Out of his belly [κοιλίας] will flow rivers of living water" (7:38; my trans.).[103] For those who believe, Jesus is the source of living water and true life. The issue of blood and

---

101. There is the possibility that the Johannine community is unaware of the sacramental tradition altogether, in which case the imagery obviously carries no eucharistic overtones. Kysar identifies a number of scholarly viewpoints with respect to the sacraments in the Fourth Gospel and contemplates the possibility that the Johannine church simply does not have any knowledge of the sacramental traditions practiced in the early Christian movement. See Kysar, *Maverick Gospel*, 143-47.

102. Culpepper says that water, along with light and bread, is one of the three core symbols of the Fourth Gospel (*Anatomy*, 189).

103. As O'Day notes, punctuational ambiguity makes translation of 7:37-38 problematic ("Gospel of John: Introduction," 622-23). Two main options are possible: rivers of living water flow out of the believer, or they flow from Jesus. Because Jesus is presented as the giver of living water in 4:10-14, and because water gushes forth from his wound in 19:34, it is best to interpret Jesus as the source of living water in 7:37-38 as well. Furthermore, translating κοιλίας as "womb" rather than "belly" or "stomach" brings even richer meaning to the life-giving potential that flows forth from Jesus. For a discussion of which Scripture seems to be in view here, see Michaels, *Gospel of John*, 465-66. He proposes that Zech 14:8 is the most plausible source: "On that day living waters shall flow out from Jerusalem, half of them to the eastern sea and half of them to the western sea; it shall continue in summer as in winter."

water in 19:34 makes this a reality: living water flows forth from Jesus' pierced torso. Out of his death—and his dead body itself—comes life.[104]

3. Evoking Scripture

The evangelist states explicitly in vv. 36-37 that the events that accompany Jesus' death take place in order to conjure up two Scriptures: "[n]one of his bones shall be broken" (v. 36) and "[t]hey will look on the one whom they have pierced" (v. 37). Whatever the motives of the Jewish authorities, and whatever the agenda of the Romans, they are contextualized and relativized by God's plans, for they fit into the paradigmatic framework of Scripture. Furthermore, attention to the unbroken bones of Jesus and the piercing of his side primarily emphasizes a number of themes that would resonate powerfully with the Johannine audience.

But what Scripture does the evangelist have in mind in v. 36? Scholars disagree on this matter. There is no exact match between the Greek text in 19:36 and any one verse in the LXX. On the one hand, many scholars point to Exod 12:10 (LXX), which describes how the Passover lamb is to be prepared on the eve of the tenth plague in Egypt: "You shall not let any of it remain until morning and you shall not break a bone of it" (cf. Exod 12:46; Num 9:12; *Jub.* 49:13-14). Those who find Passover symbolism in Jesus' crucifixion tend to favor this verse as the probable source of John's citation, as it strengthens the connection between Jesus and the slaughtered paschal lamb.[105] On the other hand, some contend that that Ps 34:20 (33:21 LXX) is in view: "He keeps all their bones; not one of them will be broken." Those who do not equate Jesus with the Passover lamb tend to favor this second option. O'Day, for example, contends that "Psalm 34 is a hymn of thanksgiving and praise for deliverance, and v. 20 praises God's protection of the righteous ones."[106]

The citation in John 19:36 has points of contact with both of these proposed intertexts. The noun "bone" (ὀστοῦν) is singular in the

---

104. The contrast between the Fourth Gospel and the Synoptics is striking. In the Synoptics, miraculous signs accompany Jesus' death: the sky darkens (Mark 15:33; Matt 27:45; Luke 23:44-45), the temple curtain is ripped in two (Mark 15:38; Matt 27:51; Luke 23:45), an earthquake occurs (Matt 27:51), and tombs open and the dead are raised (Matt 27:52-53). In the Fourth Gospel, the miraculous issue of blood and water accompanies Jesus' death, but it is localized in his body. No external signs occur.

105. E.g., Brown, *Gospel According to John*, 2:952-53; Barrett, *Gospel According to St. John*, 553, 558; Crossan, *Cross That Spoke*, 168-69.

106. O'Day, "Gospel of John: Introduction," 834.

Fourth Gospel, as in the Pentateuchal texts. However, the verb is passive (συντριβήσεται), as in Ps 34. The evangelist may have combined these two references to present Jesus both as the paschal lamb and as the righteous sufferer who will be delivered by God.[107] Whatever the case may be, it is likely that the Johannine audience would recall both references at 19:36. Both have implications for Roman power.

As we have observed, significant connections between Jesus and lamb imagery are found throughout the Fourth Gospel. Very early in the Gospel, John the Baptist declares Jesus the "Lamb of God" (1:29). Toward the end of the Roman show trial, the narrator explicitly mentions the time of their encounter: it is "about noon" on the day of preparation for Passover, approximately the time when paschal lambs would begin to be slaughtered (19:14). In this scene, Jesus' bones, like those of the paschal lambs, remain unbroken. In the exodus tradition, the Israelites slaughtered unblemished lambs and spread their blood on the entryways to their houses to identify them as Israelites and protect them from the tenth plague. The Passover observance and the ensuing festival of unleavened bread celebrated the liberation of God's people and the divine triumph over Egyptian power. As the slaughtered paschal lamb, Jesus effects liberation and the formation of the new people of God. Furthermore, the Johannine audience, living under the domination of the Roman Empire, is reminded of God's ability to overcome imperial power.[108]

By alluding to Ps 34:20 as well, the evangelist evokes images of divine protection and deliverance. The psalmist repeatedly declares the certainty of God's rescue in the midst of afflictions (e.g., 34:4, 6, 17), a theme that is expressed most powerfully in vv. 19–20: "Many are the afflictions of the righteous, but the LORD rescues them from them all. He keeps all their bones; not one of them will be broken." The psalm ends with this hopeful note, affirming that "[t]he LORD redeems the life of his servants; none of those who take refuge in him will be condemned" (34:22). This allusion conveys that God will deliver Jesus from suffering and death. The Fourth Evangelist has already explicitly declared that Jesus will be

---

107. See Menken, *Old Testament Quotations*, 147–66. He argues that the evangelist adapted the psalm by adding elements of Exod 12:10 to it so that both roles of Jesus are in view. Moloney takes a similar "both/and" perspective (*Gospel of John*, 509).

108. Note that this is yet another example of mimicry. The Passover imagery envisions divine might sufficient to overcome imperial power. In the Passover event, Egypt's might is overcome by Israel's God. Likewise, through Jesus, God will overcome Roman imperial might.

resurrected (2:19-22). By evoking Ps 34, the evangelist signals once again that Jesus' death on the cross is not the utter defeat that Roman imperial transcripts would suggest. Because the soldiers do not break Jesus' legs, they unwittingly and ironically evoke both Exod 12:10 and Ps 34:20, conveying the liberating potential of Jesus' death, the power of God to overcome empire, and the certainty that God will deliver God's faithful.[109]

The evangelist follows the first fulfillment formula with a second: "And again another passage of scripture says, 'They will look on the one whom they have pierced'" (19:37). The text in view here is certainly Zech 12:10.[110] O'Day observes that "Zechariah 12:10-14 portrays Jerusalem's lament over the death of the king it has martyred," but the figure envisioned by Zech 12:10 is not entirely clear.[111] The broader context of Zech 12:10-14 imagines widespread mourning among the inhabitants of Jerusalem.[112] The end of war leads to lament for the violence that has been inflicted and the blood that has been spilt. In John, those who "look on the one whom they have pierced" are the agents of the ruling authorities, yet the ruling elite extend to Jesus no such compassion or remorse in the Fourth Gospel.

4. Summary

By abstaining from breaking Jesus' legs and by piercing his side, Roman soldiers unknowingly evoke Scripture: they are unwitting participants in the divine plan. The evangelist subverts any understanding of the cross as a moment of defeat by reframing Jesus' death in terms of Exod 12:10, Ps 34:20, and Zech 12:10. While the motives of the Jewish authorities and the actions of the Roman soldiers appear to serve their own concerns (namely, to observe cultic purity regulations and to ensure Jesus' death), they actually bear witness to the unfolding of God's plan and promote

---

109. Heil, *Blood and Water*, 112.

110. Because the quotation does not match the text of the LXX, it may be that the evangelist is quoting from the Hebrew text. Alternatively, Menken supposes that the author is quoting from an early Christian translation of the Hebrew text into Greek (*Old Testament Quotations*, 185). Zechariah 9-14 was certainly a rich source for early Christian reflection on the meaning of Jesus' death; it is quoted or alluded to at a number of places in the Gospels, including John. Zech 9:9 is used in Matt 21:5; Mark 11:12; and John 12:15. Zech 13:7 is quoted or alluded to in Matt 26:31; Mark 14:27; and John 16:32. Rev 1:7 also contains a reference to Zech 12:10.

111. O'Day, "Gospel of John: Introduction," 834.

112. Nogalski, *Book of the Twelve*, 955-56.

belief. Furthermore, Jesus dies in a dignified, rather than tragic, fashion; his legs are not broken. A major irony threaded throughout the passion narrative undergirds this passage too: as the waters of eternal life spring forth from Jesus' pierced side, John's audience is reminded that Jesus' death is ultimately life-giving. Furthermore, the quotation from Zech 12:10 evinces regret over violence inflicted, pointing a critical finger toward the Jewish and Roman elites who employ imperial violence to maintain their status quo.

Scene 7: Interment of the King (19:38–42)

In the final scene of the passion narrative, two unlikely admirers appear to bury Jesus. Although the Jewish authorities requested that Pilate have the bodies of the crucified men removed (αἴρω) in 19:31, the narrative never explicitly states the accomplishment of this request. Instead, Joseph of Arimathea arrives in 19:38 to carry out this task. He petitions Pilate, is granted permission, and removes (αἴρω) the body. Joseph, with the help of Nicodemus, carries the task one step further, however, by granting Jesus a dignified, kingly burial. In doing so, both reluctant disciples reveal their devotion to Jesus.

1. Burial of Crucifixion Victims

In and of itself, the act of burial is significant. Burial was certainly not guaranteed for victims of crucifixion in the ancient world. Accompanying crucifixion's "symbolic annihilation" of the body was the very real possibility of complete, physical destruction of the body.[113] Hengel cites a number of quotations from the ancient world that indicate that the bodies of the crucified were often left to be consumed by animals. Pseudo-Manetho, for example, identifies types of criminals who should expect to be "fastened [and] nailed to [a cross] in the most bitter torment, [as] evil food for birds of prey and grim pickings for dogs" (*Apotelesmatica* 4.198–200).[114] Horace tells a hypothetical slave, "You will not feed crows on a cross" (*Epistles* 1.16.48; my translation), yet this seems to be an exception to the rule, indicating that most victims could expect to become carrion for birds. Finally, Hengel cites an inscription that records an incident in

---

113. Thatcher, *Greater Than Caesar*, 93. See also p. 189 for Thatcher's comments describing the cross as a means of "symbolic annihilation" of Rome's opponents.

114. Quoted from Hengel, *Crucifixion*, 9.

which citizens "hung the murderer alive for the wild beasts and birds of prey."[115] Although there was no doubt diversity of practice among the provinces regarding the disposal of crucified corpses, the bodies of those charged with treason were less likely to be turned over to family members or supporters, for "Roman governors were anxious that the convicted criminal not be regarded as a hero to be imitated."[116] Philo mentions an occasion on which Flaccus, the prefect of Egypt, "gave no orders to take down those who had died on the cross," denying burial of victims even on the eve of a feast (*In Flaccum* 10.85-86). Crossan, observing that only one extant skeleton of a crucified man has been recovered by modern archeologists, supposes that most crucifixion victims, including Jesus, were either buried unceremoniously by Roman soldiers or, more likely, left on the cross for scavenging animals.[117] Crossan contends that death by crucifixion meant that "there might be nothing left to bury at the end."[118] Whatever the historical outcome of Jesus' crucifixion, by portraying Jesus' burial in a marked, identifiable grave, the Fourth Gospel undermines the typical public transcripts of the Roman cross. Far from being symbolically eradicated by the Romans, Jesus is given an honorable burial in a tomb, a place that his followers can remember.

2. Joseph and Nicodemus

Two unlikely undertakers appear in this scene: Joseph of Arimathea, who makes his first appearance in the Gospel, and Nicodemus, who has appeared twice before (3:1-21; 7:50-52).[119] Both appear to be reluctant followers of Jesus, but they show courage and devotion in the wake of Jesus' death. Joseph is described as a "secret" follower of Jesus "because of his fear of the Jews" (19:38). O'Day observes that "[i]n identifying Joseph as

---

115. Quoted from Hengel, *Crucifixion*, 76. The inscription can be found in Marshall, *Collection of Ancient Greek Inscriptions*, no. 1036.

116. Brown, *Death of the Messiah*, 2:1208.

117. Crossan, *Historical Jesus*, 391-92. Crossan argues that only those with wealth and power might hope to regain the bodies of crucified loved ones for proper burial. Thus, he believes that the Second Evangelist likely invented the wealthy councilman Joseph of Arimathea as a literary fiction to explain how Jesus' followers could have recovered and buried his body (393-94).

118. Crossan, *Revolutionary Biography*, 126.

119. Brown laments the difficulty in identifying Joseph, observing that Arimathea is a "town very difficult to identify and reminiscent of no scriptural symbolism" (*Death of the Messiah*, 2:1240).

a secret disciple of Jesus, the Fourth Evangelist links him with the Jewish authorities of [12:42-43] who, because of a fear of losing their political power and position within the synagogue, will not confess their faith in Jesus."[120] However, Joseph shows considerable boldness by risking his social status, overcoming his fear, and approaching Pilate to ask for Jesus' body. He is likely a person of wealth and status because he can gain an audience with Pilate and has a new tomb at his disposal.[121]

As Nicodemus appears on the scene, the narrator explicitly reminds readers that his first encounter with Jesus was "by night" (19:39), under cover of darkness. At that time, Nicodemus, a "leader of the Jews" (3:1) and a teacher of Israel (3:10), proved unable to grasp Jesus' teachings. He then made a second appearance at 7:50-52, where he appeared sympathetic to Jesus, arguing with fellow Jewish authorities that Jesus be granted legal due process. However, his argument is made in terms of legality rather than conspicuous faith.[122] Now, following Jesus' death, Nicodemus no longer approaches him in a clandestine manner. Nor does he couch his support for Jesus in an ambiguous form. By burying Jesus, Nicodemus openly honors him.

The Fourth Gospel has presented both Joseph and Nicodemus as reluctant to express faith in Jesus. Yet Jesus' death has transformed both of them. They as yet do not seem to expect Jesus' resurrection because of their insistence on burying him, yet they both openly honor him with burial. They represent the first of those "drawn" to Jesus in his lifting up on the cross (12:32), even if they do not yet fully believe.

3. A Burial Befitting a King

The burial Jesus receives is lavish, stately, and regal, rather than the kind typically accorded to peasants. Its presentation in the Fourth Gospel is stately and regal. From a practical standpoint, spices masked the odor

---

120. O'Day, "Gospel of John: Introduction," 835.

121. The Synoptic Gospels describe Joseph as "a respected member of the council" (Mark 15:43), a "rich man" (Matt 27:57), and "a member of the council" (Luke 23:50).

122. Nicodemus is associated with Jesus in 7:52, when one of the Pharisees asks, "Surely you are not also from Galilee, are you?" The answer implied by the Greek construction is "no," although one wonders if the ironic answer might not, in fact, be "yes." Note the apparent parallel between this question and the questions asked of Peter in the courtyard of the high priest (18:17, 25-27). Like Nicodemus, Peter denies association with Jesus, although he is certainly one of Jesus' disciples.

emitted by a deceased body as it began to decompose.[123] However, the astonishing quantity of spices provided by Nicodemus shifts the emphasis in the narrative from odor control to regality.[124] Even so, the one hundred *litras* of spices that Nicodemus brings, approximately seventy-five pounds, is lavish to the point of incredulity. Some scholars attempt to explain away the excessive number by various means.[125] However, the massive quantity of spices used for Jesus' burial is best understood as another instance of Johannine hyperbole. Excessive quantities are also featured elsewhere in the Fourth Gospel: abundant wine (2:1–11), more than enough bread at the feeding of the five thousand (6:2–13), Mary's anointing of Jesus with expensive perfume (12:1–8), and the disciples' large catch of fish (153 of them; 21:6, 11). Each instance serves the theological and rhetorical interests of the Fourth Evangelist, giving expression to the lavish abundance of gifts that God makes available in Jesus. Furthermore, the hyperbolic presentation of the burial spices is wholly appropriate at the conclusion of the passion narrative. Jesus has been presented as king in both his show trial and his crucifixion and thus is buried fittingly in a royal manner.

A number of ancient sources bear witness to the extravagant use of fragrant spices for the burial of kings and other elite figures. Josephus, for example, reports that five hundred servants carried spices in observance of Herod the Great's burial (*J.W.* 1:673). Jeremiah 34:4–5 describes God's promise to King Zedekiah that, at his death, "as spices were burned for your ancestors . . . so they shall burn spices for you." Likewise, the body of King Asa is laid in a tomb filled with spices upon his death (2 Chr 16:14). The location of the tomb in which Jesus is placed—in a garden—may also signal a kingly burial. Brown notes that at least two kings of Judah were buried in garden tombs (2 Kgs 21:18, 26). He also proposes that King

---

123. Brown has a thorough discussion of the Greek terms used to describe the articles that Nicodemus brings in 19:39–40 (μίγμα, σμύρνης, ἀλόης, and ἀρωμάτων). He concludes that Nicodemus most likely brings a dry mixture of two fragrant spices—myrrh and aloes—that would mask the odor of the decomposing body. See *Death of the Messiah*, 2:1261–64.

124. Note here the contrast with the description of Lazarus's burial in the Fourth Gospel (11:38–44). Martha anticipates a "stench" from Lazarus's tomb because he has been dead for four days (11:39). Like Lazarus, at 19:40 Jesus is also "bound" (δεδεμένος; 11:44). Yet Jesus' tomb is unlikely to give off a foul stench because of the spices.

125. Lagrange, for example, suspects that a scribal error may have been made and that the original was a more modest figure. See Lagrange, *Evangile selon Saint Jean*, 503. In the extant manuscripts, however, no textual variants exist for the quantity.

David's tomb may have been in a garden (Neh 3:16 LXX) whose location was known to first-century Jewish audiences (Acts 2:29). As Brown points out, the evidence is not conclusive, but "such a [regal] symbolism would be a most appropriate conclusion" to the passion narrative.[126] F. F. Bruce is less cautious in his assessment, confidently asserting that Nicodemus and Joseph intend this as a royal burial for Jesus.[127]

The hyperbolic burial spices also signal the presence of irony in this text. The Johannine audience knows that Jesus will be raised from death; Nicodemus and Joseph apparently do not. With the great quantity of spices, they evidently prepare the corpse for a long interment.[128] Dennis D. Sylva argues that this, coupled with the fact that the two characters bind (ἔδησαν; 19:40) Jesus, reflects their failure to understand the meaning of Jesus' death or to anticipate his life beyond it. Thus, Sylva contends that they are negative figures in the narrative.[129] However, irony makes better sense of this moment. Their misunderstanding represents another striking instance of dramatic irony. They recognize that Jesus deserves to be buried in an honorable, regal fashion, but fail to understand the full implications of their actions and Jesus' death. However, the Johannine audience knows that Jesus will be raised from death, and can smile knowingly.[130] The spices will not be needed for long.

4. Summary

Once again, it is evident that Jesus' death represents not merely defeat but rather his exaltation. As Brown maintains, "John transformed the crucifixion into the triumph of Jesus; so also he has transformed the burial into a triumph. One who reigned as a king on the cross receives a burial worthy of his status."[131] Rome has publicly shamed, dishonored, and executed Jesus, yet the actions of Joseph and Nicodemus disrupt these

---

126. Brown, *Death of the Messiah*, 2:1270.
127. Bruce, *Gospel of John*, 379.
128. Howard-Brook, *Becoming Children of God*, 435.
129. Sylva, "Nicodemus and His Spices," 148–51.
130. Some might even view the enormous load of spices as humorous, in line with Brown: "such a weight would ... smother the corpse under a mound" (*Death of the Messiah*, 2:1260). Carroll and Green surmise that "the narrator may well be seen winking and the reader heard laughing as Nicodemus brings such an immense quantity of spices," but also note that, in spite of Jesus' impending resurrection, burial is necessary in the interim. See Carroll and Green, *Death of Jesus*, 108.
131. Brown, *Death of the Messiah*, 2:1268.

imperial outcomes. Furthermore, situational irony emerges as Joseph of Arimathea and Nicodemus step out of the shadows to express their devotion to Jesus by burying him, thereby bearing witness to the cross as the means by which Jesus draws all people to himself (12:32). This is far from symbolic annihilation and certainly not the outcome the Jewish authorities and the Romans sought! The Fourth Gospel's presentation of Jesus' honorable burial—befitting a king—subverts the power and symbolism of the cross in the public transcripts of the Roman Empire even while it mimics imperial practices.

Crucifixion, Burial, and Hidden Transcripts

1. The Johannine Meaning of the Cross

The Johannine presentation of Jesus' crucifixion and burial stands in stark contrast to the meaning of these events conveyed by the public transcripts of imperial Rome. For Jesus, the cross becomes layered with meaning that makes it much more than merely a place of suffering, mockery, and humiliation.[132] It does not result ultimately in his defeat or symbolic annihilation. Nor does the Johannine presentation of the cross suggest that Rome is finally the dominant power in the world, directing the course of history. And the cross does not broadcast a warning to onlookers that Rome exercises ultimate sovereignty over all subject peoples; instead, it proclaims loudly that Jesus is king. In the end, neither the cross nor Rome has the power to consign Jesus permanently to death. All of these points suggest that the Fourth Gospel's account of the crucifixion and burial forms part of a Johannine hidden transcript that contests Roman imperial sovereignty and promotes belief in Jesus.

In his death and burial, Jesus, the Son of Man, has been glorified (12:23). The Johannine presentation of these events reflects Jesus' claim earlier in the Gospel that "unless a grain of wheat falls into the earth and dies, it remains just a single grain; but if it dies, it bears much fruit" (12:24). In dying, Jesus bears much fruit. His death is a decisive moment in the Gospel which accomplishes God's plans and makes life available to all people. As O'Day claims, "Jesus' death does not abrogate God's offer

---

132. Ashton argues that the Fourth Evangelist downplays Jesus' suffering to the extent that, with respect to John's passion narrative, the term "passion" is a "misnomer." See Ashton, *Understanding the Fourth Gospel*, 489.

of life and love; rather, it brings that offer to fruition."[133] In the wake of his death, life-giving water rushes forth from his body and Joseph of Arimathea and Nicodemus find themselves among the first "drawn" to Jesus in his lifting up. Jesus' death effects both life and belief.

We have also seen that the theme of Jesus' kingship, so prominent in the Roman show trial, continues in force throughout the crucifixion and burial scenes. On the cross, Jesus is enthroned as king and surrounded by his kingly retinue. And as he reigns from the cross, he inaugurates the family of God. Even in death, Jesus receives a dignified, regal burial.

Furthermore, Jesus continues to be the principal catalyst of the events that transpire. He is in full control, carrying his cross and voluntarily laying down his own life. His death, while the result of imperial violence, springs from his intention to advance God's plans. O'Day underlines this point, drawing attention to the pronounced emphasis on Scripture throughout the crucifixion account: "The explicit references to the fulfillment of Scripture, the highest concentration of fulfillment formulas anywhere in the Fourth Gospel, repeatedly reinforce that the drama being acted out in Jesus' death belongs to God's plan and work of salvation."[134] The Scriptures that the evangelist evokes emphasize in particular the surety that God will deliver Jesus, the faithful one, from suffering and from his opponents. In his death, Jesus has triumphed, finally accomplishing all that his Father has given him to do.

2. Irony, Mimicry, and the Cross

Within the narrative world of the Fourth Gospel, things hardly could have gone better from the perspective of the Jewish and Roman elites. Jesus has been killed and the threat that he posed eliminated. Carter argues that Jesus has been "mocked as a kingly pretender." The elites have "silenced his critique, claims, and challenge to their societal order. They have defended their hierarchical societal system and preserved their place in it. The elite have prevailed, reducing his claims to naught."[135] Jesus is dead and Rome would appear to have won. Yet irony prevails; they will not have the last word. Jesus will soon be resurrected, a "surprising reversal" for those who do not anticipate Jesus' resurrection.[136] As we have

---

133. O'Day, "Gospel of John: Introduction," 836.
134. O'Day, "Gospel of John: Introduction," 836.
135. Carter, *John and Empire*, 168.
136. Carter, *John and Empire*, 168. Of course, the Johannine audience already knows

demonstrated, the Johannine presentation ironizes the Roman meaning of the cross, presenting an alternative view that contrasts sharply with the public meaning of crucifixion. The elite characters in the narrative cannot grasp the Johannine meaning. Even casual readers of the Gospel might find it ambiguous. The evangelist invites the informed reader, however, to grasp the true meaning of the events. The evangelist's ironic presentation appeals to readers and hearers to share the vision of Jesus' crucifixion as his triumph and his enthronement.[137] This irony finds sharpest expression in the crucifixion scene by means of the inscription that Pilate places upon the cross: Jesus is king.[138]

For the Johannine audience, the account of Jesus' crucifixion and burial also provides comfort and a reminder that Rome does not exercise true sovereignty. In spite of Rome's public transcripts, the empire does not ultimately hold power over life and death; Jesus' Father does. The Fourth Gospel also conveys that Rome's dominance is temporary; Jesus' identity as the "Lamb of God" recalls the Passover and the deliverance of God's people from imperial oppression in Egypt.

There is mimicry in John's vision, however. Even as it imagines an alternative vision, the Gospel imitates imperial language and structures. The Gospel inevitably constructs its own vision and ideology by borrowing elements from the Roman imperial worldview. Jesus takes on the emperor's title, *basileus*, and intends to replace Rome's dominion with the worldwide, unending dominion of the Son of Man. On the cross, Jesus symbolically dethrones Caesar and takes his place as the new king and true sovereign of the world. In his "lifting up" and return to the Father, Jesus ironically imitates the apotheosis of Roman emperors through crucifixion.[139] Thus, we cannot say that the Fourth Gospel unequivocally rejects imperial power structures and ideology; it co-opts some of them. Still, Jesus' kingdom remains distinct from Rome's in at least one way: his reign is not characterized by imperial violence but by self-giving love.

---

that Jesus will be resurrected.

137. Interestingly enough, early Christians, including the Fourth Evangelist, were apparently so effective in subverting the message and meaning of the Roman cross that nowadays it is common and socially acceptable for Christians to wear tiny golden crosses—instruments of Roman imperial domination, torture and death—affixed to necklaces.

138. Once again, Pilate ironically emerges as the most vocal proponent of Jesus' kingship within the narrative.

139. Carter, *John and Empire*, 327.

3. Resurrection

Jesus' death and burial do not mark the end of the Fourth Gospel. As we have seen, both accounts point discreetly toward the resurrection, narrated in the very next chapter of the Gospel. The resurrection represents the fullest, most decisive triumph over the cross and Rome's power to enact violence and death. Rome and its allies may have executed Jesus, but in three days he will live again.

CHAPTER 6

Conclusion

IN THIS DISSERTATION, I have argued that the passion narrative of the Fourth Gospel displays part of a Johannine hidden transcript that resists, contests, and in places mimics elements of Roman imperial power. This hidden transcript, while not limited to the Gospel itself, is part of the political discourse of the Johannine community that assists them in negotiating life within the Roman Empire. It mocks the representatives of Rome, including Pilate, eroding confidence in the empire and its agents. It also subverts imperial dominance, authority, and power, while bolstering faith in the sovereignty of Jesus and God. As such, it fosters an alternative worldview and community, and serves as a means of distancing Johannine Christians from the Roman imperial world—especially those who are too comfortably accommodated. I have demonstrated that this hidden transcript is especially evident in the literary feature of irony that is so prevalent in the passion narrative.

SUMMARY AND CONCLUSIONS

The first chapter introduced the study by situating it within the context of Johannine scholarship. It noted a general lack of attention in the history of scholarship to political dimensions of the Fourth Gospel. Yet the chapter also reviewed several recent efforts on the part of Johannine scholars to read and interpret the Gospel within its first-century Roman imperial context with an eye on how it assists believers in their negotiation of life within the empire.

This chapter attended to the historical context of the Fourth Gospel, dating it sometime around the end of the first century CE, but without settling conclusively upon a location. I contended that the membership of the Johannine community, in all probability, was diverse, with some members happily entrenched within the broader synagogue community, while others, including the Fourth Evangelist, found themselves in a more tensive stance. The relationship between Johannine Christians and the broader Roman imperial world was probably also complex. Some Christians within the Johannine community, like some synagogue communities, were accommodated to life within the empire. However, I proposed that the evangelist and his supporters opposed elements of Roman imperialism.

The first chapter also introduced and described James C. Scott's model of hidden transcripts, which proposes that groups under domination develop discourse and actions out of the sight of the dominant that express perspectives and worldviews that differ and often contest their interactions with the dominant. Scott's model of hidden transcripts is useful for the study of New Testament texts because it provides a lens through which we can discern resistance to empire, even in the absence of overt opposition and open, violent revolution. I have argued that that the Fourth Gospel is part of such a "hidden transcript" of resistance in that it does not advocate violent revolution, nor does it accept unqualified accommodation to Roman domination.

The first chapter also introduced the literary device of irony. Irony expresses multiple levels of meaning which stand in some opposition to one another and are communicated to perceptive readers. Three types of irony were set forth: verbal, dramatic, and situational. Irony's function as both appeal and weapon was also considered. I proposed that irony in the Fourth Gospel, as part of a Johannine hidden transcript, informs and affects the community's negotiation of life under Roman imperial domination. It critiques and subverts—even as it occasionally imitates—aspects of Roman rule while promoting the Johannine worldview.

In the second chapter, I provided a sketch of significant features of the Roman imperial world that bear upon an interpretation of the Johannine passion narrative. I adopted the sociological models of Gerhard E. Lenski and John H. Kautsky in order to better understand the socioeconomic stratification and power dynamics among elites and non-elites in the first-century Roman Empire. I also discussed other imperial realities, such as Roman alliances with local elites, governance, and justice, which inform a reading of the passion narrative.

The third chapter directed attention to the passion narrative itself, starting with the Johannine arrest scene (18:1–12). Irony pervades the scene and mocks the agents of Roman imperialism as they attempt to seize Jesus. I stressed two major ironies that surface in the scene: first, that Jesus is the one in control of events from the outset of his passion; and second, that the arresting party acts in woeful ignorance of Jesus' true identity. These two central ironies, supported by a number of other ironies and features in the text, exhibit a hidden transcript that resists Roman dominance. The arrest scene contests public transcripts that declare Rome's direction of history and the emperor as the agent of the divine will on the earth. In contrast, Jesus is presented as the legitimate agent of the divine will who intends to lay down his life willingly.

The threat of violence pervades the arrest scene, and the overwhelming show of force by the Roman and Jewish elites reminds readers that Rome uses this threat to maintain dominance and "peace" throughout the empire. Yet a staggering display of Roman power is trumped by the reality of Jesus' nonviolent power. The scene resists violence as an appropriate strategy for responding to imperial domination and brutality.

Furthermore, I argued that the arrest scene has the capacity to restore or inspire dignity in Johannine Christians who experience forms of Roman domination by providing an account of their crucified lord as one in command of all the events leading to his death. It supplies a fantasy of imagined revenge: hundreds of Roman soldiers fall pathetically to the ground when Jesus utters the divine name. It also functions as a coping mechanism—a "safety valve"—by allowing Johannine believers to express anger through the narrative without having to channel their frustration into overt resistance.

The fourth chapter examined the complex interactions of Jesus, Pilate, and members of the Jewish elite during Jesus' interrogation before the Roman procurator (18:28—19:16a). I argued that the theme of sovereignty assumes central focus as Jesus comes face-to-face with Pilate, the chief representative of imperial power in Judea. Major ironies develop this theme: Jesus is presented as a king undergoing coronation, whose kingdom/empire presents an alternative to Rome's; his empire mimics Rome's, yet his is marked by nonviolence and life. Jesus is also depicted as judge of the proceedings and the paschal lamb who effects liberation from imperial domination.

The agents of imperial power—the Jewish authorities, Pilate, and the Roman soldiers—are presented in an extremely negative light throughout the Roman interrogation of Jesus. Irony exposes their preference for "darkness" over "light" and their opposition to Jesus, the agent of God's divine purposes, because they cannot grasp his true identity. The Jewish authorities are marked by irony as hypocrites, liars, murderers, and imperial collaborators. Pilate does not fare much better: he is callous and impervious to the truth even as he unwittingly espouses Jesus' kingship as an alternative to that of Caesar's. Both Pilate and the Jewish authorities attempt to further their own purposes but ironically end up advancing God's plans instead; Jesus will be "lifted up" and thereby draw all people to himself (12:32). The irony works to distance the Johannine audience from the agents of Roman imperialism while fostering belief in Jesus.

The hidden transcript that emerges proposes that Jesus is the true king and that the God of the Jews exercises true power and authority. It also envisions the end of all worldly empires and the establishment of Jesus' everlasting dominion as the Son of Man. These claims contest and undermine (even while they mimic) Roman imperial assertions of ultimate sovereignty, power, and unending rule.

The fifth chapter addressed the events surrounding Jesus' crucifixion and burial. With the presentation of Jesus as king, accentuated in the inscription affixed to the cross (19:19–22), the Fourth Evangelist casts an ironic shroud over the entire crucifixion account: the one crucified by Rome is the world's true sovereign. In this chapter, I maintained that the Fourth Gospel ironizes the meaning of the Roman cross by layering on an alternative vision of its significance. According to Rome's public transcripts, crucifixion is a shameful, humiliating death that proclaims Roman domination and eliminates threats to the imperial status quo. Yet the cross does not annihilate Jesus; he is "lifted up" and exalted as king, and the cross becomes the means by which he draws all people to himself (cf. 12:32) as well as the place where he establishes a new family of God (19:26–27). The inscription on the cross serves not as a warning to other would-be dissidents, but rather as a worldwide proclamation of Jesus' sovereignty. Furthermore, with his death, Jesus completes the work that the Father has given to him to do. Having done so, he lays down his life willingly; he is the sole master of his life and death. In spite of the violence inflicted by the agents of Rome, Jesus' death is life-giving and leads to belief.

Jesus' burial reaffirms these claims. Jesus is buried in a manner befitting a king by two reluctant followers who are drawn to him by his death. Joseph of Arimathea and Nicodemus provide a lavish burial for the one whom Rome has dishonored with crucifixion. Yet neither crucifixion nor burial has the last word. Roman imperial power, in the end, is limited and cannot annihilate Jesus; he will soon be resurrected, proving that Rome holds no power over him at all.

Thus, as part of the Johannine hidden transcript, the crucifixion and burial accounts disrupt the imperial meaning of the cross. God's will, not Rome's, is accomplished by Jesus' obedient death on the cross. The Fourth Gospel contests claims of Roman hegemony and power and advances an alternative vision focused on Jesus' sovereignty and the life made available through him.

Throughout this project, we have seen how irony in the passion narrative has presented to a perceptive Johannine audience multiple levels of meaning which have ramifications for negotiating life within the Roman Empire. Irony functions positively by promoting belief in Jesus as sovereign and God's agent on earth. Such irony has the capacity to advance the overall purpose of the Gospel of promoting and sustaining belief in Jesus (20:31). Irony functions negatively by conveying strong ideological resistance to the imperial system and public transcripts that attest Roman sovereignty. For Johannine Christians who are too comfortable or too accommodated to life within the Roman Empire, such irony pressures them to distance themselves. For those already wary, the Gospel reinforces such distance.

I contended that the Fourth Gospel itself constitutes Scott's second mode of political discourse: the hidden transcript itself.[1] Yet it also provides insight into the Johannine community's implementation of the third mode of discourse, the politics of disguise and anonymity. The Gospel's use of irony provides a strategy for insinuating the hidden transcript of the Johannine community into the public sphere by providing a tool with multiple levels of meaning that is able to convey ambiguous mean-

---

1. Recall Scott's four modes of political discourse among subject groups. The first mode represents the open appeal of subordinates via flattery or ideological justification to the dominant elite in order to elicit benefits or favors. The second is the hidden transcript, in which subject people speak and act freely while out of sight of the dominant. The third is what Scott calls the "politics of disguise and anonymity," in which subordinates express the hidden transcript in public, yet in ambiguous or coded fashion. Finally, the fourth mode is the volatile disclosure of the hidden transcript in open, overt fashion. See pp. 26-27 above.

ing discernible only to "insiders." Such a strategy would allow Johannine Christians to give voice to their perspectives while safely cloaking them in ambiguous language. This cannot be demonstrated conclusively from evidence of the Gospel alone, but it remains an intriguing possibility.

Finally, I have also argued that as Fourth Gospel resists Roman imperialism, it also mimics and reinscribes elements of the Roman imperial system. For example, Jesus is presented throughout the passion narrative as the king/emperor. As Dube wittily quips, "The Johannine Jesus now emerges fully clothed in the emperor's titles."[2] The Gospel contests and attempts to subdue Caesar's sovereignty by asserting the opposing sovereignty of Jesus and God. Jesus' kingdom/empire is held up as an alternative, more powerful empire than Rome's. The Fourth Gospel envisions the end of Rome and all empires by means of the Son of Man figure, yet conveys God's intention to replace them with the worldwide dominion of Jesus. Horsley notes a propensity toward mimicry of this type present within many sacred Jewish and Christian texts: "In imagining how the one true God would finally bring judgment upon oppressive imperial rulers, many biblical texts portrayed God and the heavenly armies as exercising violence, whether figurative or literal."[3] However, the Fourth Gospel steadfastly resists violence as an appropriate strategy for imperial negotiation. Jesus' kingdom, as we have seen, is distinct in this respect from Rome's: his reign is characterized by nonviolent, self-giving love.

Suggestions for Further Study

This study is significant because it revisits the discussion of irony that was prominent in Johannine studies in the early 1980s and brings it into conversation with contemporary research in imperial criticism.[4] The results of the study suggest further avenues for research likely to prove fruitful. I have focused on the presence of irony and hidden transcripts in the passion narrative, where Jesus comes most directly into contact and conflict with the face of Roman imperialism. Clearly, the use of irony throughout John's Gospel as a whole needs revisiting, to see if there are other points

---

2. Dube, "Reading for Decolonization," 66. Looking elsewhere in the Fourth Gospel, we could add other imperial titles accorded to Jesus, including "Lord" (e.g., 1:23) and "Savior of the World" (4:42).

3. Horsley, *In the Shadow of Empire*, 182.

4. For studies of Johannine irony, see especially Culpepper, *Anatomy*; Duke, *Irony in the Fourth Gospel*; O'Day, *Revelation in the Fourth Gospel*.

at which it assists its readers with the challenges of negotiating life under Roman imperial domination. Because the Jewish authorities are local elites who are allied with Rome, scenes in which they appear and come into contact with Jesus in the narrative merit further exploration.

For example, the Fourth Evangelist pokes fun at the Jewish authorities in 7:26 when some in the crowd wonder, "[h]ere he is, speaking openly, but they say nothing to him! Can it be the authorities really know that this is the Christ?" It is unlikely that many of the authorities believe that Jesus is the Messiah, given the hostility toward him that continues to develop throughout the narrative. Furthermore, the Good Shepherd discourse is sharply critical of the Jewish authorities (10:1–18). However, some will come to belief (12:42). The Fourth Gospel seems to hold out hope that Jewish elites who are allied with Rome might participate in God's reign: Nicodemus, a "ruler of the Jews" (3:1) and Joseph of Arimathea, a "member of the Council," bury Jesus. The story of the man born blind also provides significant encounters between Jesus, the blind man, and the Jewish authorities (John 9). Duke observes of that story that "[t]he man born blind is the one who sees with increasing clarity; the ones who claim sight plunge into progressively thickening night."[5] The story is filled with moments of dramatic irony. It also begs the audience to consider questions related to access to truth and Jesus' identity, and it presents Jesus as the Son of Man who will execute judgment (9:35, 39). The triumphal entry scene, in which Jesus enters Jerusalem upon a donkey, imitating and satirizing an imperial victory parade, brings issues of sovereignty to the fore and may also prove fruitful for further study (12:12–19).

There are no doubt other ways in which the Fourth Gospel assists Johannine believers in negotiating life in the Roman Empire. For example, matters of scarcity and abundance would have resonated with first-century audiences who lived at subsistence levels as a result of the economic realities of Roman domination. Such issues surface in the wedding at Cana (2:1–12) and the feeding of the 5,000 (6:1–15) and merit further research. Finally, the resurrection account and Jesus' appearances to his disciples following it (chapters 20–21) ought to prove fruitful for further study. Jesus' resurrection is a decisive response to Rome's use of violence and death to maintain the imperial status quo. Rome does not have the final word.

5. Duke, *Irony in the Fourth Gospel*, 118.

Negotiating Empire Today

This study of the way in which the Fourth Gospel assists Johannine believers in negotiating life in the imperial world raises important questions for life in our own contexts of imperial power. In this respect, we can be instructed by dangers, as well as insights, that the Fourth Gospel presents. For instance, at points throughout this dissertation I have called attention to instances in which the Fourth Gospel mimics aspects of Roman imperialism. The Gospel envisions an expansion of belief in Jesus, who has "conquered the world" (16:33) and whose kingship is announced to all of humanity (19:20). As Dube notes in her study of the story of the Samaritan woman and the missionary vision of the Johannine community, "the alternative vision of the Johannine community ironically embraces an ideology of expansion, despite the fact that it, itself, is the victim of imperial expansion and is struggling for its own liberation."[6] Johannine Christianity thus has a deep-rooted imperializing impulse within it. The dangers of this impulse are limited when they are expressed by a small, marginalized, relatively powerless religious group in the early centuries of the Roman Empire. However, when Christianity is the dominant religion of a global superpower such as the United States, it has the potential to be much more dangerous. Marcus Borg notes the dramatic shift in the history of Christianity when it was adopted as the official religion of the Roman Empire: "In one of the most remarkable reversals in history, within three hundred years Jesus had become lord of the empire that had executed him. He became the central figure of the dominant religion of Western culture, and thereby also became the central figure of Western history. That is a remarkable achievement for a Galilean Jewish peasant."[7] Yet this development has proved problematic, for Christianity has become one of the most dominant imperializing forces of the last two millennia, with consequences that continue to this day.

The Christian religion has spread to the four corners of the world and Jesus truly has become, in many respects, the "Savior of the World" (4:42). But inherent propensity toward expansion and conquest within Christianity has caused much suffering, violence, and destruction throughout history. Howard-Brook notes how "imperial Christianity" has resulted in "wars, economic exploitation, and countless varieties of

---

6. Dube, "Reading for Decolonization," 63.
7. Borg and Wright, *Meaning of Jesus*, 59.

domination 'in the name of Jesus.'"[8] A number of programs of colonization throughout history, such as the sixteenth-century conquest of the Aztec Empire by Spanish *conquistador* Hernán Cortés, have been motivated and "legitimized" by the desire to spread the Christian faith. Various expressions of Christianity within America today have imperialistic tendencies on a smaller, but no less significant scale—they assert opinions, doctrines, and ideologies that seek to subdue, vanquish, or politically marginalize those who disagree. Carter offers a scathing critique of imperial Christianity, observing that "Christianity has become and continues to be imperial Rome, intolerant of, vindictive toward, and heaping destruction upon those who do not fall into line."[9] Christians today continue to find themselves enmeshed in empire, but now many—especially in America—find themselves closer to centers of power rather than on the margins. In many countries, Christians still enjoy majority status, occupy positions of authority, and have forceful voices on national and world stages. Contemporary Christians must consider carefully how they negotiate modern imperial realities and examine critically the ways in which they, too, participate in empire.

Indeed, the overwhelming display of military force in John's arrest scene should make American readers uncomfortable. At present, military expenditures in the United States vastly exceed those of any other country in the world, and American military bases encircle the globe. Kahl notes that, "[i]n the past several years, we have become critically uneasy about issues of empire, as the United States has aggressively asserted its power in the world after the tragedy of 9/11."[10] Yet plenty of Americans, Christians among them, continue to champion the imperial might and political right of the United States.

It is also imperative that Christians be mindful of the economic practices and systems they participate in, and often unintentionally support. Howard-Brook and Gwyther contend that, through economic globalization, a number of massive transnational corporations and financial institutions have gained such economic power that they represent a modern form of imperialism.[11] Powerful media and marketing forces espouse the benefits of these contemporary empires, including wealth,

---

8. Howard-Brook, *Come Out*, 473.
9. Carter, *John and Empire*, 342.
10. Kahl, "Acts of the Apostles," 138.
11. Howard-Brook and Gwyther, *Unveiling Empire*, 236–60.

modern comforts and luxuries, and ease of living, all while they exploit the cheap labor and unethical work conditions of developing countries.

The Fourth Gospel requires that we be wary of participation in such violent, exploitative imperial practices. The way forward is difficult, however. We do not always recognize empire or our participation in it. Nevertheless, the Fourth Gospel urges us to be mindful of our loyalties and the objects of our worship. Howard-Brook proposes that Christians must "offer our embodied witness to the reality of God's compassionate love for all people and all creation."[12] This outlook has the capacity to undermine the impulse toward social and economic hierarchies, exclusion or exploitation of outsiders, consolidation of power, domination, and systems of patronage and debt. In its place it offers an egalitarian social structure, inclusion of outsiders, and an economy based on shared abundance, not patronage and debt.[13] Empire is replaced with community, compassion, solidarity, nonviolence, and self-giving love.

---

12. Howard-Brook, *Come Out*, 474.
13. Howard-Brook, *Come Out*, 11.

Bibliography

Abrams, M. H. *A Glossary of Literary Terms*. 3rd ed. New York: Holt, Rinehart & Winston, 1971.
Agosto, Efrain. "Patronage and Commendation: Imperial and Anti-Imperial." In *Paul and the Roman Imperial Order*, edited by Richard A. Horsley, 103–23. Harrisburg: Trinity, 2004.
Anderson, Paul J., et al., eds. *John, Jesus, and History, Volume 1: Critical Appraisals of Critical Views*. Society of Biblical Literature Symposium Series 44. Atlanta: Society of Biblical Literature, 2007.
———. *John, Jesus, and History, Volume 2: Aspects of Historicity in the Fourth Gospel*. Atlanta: Society of Biblical Literature, 2009.
Ando, Clifford. *Imperial Ideology and Provincial Loyalty in the Roman Empire*. Berkley: University of California Press, 2000.
Apuleius. *The Golden Ass: Being the Metamorphoses of Lucius Apuleius*. Edited by William Adlington. New York: Putnam, 1922.
Ashton, John. *Understanding the Fourth Gospel*. Clarendon: Oxford, 1991.
Aubert, Jean-Jacques. "A Double Standard in Roman Criminal Law? The Death Penalty and Social Structure in Late Republican and Early Imperial Rome." In *Speculum Iuris: Roman Law as a Reflection of Social and Economic Life in Antiquity*, edited by Jean-Jacques Aubert and Boudewijn Sirks, 94–133. Ann Arbor: University of Michigan Press, 2002.
Augustine. *The City of God*. Translated by George E. McCracken et al. 7 vols. Loeb Classical Library. Cambridge: Harvard University Press, 1957–72.
Azevedo, Neil. "Pontius Pilate." In *Ocean*, 45. Grove Press Poetry Series. New York: Grove, 2005.
Bajsić, Alois. "Pilatus, Jesus und Barabbas." *Biblica* 48 (1967) 7–28.
Bammel, Ernst. "*Philos tou Kaisaros*." *Theologische Literaturzeitung* 77 (1952) 205–10.
Barrett, C. K. *The Gospel According to St. John: An Introduction with Commentary and Notes on the Greek Text*. London: SPCK, 1958.
Bauckham, Richard, ed. *The Gospels for All Christians: Rethinking the Gospel Audiences*. Grand Rapids: Eerdmans, 1998.
Beasley-Murray, George R. *John*. Word Biblical Commentary 36. Waco: Word, 1987.
Benoit, Pierre. *Jesus and the Gospel*. Translated by Benet Weatherhead. 2 vols. New York: Herder & Herder, 1973.
———. *The Passion and Resurrection of Jesus Christ*. New York: Herder & Herder, 1969.

Bernard, J. H. *A Critical and Exegetical Commentary on the Gospel According to St. John*. Edited by A. H. McNeile. Edinburgh: T. & T. Clark, 1928.

Bhabha, Homi K. *The Location of Culture*. London: Routledge, 1994.

Blank, Josef. "Die Verhandlung vor Pilatus: John 18:28—19:16 im Lichte johanneisher Theologie." *Biblische Zeitschrift* 3 (1959) 60–81.

Blass, Friedrich, et al. *A Greek Grammar of the New Testament and Other Early Christian Literature*. Chicago: University of Chicago Press, 1961.

Blinzler, Josef. "Der Entscheid des Pilatus—Exekutionsbefehl oder Todesurteil?" *Münchener theologische Zeitschrift* 5 (1954) 171–84.

———. *The Trial of Jesus*. Translated from 2nd German ed. Westminster: Newman, 1959.

Bond, Helen K. *Pontius Pilate in History and Interpretation*. Society for New Testament Studies Monograph Series 100. Cambridge: Cambridge University Press, 1998.

Bonsirven, Joseph. "Hora Talmudica: La notion chronologique de Jean 19:14, aurait-elle un sens symbolique?" *Biblica* 33 (1952) 511–15.

Booth, Wayne C. *A Rhetoric of Irony*. Chicago: University of Chicago Press, 1974.

Borg, Marcus J., and John Dominic Crossan. *The Last Week: The Day-by-Day Account of Jesus' Final Week in Jerusalem*. San Francisco: HarperSanFrancisco, 2006.

Borg, Marcus J., and N. T. Wright. *The Meaning of Jesus: Two Visions*. San Francisco: HarperSanFrancisco, 1999.

Brown, Raymond E. *The Community of the Beloved Disciple*. New York: Paulist, 1979.

———. *The Death of the Messiah: From Gethsemane to the Grave: A Commentary on the Passion Narratives in the Four Gospels*. 2 vols. The Anchor Bible Reference Library. New York: Doubleday, 1994.

———. *The Gospel According to John*. 2 vols. Anchor Bible Commentary Series 29–29A. New York: Doubleday, 1966–70.

———. *An Introduction to the New Testament*. New York: Doubleday, 1997.

Bruce. F. F. *The Gospel of John: Introduction, Exposition and Notes*. Grand Rapids: Eerdmans, 1983.

Brunt, P. A. "Laus Imperii." In *Paul and Empire: Religion and Power in Roman Imperial Society*, edited by Richard A. Horsley, 25–35. Harrisburg: Trinity Press International, 1997.

Bultmann, Rudolf Karl. *The Gospel of John: A Commentary*. Philadelphia: Westminster, 1971.

———. *Theology of the New Testament*. 2 vols. Translated by Kendrick Grobel. New York: Charles Scribner's Sons, 1955.

Burkett, Delbert. *The Son of Man in the Gospel of John*. Journal for the Study of the New Testament: Supplement Series 56. Sheffield: Sheffield Academic, 1991.

Caird, G. B. *The Language and Imagery of the Bible*. Philadelphia: Westminster, 1980.

Carnazzo, Sebastian A. *Seeing Blood and Water: A Narrative-Critical Study of John 19:34*. Eugene, OR: Pickwick, 2012.

Carroll, John T., and Joel B. Green. *The Death of Jesus in Early Christianity*. Peabody: Hendrickson, 1995.

Carson, D. A. *The Gospel According to John*. Grand Rapids: Eerdmans, 1991.

Carter, Warren. "Church Bible Studies, Ancient and Modern Empires, and the Gospel according to John." In *The Bible in the Public Square: Reading the Signs of the Times*, edited by Cynthia Briggs Kittredge et al., 13–24. Minneapolis: Fortress, 2008.

———. "Going All the Way? Honoring the Emperor and Sacrificing Wives and Slaves in 1 Peter." In *A Feminist Companion to the Catholic Epistles and Hebrews*, edited by Amy-Jill Levine with Maria Mayo Robbins, 14–33. Feminist Companion to the New Testament and Early Christian Writings 8. New York: T. & T. Clark, 2004.

———. *John and Empire: Initial Explorations.* New York: T. & T. Clark, 2008.

———. *John: Storyteller, Interpreter, Evangelist.* Peabody: Hendrickson, 2006.

———. *Matthew and Empire: Initial Explorations.* Harrisburg: Trinity Press International, 2001.

———. *Pontius Pilate: Portraits of a Roman Governor.* Collegeville: Liturgical, 2003.

———. *The Roman Empire and the New Testament: An Essential Guide.* Nashville: Abingdon, 2006.

Cassidy, Richard J. *Jesus, Politics, and Society: A Study of Luke's Gospel.* Maryknoll: Orbis, 1978.

———. *John's Gospel in New Perspective: Christology and the Realities of Roman Power.* Maryknoll: Orbis, 1992.

Champion, Craige Brian. *Roman Imperialism: Readings and Sources.* Malden: Blackwell, 2004.

Chevalier, Haakon. *The Ironic Temper.* New York: Oxford University Press, 1932.

Cicero. *On the Orator.* Translated by E. W. Sutton. 2 vols. Loeb Classical Library. Cambridge: Harvard University Press, 1942–48.

———. *The Speeches.* Translated by H. Grose Hodge et al. 7 vols. Loeb Classical Library. Cambridge: Harvard University Press, 1931–58.

———. *The Verrine Orations.* Translated by L. H. G. Greenwood. 2 vols. Loeb Classical Library. Cambridge: Harvard University Press, 1935.

Clark-Soles, Jaime. *Death and the Afterlife in the New Testament.* New York: T. & T. Clark, 2006.

Colson, F. H., and G. H. Whitaker, trans. *Philo.* 10 vols. Loeb Classical Library. Cambridge: Harvard University Press, 1929–1962.

Crossan, John Dominic. *The Cross That Spoke: The Origins of the Passion Narrative.* San Francisco: Harper & Row, 1988.

———. *The Historical Jesus: The Life of a Mediterranean Jewish Peasant.* San Francisco: HarperSanFrancisco, 1991.

———. *Jesus: A Revolutionary Biography.* San Francisco: HarperSanFrancisco, 1994.

———. *Who Killed Jesus? Exposing the Roots of Anti-Semitism in the Gospel Story of the Death of Jesus.* San Francisco: HarperSanFrancisco, 1995.

Conway, Colleen M. "There and Back Again: Johannine History on the Other Side of Literary Criticism." In *Anatomies of Narrative Criticism: The Past, Present, and Future of the Fourth Gospel as Literature*, edited by Tom Thatcher and Stephen D. Moore, 77–91. Atlanta: Society of Biblical Literature, 2008.

Conzelmann, Hans. *The Theology of St. Luke.* Translated by Geoffrey Buswell. London: Faber & Faber, 1960.

Cotter, Wendy. "Greco-Roman Apotheosis Traditions and the Resurrection Appearances in Matthew." In *The Gospel of Matthew in Current Study*, edited by David E. Aune, 127–53. Grand Rapids: Eedrmans, 2001.

Culpepper, R. Alan. *Anatomy of the Fourth Gospel: A Study in Literary Design.* Philadelphia: Fortress, 1983.

Danker, Frederick William, et al., eds. *A Greek-English Lexicon of the New Testament and Other Early Christian Literature.* Chicago: University of Chicago Press, 2000.

Dio Chrysostom. Translated by J. W. Cohoon and H. Lamar Crosby. 5 vols. Loeb Classical Library. Cambridge: Harvard University Press, 1932–51.

Dodd, C. H. *Historical Tradition in the Fourth Gospel*. Cambridge: Cambridge University Press, 1963.

———. *The Interpretation of the Fourth Gospel*. Cambridge: Cambridge University Press, 1953.

Dube, Musa W. "Reading for Decolonization (John 4:1–42)." In *John and Postcolonialism: Travel, Space and Power*, edited by Musa W. Dube and Jeffrey L. Staley, 51–75. New York: Sheffield Academic, 2002.

Dube, Musa W., and J. Staley, eds. *John and Postcolonialism: Travel, Space, and Power*. London: Continuum, 2002.

Duke, Paul D. *Irony in the Fourth Gospel*. Atlanta: John Knox, 1985.

Duling, Dennis C. "Empire: Theories, Methods, Models." In *The Gospel of Matthew in its Roman Imperial Context*, edited by John Riches and David C. Sim, 49–74. Journal for the Study of the New Testament 276. London: T. & T. Clark International, 2005.

Ehrman, Bart. "Jesus' Trial Before Pilate: John 18:28—19:16." *Biblical Theology Bulletin* 13 (1983) 124–31.

Esler, Philip Francis. *Community and Gospel in Luke-Acts: The Social and Political Motivations of Lucan Theology*. Society for New Testament Studies Monograph Series 57. Cambridge: Cambridge University Press, 1987.

Fears, J. Rufus. "The Cult of Jupiter and Roman Imperial Ideology." In *Aufstieg und Niedergang der römischen Welt*, 2:17.1, 3–141. Berlin: Walter de Gruyter, 1981.

Feuillet, A. "Les adieux du Christ à sa Mère (Jn 19:25–27) et la maternitè spirituelle de Marie." *Nouvelle Revue Théologique* 86 (1964) 469–89.

Fischer, Michael M. J. "Ethnicity and the Post-Modern Arts of Memory." In *Writing Culture: The Poetics and Politics of Ethnography*, edited by J. Clifford and G. E. Marcus, 194–233. Berkeley: University of California Press, 1986.

Fischer, Michael M. J., ed. *In the Shadow of Empire: Reclaiming the Bible as a History of Faithful Resistance*. Louisville: Westminster John Knox, 2008.

———. *Paul and the Roman Imperial Order*. Harrisburg: Trinity, 2004.

Fludernik, Monika, and Greta Olson. "Introduction." In *In the Grip of the Law: Trials, Prisons and the Space Between*, edited by Monika Fludernik and Greta Olson, xiii–liv. Frankfurt am Main: Lang, 2004.

Friesen, Steven J. "Poverty in Pauline Studies: Beyond the So-called New Consensus." *Journal for the Study of the New Testament* 26 (2004) 323–61.

———. *Twice Neokoros: Ephesus, Asia and the Cult of the Flavian Imperial Family*. Etudes Préliminaires aux religions orientales dans l'Empire romain 116. Leiden: Brill, 1993.

Garnsey, Peter. *Social Status and Legal Privilege in the Roman Empire*. Oxford: Clarendon, 1970.

Garnsey, Peter, and Richard Saller. *The Roman Empire: Economy, Society, and Culture*. Berkeley: University of California Press, 1987.

Giblin, Charles Homer. "John's Narration of the Hearing before Pilate." *Biblica* 66 (1985) 221–39.

Glancy, Jennifer A. "Torture: Flesh, Truth, and the Fourth Gospel." *Biblical Interpretation* 13 (2005) 107–36.

Goodman, Martin. *The Ruling Class of Judea: The Origins of the Jewish Revolt Against Rome A.D. 66–70*. New York: Cambridge University Press, 1987.

Haenchen, Ernst. *John 2: A Commentary on the Gospel of John Chapters 7–21*. Translated by Robert W. Funk. Hermeneia: A Critical and Historical Commentary on the Bible. Philadelphia: Fortress, 1984.

Hanson, K. C., and Douglas E. Oakman. *Palestine in the Time of Jesus: Social Structures and Social Conflicts*. 2nd ed. Minneapolis: Fortress, 2008.

Harnack, Adolf von. *Bruchstücke des Evangeliums und der Apokalypse des Petrus*. Leipzig: Hinrichs, 1893.

Heil, John Paul. *Blood and Water: The Death and Resurrection of Jesus in John 18–21*. Catholic Biblical Quarterly Monograph Series 27. Washington: Catholic Biblical Association of America, 1995.

Hengel, Martin. *Crucifixion in the Ancient World and the Folly of the Message of the Cross*. Philadelphia: Fortress, 1977.

Hengstenberg, Ernst Wilhelm. *Commentary on the Gospel of St. John*. 2 vols. Edinburgh: T. & T. Clark, 1865.

Herzog, William R. *Jesus, Justice, and the Reign of God: A Ministry of Liberation*. Louisville: Westminster John Knox, 2000.

Horace. *Satires, Epistles, Ars Poetica*. Translated by H. Rushton Fairclough. Loeb Classical Library. Cambridge: Harvard University Press, 1947.

Horsley, Richard A. "High Priests and the Politics of Roman Palestine: A Contextual Analysis of the Evidence in Josephus." *Journal for the Study of Judaism in the Persian, Hellenistic, and Roman Periods* 17 (1986) 23–55.

———. "Introduction: Jesus, Paul, and the 'Arts of Resistance': Leaves from the Notebook of James C. Scott." In *Hidden Transcripts and the Arts of Resistance: Applying the Work of James C. Scott to Jesus and Paul*, edited by Richard A. Horsley, 1–28. Semeia Studies 48. Atlanta: Society of Biblical Literature, 2004.

———. *Jesus and Empire: The Kingdom of God and the New World Disorder*. Minneapolis: Fortress, 2003.

Horsley, Richard A., ed. *Paul and Empire: Religion and Power in Roman Imperial Society*. Harrisburg: Trinity, 1997.

Horsley, Richard A., with John S. Hanson. *Bandits, Prophets, & Messiahs: Popular Movements in the Time of Jesus*. Harrisburg: Trinity, 1999.

Howard-Brook, Wes. *Becoming Children of God: John's Gospel and Radical Discipleship*. Eugene, OR: Wipf & Stock, 1994.

———. *"Come Out, My People!": God's Call out of Empire in the Bible and Beyond*. Maryknoll: Orbis, 2010.

Howard-Brook, Wes, and Anthony Gwyther. *Unveiling Empire: Reading Revelation Then and Now*. Maryknoll: Orbis, 2008.

Huskinson, Janet, ed. *Experiencing Rome: Culture, Identity, and Power in the Roman Empire*. London: Routledge, 2000.

Hutcheon, Linda. *Irony's Edge: The Theory and Politics of Irony*. New York: Routledge, 1994.

Kahl, Brigitte. "Acts of the Apostles: Pro(to)-Imperial Script and Hidden Transcript." In *In the Shadow of Empire: Reclaiming the Bible as a History of Faithful Resistance*, edited by Richard A. Horsley, 137–56. Louisville: Westminster John Knox, 2008.

Kautsky, John H. *The Politics of Aristocratic Empires*. New Brunswick: Transaction, 1997.

Keener, Craig S. *The Gospel of John: A Commentary*. 2 vols. Peabody: Hendrickson, 2003.
Kelly, Christopher. *The Roman Empire: A Very Short Introduction*. New York: Oxford University Press, 2006.
Kim, Seyoon. *Christ and Caesar: The Gospel and the Roman Empire in the Writings of Paul and Luke*. Grand Rapids: Eerdmans, 2008.
Kirk, Alan. "The Memory of Violence and the Death of Jesus in Q." In *Memory, Tradition, and Text: Uses of the Past in Early Christianity*, edited by Alan Kirk and Tom Thatcher, 191–206. Atlanta: Society of Biblical Literature, 2005.
Koester, Craig R. "Savior of the World (John 4:42)." *Journal of Biblical Literature* 109 (1990) 665–80.
———. *Symbolism in the Fourth Gospel: Meaning, Mystery, Community*. Minneapolis: Fortress, 1995.
———. *The Word of Life: A Theology of John's Gospel*. Grand Rapids: Eerdmans, 2008.
Koskenniemi, Erkki, et al. "Wine Mixed with Myrrh (Mark 15.23) and Crurifragium (John 19.31–32) Two Details of the Passion Narratives." *Journal for the Study of the New Testament* 27 (2005) 379–91.
Kunzle, David. "World Upside Down: The Iconography of a European Broadsheet Type." In *The Reversible World: Symbolic Inversion in Art and Society*, edited by Barbara A Babcock, 39–94. Ithaca: Cornell University Press, 1978.
Kysar, Robert. "Expulsion from the Synagogue: The Tale of a Theory." In *Voyages with John: Charting the Fourth Gospel*, 237–45. Waco: Baylor University Press, 2005.
———. *John*. Augsburg Commentary on the New Testament. Minneapolis: Augsburg, 1986.
———. *John, the Maverick Gospel*. Rev. ed. Louisville: Westminster John Knox, 1993.
Lagrange, Marie-Joseph. *Evangile selon Saint Jean*. Paris: Gabalda, 1948.
La Potterie, Ignace de. "Jesus: King and Judge According to John 19:13." Translated by J. O'Hara. *Scripture* 13 (1961) 97–111.
———. "Jésus, roi et juge d'après Jn 19:13: *ekathisen epi bēmatos*." *Biblica* 41 (1960) 217–47.
Lémonon, Jean-Pierre. *Pilate et le gouvernement de la Judée: Textes et Monuments*. Paris: Gabalda, 1981.
Lenski, Gerhard E. *Power and Privilege: A Theory of Social Stratification*. Chapel Hill: University of North Carolina Press, 1984.
Lincoln, Andrew T. *Truth on Trial: The Lawsuit Motif in the Fourth Gospel*. Peabody: Hendrickson, 2000.
Lindars, Barnabas. *The Gospel of John*. NCB. London: Oliphants, 1972.
Lohse, Eduard. *History of the Suffering and Death of Jesus Christ*. Translated by Martin O. Dietrich. Philadelphia: Fortress, 1967.
Louw, Johannes P., and Eugene. A. Nida, eds. *Greek-English Lexicon of the New Testament: Based on Semantic Domains*. 2 vols. 2nd ed. New York: United Bible Societies, 1989.
MacMullen, Ramsay. *Roman Social Relations: 50 B.C. to A.D. 284*. New Haven: Yale University Press, 1974.
Malamat, Abraham, and Haim Hillel Ben-Sasson. *A History of the Jewish People*. Cambridge: Harvard University Press, 1976.
Marshall, F. H., ed. *The Collection of Ancient Greek Inscriptions in the British Museum*, vol. 4. Oxford: Clarendon, 1916.

Martial. *Epigrams*. Translated by D. R. Shackleton Bailey. 3 vols. Loeb Classical Library. Cambridge: Harvard University Press, 1993.

Martyn, J. Louis. *History and Theology in the Fourth Gospel*. New York: Harper & Row, 1968.

McGing, Brian Charles. "Pontius Pilate and the Sources." *Catholic Biblical Quarterly* 53.3 (1991) 416–38.

Meeks, Wayne. "The Divine Agent and His Counterfeit in Philo and the Fourth Gospel." In *Aspects of Religious Propaganda in Judaism and Early Christianity*, edited by Elisabeth Schussler Fiorenza, 43–67. Notre Dame: University of Notre Dame Press, 1976.

———. *The Prophet-King: Moses Traditions and the Johannine Christology*. Leiden: Brill, 1967.

Menken, Maarten J. J. *Old Testament Quotations in the Fourth Gospel: Studies in Textual Form*. Kampen, Netherlands: Kok Pharos, 1996.

Michaels, J. Ramsey. *The Gospel of John*. The New International Commentary on the New Testament. Grand Rapids: Eerdmans, 2010.

———. "John 18:31 and the 'Trial' of Jesus." *New Testament Studies* 36 (1990) 474–79.

Minns, Denis, and P. M. Parvis. *Justin, Philosopher and Martyr: Apologies*. Oxford: Oxford University Press, 2009.

Moloney, Francis J. *The Gospel of John*. Sacra Pagina 4. Collegeville: Liturgical, 1998.

———. *The Johannine Son of Man*. 2nd ed. Biblioteca di Scienze Religiose 14. Rome: Libreria Ateneo Salesiano, 1978.

Moo, Douglas J. *The Old Testament in the Gospel Passion Narratives*. Sheffield: Almond, 1983.

Moore, Stephen D. *Empire and Apocalypse: Postcolonialism and the New Testament*. Sheffield: Sheffield Phoenix, 2006.

Morley, Neville. *Metropolis and Hinterland: The City of Rome and the Italian Economy 200 B.C.–A.D. 200*. Cambridge: Cambridge University Press, 2002.

Moule, C. F. D. "Fulfillment-Words in the New Testament: Use and Abuse." *New Testament Studies* 14 (1968) 293–320.

Muecke, D. C. *The Compass of Irony*. New York: Methuen, 1969.

———. "Irony Markers." *Poetics* 7 (1978) 363–75.

Nogalski, James D. *The Book of the Twelve: Micah–Malachi*. Smyth & Helwys Bible Commentary. Macon, GA: Smyth & Helwys, 2011.

Oakes, Peter. *Rome in the Bible and the Early Church*. Grand Rapids: Baker Academic, 2002.

O'Day, Gail R. "Gospel of John." In *Women's Bible Commentary*, edited by Carol A. Newsom et al., 517–30. 3rd ed. Louisville: Westminster John Knox, 2012.

———. "The Gospel of John: Introduction, Commentary, and Reflections." In *Luke, John. The New Interpreter's Bible Commentary 9*, edited by Leander E. Keck, 491–865. Nashville: Abingdon, 1995.

———. "I Have Called You Friends." *Christian Reflection: A Series in Faith and Ethics* 27 (2008) 20–27.

———. *Revelation in the Fourth Gospel: Narrative Mode and Theological Claim*. Philadelphia: Fortress, 1986.

Papias. "Fragments of Papias and Quadratus." In *Apostolic Fathers: Volume II*, translated by Bart D. Ehrman, 85–119. Loeb Classical Library. Cambridge: Harvard University Press, 2003.

Pliny. *Letters and Panegyricus*. Translated by Betty Radice. 2 vols. Loeb Classical Library. Cambridge: Harvard University Press, 1969–75.

Plutarch. *Lives*. Translated by Bernadotte Perrin. 11 vols. Loeb Classical Library. New York: Putnam's Sons, 1914–28.

Price, Simon R. F. "From Noble Funerals to Divine Cult: The Consecration of Roman Emperors." In *Rituals of Royalty: Power and Ceremonial in Traditional Societies*, edited by David Cannadine and Simon Price, 56–105. Cambridge: Cambridge University Press, 1987.

———. *Rituals and Power: The Roman Imperial Cult in Asia Minor*. Cambridge: Cambridge University Press, 1984.

Quintillian. *The Lesser Declamations*. Edited and translated by D. R. Shackleton Bailey. 2 vols. Loeb Classical Library. Cambridge: Harvard University Press, 2006.

Reed, David. "Rethinking John's Social Setting: Hidden Transcript, Anti-language, and the Negotiation of Empire." *Biblical Theology Bulletin* 36 (2006) 93–106.

Reinhartz, Adele. *Befriending the Beloved Disciple: A Jewish Reading of the Gospel of John*. New York: Continuum, 2001.

Rensberger, David K. *Johannine Faith and Liberating Community*. Philadelphia: Westminster, 1988.

———. "The Politics of John: The Trial of Jesus in the Fourth Gospel." *Journal of Biblical Literature* 103 (1984) 395–411.

Retief, Cilliers L. "The History and Pathology of Crucifixion." *South African Medical Journal* 93 (2003) 938–41.

Rhea, Robert. *The Johannine Son of Man*. Abhandlungen zur Theologie des Alten und Neuen Testaments 76. Zürich: Theologischer, 1990.

Richey, Lance Byron. *Roman Imperial Ideology and the Gospel of John*. The Catholic Biblical Quarterly Monograph Series 43. Washington, DC: Catholic Biblical Association of America, 2007.

Rives, James. "Religion in the Roman World." In *Experiencing Rome: Culture, Identity, and Power in the Roman Empire*, edited by Janet Huskinson, 245–76. London: Routledge, 2000.

Robbins, Vernon K. "Luke–Acts: A Mixed Population Seeks a Home in the Roman Empire." In *Images of Empire*, edited by Loveday Alexander, 202–21. Journal for the Study of the Old Testament Supplement Series 122. Sheffield: Sheffield Academic Press, 1991.

Robinson, O. F. *Penal Practice and Penal Policy in Ancient Rome*. New York: Routledge, 2007.

Rolfe, J. C., trans. *Suetonius*. 2 vols. Loeb Classical Library. Cambridge: Harvard University Press, 1979.

Saldarini, Anthony J. *Pharisees, Scribes and Sadducees in Palestinian Society: A Sociological Approach*. Wilmington, DE: Glazier, 1988.

Schnackenburg, Rudolf. *The Gospel According to St. John*. 3 vols. New York: Seabury, 1968–82.

Schneiders, Sandra M. *Written That You May Believe: Encountering Jesus in the Fourth Gospel*. Rev. ed. New York: Crossroad, 2003.

Schwartz, Saundra Charlene. "Courtroom Scenes in the Ancient Greek Novels." Ph.D. diss., Columbia University, 1998.

Scott, James C. *Domination and the Arts of Resistance: Hidden Transcripts*. New Haven: Yale University Press, 1990.

———. *Weapons of the Weak: Everyday Forms of Peasant Resistance*. New Haven: Yale University Press, 1985.
Scott, Kenneth. *The Imperial Cult under the Flavians*. New York: Arno, 1975.
Sedgewick, Garnett Gladwin. *Of Irony: Especially in Drama*. 3rd ed. Vancouver, BC: Ronsdale, 2003.
Seneca. *Moral Essays*. Translated by John W. Basore. 3 vols. Loeb Classical Library. Cambridge: Harvard University Press, 1928–35.
Senior, Donald. *The Passion of Jesus in the Gospel of John*. Collegeville: Liturgical, 1991.
Sharp, Carolyn J. *Irony and Meaning in the Hebrew Bible*. Bloomington: Indiana University Press, 2009.
Sherwin-White, A. N. *Roman Society and Roman Law in the New Testament*. Oxford: Clarendon, 1963.
Skinner, Matthew L. *The Trial Narratives: Conflict, Power, and Identity in the New Testament*. Louisville: Westminster John Knox, 2010.
Smallwood, E. Mary. "High Priests and Politics in Roman Palestine." *Journal of Theological Studies* 13 (1962) 14–34.
Smith, D. Moody. *John Among the Gospels: The Relationship in Twentieth-Century Research*. Minneapolis: Fortress, 1992.
Staley, Jeffrey Lloyd. *The Print's First Kiss: A Rhetorical Investigation of the Implied Reader in the Fourth Gospel*. SBL Dissertation Series 82. Atlanta: Scholars, 1988.
Stauffer, Ethelbert. *Jesus and His Story*. London: SCM, 1960.
Steele, John Aulay. "The Pavement." *Expository Times* 34 (1922–23) 562–63.
Stibbe, Mark W. G. *John As Storyteller: Narrative Criticism and the Fourth Gospel*. Cambridge: Cambridge University Press, 1992.
Strachan, R. H. *The Fourth Gospel*. 3rd ed. London: SCM, 1941.
Sylva, Dennis D. "Nicodemus and His Spices (John 19:39)." *New Testament Studies* 34 (1988) 148–51.
Tacitus. *The Histories and The Annals*. Translated by Clifford H. Moore and J. Jackson. 4 vols. Loeb Classical Library. Cambridge: Harvard University Press, 1931–37.
Terdiman, Richard. *Discourse/Counter-Discourse: The Theory and Practice of Symbolic Resistance in Nineteenth-Century France*. Ithaca: Cornell University Press, 1985.
Thackeray, H. St. J., et al., trans. *Josephus*. 10 vols. Loeb Classical Library. Cambridge: Harvard University Press, 1926–65.
Thatcher, Tom. "Anatomies of the Fourth Gospel: Past, Present, and Future Probes." In *Anatomies of Narrative Criticism: The Past, Present and Future of the Fourth Gospel as Literature*, edited by Tom Thatcher and Stephen D. Moore, 1–35. Atlanta: Society of Biblical Literature, 2008.
———. *Greater Than Caesar: Christology and Empire in the Fourth Gospel*. Minneapolis: Fortress, 2009.
———. "The Sabbath Trick: Unstable Irony in the Fourth Gospel." *Journal for the Study of the New Testament* 76 (1999) 53–77.
Thatcher, Tom, and Stephen D. Moore, eds. *Anatomies of Narrative Criticism: The Past, Present and Future of the Fourth Gospel as Literature*. Atlanta: Society of Biblical Literature, 2008.
Tilborg, Sjef van. *Reading John in Ephesus*. Supplements to Novum Testamentum 83. New York: Brill, 1996.
Vaux, Roland de. *Ancient Israel: Its Life and Institutions*. Translated by John McHugh. New York: McGraw-Hill, 1961.

Versnel, H. S. *Inconsistencies in Greek and Roman Religion II: Transition and Reversal in Myth and Ritual*. Studies in Greek and Roman Religion 6. Leiden: Brill, 1993.

Walaskay, Paul W. *And So We Came to Rome: The Political Perspective of St. Luke*. Society for New Testament Studies Monograph Series 49. Cambridge: Cambridge University Press, 1983.

Wallace, Daniel B. *Greek Grammar Beyond the Basics: An Exegetical Syntax of the New Testament*. Grand Rapids: Zondervan, 1996.

Walsh, Brian J., and Slyvia C. Kesmaat. *Colossians Remixed: Subverting the Empire*. Downers Grove: InterVarsity, 2004.

Wengst, Klaus. *Pax Romana and the Peace of Jesus Christ*. Philadelphia: Fortress, 1987.

Wheelwright, Philip Ellis. *Metaphor and Reality*. Bloomington: Indiana University Press, 1962.

Winter, Paul. *On the Trial of Jesus*. Edited by T. A. Burkill and and Géza Vermès. 2nd ed. New York: Walter de Gruyter, 1974.

Wolfsdorf, David. *Trials of Reason: Plato and the Crafting of Philosophy*. Oxford: Oxford University Press, 2008.

Zugibe, Frederick T. "Two Questions about Crucifixion: Does the Victim Die of Asphyxiation? Would Nails in the Hand Hold the Weight of the Body?" *Bible Review* 5 (1989) 34–43.

www.ingramcontent.com/pod-product-compliance
Lightning Source LLC
Chambersburg PA
CBHW050348230426
43663CB00010B/2031